Language as Discourse

APPLIED LINGUISTICS AND LANGUAGE STUDY

General Editor
Professor Christopher N Candlin, Macquarie University

For a complete list of books in this series see pages xvi and xvii

Language as Discourse: Perspectives for Language Teaching

Michael McCarthy and Ronald Carter

Longman

An imprint of **Pearson Education**

Harlow, England · London · New York · Reading, Massachusetts · San Francisco
Toronto · Don Mills, Ontario · Sydney · Tokyo · Singapore · Hong Kong · Seoul
Taipei · Cape Town · Madrid · Mexico City · Amsterdam · Munich · Paris · Milan

Pearson Education Limited
Edinburgh Gate
Harlow
Essex CM20 2JE
England

and Associated Companies throughout the world.

Visit us on the World Wide Web at:
http://www.pearsoneduc.com

First published 1994

ISBN 0–582–084245 PPR

British Library Cataloguing-in-Publication Data
A catalogue record for this book is
available from the British Library

Library of Congress Cataloging-in-Publication Data
McCarthy, Michael, 1947–
    Language as discourse : perspectives for language teaching / M J
McCarthy and R A Carter.
        p.   cm. — (Applied linguistics and language study)
    Includes bibliographical references and index.
    ISBN 0–582–08424–5
    1. Discourse analysis.   2. Language and languages—Study and
teaching.   I. Carter, Ronald.   II. Title.   III. Series.
P302.M3916   1994
401'.41—dc20   92–40126
                                                                CIP

10 9   8   7   6
05 04 03 02

Set by 8H in 10/12pt Ehrhardt
Printed and bound by Antony Rowe Ltd, Eastbourne

Contents

General Editor's Preface

This is an uncomfortable book. It disturbs a set order, and it challenges orthodoxies. At the same time it gives comfort to those concerned with the future of its discipline as it sets out what is in a sense a manifesto for fundamental change. How is this achieved?

We could begin with the book's ending. In their final Chapter, the authors have this to say: *'The moment one starts to think of language as discourse, the entire landscape changes, usually, forever.'* What is this novel landscape, how is it drawn? What is involved in such a change?

Taking first its basic construct, its understanding of language, what does it mean for the authors to adopt a discourse-based view? It may help to take a painter's perspective. Recall how in the innovation of Impressionist painting images emerge from a landscape as component strokes and brushwork assume recognisable yet still uncertain forms which then, on closer inspection, dissolve back into unidentifiable and insignificant items of colour. Post-impressionist *pointillisme* captures this exactly. In a sense so it is with language. We can train our eye or ear on the phonological and lexicogrammatical forms as primes or we can seek to discern the texts which so to speak emerge from the detail of the features. It's a matter of perspective. What do we gain from taking the landscape of the text as our starting point rather than a focus on these constituent forms? At once we are compelled to recognize that such a landscape is not just an assemblage of linguistic strokes but a coherent entity purposefully constructed by identifiable participants in response to particular exigencies of time and place and subject matter, reflecting contexts which can be recognized and reconstructed. A landscape moreover, which is sited in a particular historical moment and social circumstance and not an adventitiously constructed object taken from some anonymous inventory; a text with identity, ownership, audience and purpose. Nonetheless such texts *are* composed, like paintings they make significant and appropriate choices, here from the lexicogrammar or the phonology. There is no landscape without form and without component features. Again, like painting, it's a matter of perspective. What the authors argue is that if we want to comprehend the landscape then language teaching has to begin with texts and to recognize through them the forms of lexicogrammar and phonology and how these wordings and these soundings function in their particular patternings to represent and reveal to the critical observer the cultural and ideological meanings of the landscape.

Why would this view be uncomfortable? Primarily, because it alters the basis of teaching and learning. If one begins with forms, there is no ground for much participation by the learner, no ground for personal or collective assessment of their putative significance in the meaning-making process, no opportunity for considered choice. The forms remain the convenient property of the textbook or the teacher, unreal and inauthenticatable objects for display and empty acquisition. To focus on texts, however, raises disturbing questions, one that cannot be answered by reference only to the authority of the textbook or the teacher. Questions which would not be appropriately addressed to forms alone. How are such texts constructed? Why are these wordings and soundings chosen? How can such texts be classified? To what extent are such texts unitary and to what extent intertextual? Where does a particular text stand on the continuum of spokenness to writingness? How does a text display its underlying arguments? How is a text representative of a particular authorship and socio-cultural position? These are in turn all questions which both widen the scope of the curriculum and alter the nature of the role and the professional competency of the language teacher. Therein lies their uncomfortableness. Furthermore, beginning with texts is not merely a matter of topography. Texts like landscapes are open to interpretation. Their significance is not only a matter of contour. Observers see them through different eyes, from different perspectives. What Halliday calls the *texture* of texts has to be related to equally apposite questions of how texts are variably interpreted. There is a strategic aspect to the understanding of texts: what ways of seeing are there? How is the viewer positioned to adopt this rather than that perspective? How are texts best understood, from an awareness of the overall landscape, so to speak top down, or bottom up from the component features? As in Greenway's film, the teacher like the draughtsman has particular devices to chart the topography but his contrivance is always less than the landscape he seeks to capture. Are different texts interpreted in different ways? What part does the cultural and social background of the learner play in modes of interpretation? As much as a redrawing of its perspective on language such cognitive questions are at the heart of this latest contribution to the *Applied Linguistics and Language Study Series*. They are questions which clearly entail reassessment of more than language. They go to the heart of teaching and learning. They compel a combining in the teacher and the learner of the roles of analyst and interpreter, integrating classification with making the meaningful intelligible. In the authors' words, they provide a basis for language learning to become language education. In that sense this book makes uncomfortable yet challenging reading for the curriculum designer for what it does is to offer to language education some of the exciting intertextual complexity of its textual subject-matter. Language education becomes interdisciplinary. While its focus remains in the description of language, grammar, lexis, phonology and discourse, an understanding of the curriculum landscape now requires insights from cognitive psychology and sociology, from studies in ideology and media studies, from conversational analysis and ethnography and from cultural history. It widens the scope of language learner education but also, perhaps more uncomfortable, of language teacher education. Characteristically new here is the insistence on a continuum and a community of teachers of foreign and second languages and teachers of the mother tongue.

To be effective as agents of change, however, curricula need to be turned into practical action. Their realisation, and in a sense their justification, occurs in the activities of the classroom. Here, as elsewhere we have innovation, but now in relation to the contour of the landscape itself. Three areas of redrawing of the language educational curriculum stand out: the first is the authors' catholic approach to the selection of texts, eschewing sharp boundaries of genre, between, for example, the literary, the conversational and the informational. A second realignment is that of the raising of the teaching of strategy and process, in terms of both language learning and discourse analysis, to be central parts of the curriculum content and classroom procedure. In stressing the importance, for example, of consciousness-raising as a way of developing the learner's metalinguistic knowledge the authors link this to the value of critical awareness more generally, both for language and learning. Finally here (though there are many other similar innovations), the book elevates the development of interpersonal and interactional skills, in writing and in speech to a par with the current and overwhelming emphasis in many curricula on the transactional, arguing that both planes of discourse need equal treatment in a communicative curriculum. Above all what is so exciting about Mike McCarthy's and Ron Carter's book is the extraordinary richness of their illustration of how such practical action can be achieved. Each Chapter is not only thoroughly and very widely referenced internally but is accompanied by imaginative Reader Activities, each glossed with suggestive Notes and linked to annotated Further Readings. Thus all of the necessary apparatus is provided but in a way in which the roles of teacher and learner are subtly interchanged. Tasks for teachers can equally be tasks for learners, and this is entirely in keeping with the view taken here of the landscape of language and how it can be perceived. Like writers and readers, speakers and hearers, teachers and learners cooperatively engage in co-construction of the landscape of texts and together are enabled by the processes of this book to combine resources in exploring their significance in particular time and space.

Professor Christopher N Candlin
Macquarie University, Sydney
General Editor

Introduction

This book focuses on a description of the discourse properties of language and on the relevance of such description for language teaching. In the book we challenge some prevailing assumptions. One main assumption that we challenge is that English language teachers already know enough about the language. It is often said that such teachers are surrounded by an array of well-researched and thoroughly tested grammars and dictionaries which provide extensive coverage, and that learning more about the language need not be something to consume too much of their valuable time. Instead, it is also often said, their main concern should be with how to teach the language more effectively. We challenge this main assumption that methodology is all. Another assumption that we challenge is that there are discontinuities between first and second language learning. We prefer to underline the continuities and connections and argue that our discourse-based approach to language learning and teaching applies to both L1 and L2.

Since the early 1970s there has been a rapid expansion of descriptive work on the discourse properties of language. In their own way each of the disciplines of discourse analysis, pragmatics and text linguistics has explored how language is used across stretches of language. This has frequently involved examining language in naturally occurring contexts, both spoken and written, and has sometimes involved the study of complete texts. Such an orientation contrasts with dominant paradigms for the description of, for example, grammar, vocabulary and the sound system of English, which have tended to concentrate on decontextualized units of language. Thus, grammar is studied in relation to sentences which are often made up by the analyst or taken from unrepresentative contexts. The practice is useful, of course, for illustrative and analytical purposes. It has certainly influenced language teaching in that the emphasis in many language course books is on single sentences or minimal units of language and on practising forms of language within such a framework.

One of the main aims of this book is to examine what insights from language study at the level of discourse have to offer to the language teacher and student. Given that most real language use involves the production and reception of connected stretches of spoken and written language, we assert that this kind of description is of considerable potential value. Indeed, we go further and assert that the functions of language are often best understood in a discourse environment and that exploring language in context forces us to revise some commonly held understandings about the forms and meanings of language. In the case of grammar, in particular, the focus on text and discourse can help us to notice and analyse aspects of usage which have previously gone unnoticed and untaught. One connected argument here is that the better a text analyst the teacher can be, the better equipped – all other things being equal – his or her students are likely to be in using the language appropriately.

Paradoxically, in our view, some versions of communicative language teaching give insufficient attention to the actual processes of communication. For this reason in this book we normally cite only examples of real language use in a variety of naturally occurring contexts and we devote a lot of space to exploring the centrality of language to the construction of meaning in such contexts. One particular aspect of language use we explore in some detail is the way in which meanings are not wholly stable, that they vary according to the context, purpose and audience for the communication and that the same forms of language can have different meanings in different contexts. We place great stress on the interpersonal, variational and negotiable aspects of language in contrast to conventional concerns with more ideational, content-based and stable relations between forms and meanings. We consider the implications for language teaching of such an approach.

In our emphasis on language variety we do not privilege any particular texts and set up no hierarchy of values. All naturally occurring texts are of equal value. We argue for the value of literary texts in language development but argue at the same time that certain aspects of literary discourse may be both best illuminated and taught by a consideration of what are conventionally regarded as non-literary texts. The focus we provide on the continuum from non-literary to literary texts also enables us to give attention to other relatively neglected areas of language study and teaching: the role of aspects of culture and cultural presuppositions in language description and teaching and the relationship between language and ideology. Once again our argument is that the relevant issues at the interface of literature, ideology, culture and language teaching can be best located by concentrating on the discourse properties of language in a variety of texts. Our emphasis on the relevance for learners of increased learning about language is part of the same process of integrating a study of text and discourse with an increased competence in using the language communicatively.

The subtitle to this book is deliberately chosen. The book is not a survey. The field of discourse analysis now offers a number of fine introductions which lay out the main issues, review work in the field and discuss applications (eg Brown and Yule 1983; Stubbs 1983; Coulthard 1985; Cook 1989; McCarthy 1991; Hatch 1992). We therefore make no claim to complete coverage of all the potentially relevant aspects of discoursal and textual organization. For example, we have little to say about discourse-based aspects of phonology and intonation. We have little to say about discourse as a cognitive process, although we do explore some conditions for the production and interpretation of text as a socio-cognitive process. We could have more to say about theories of learning. We do not cover in detail areas of discourse description covered in other books. Though we do not neglect methodology, we also recognize that more space could be devoted to methodology. Our purpose, however, is to offer perspectives. We do so in places in a quite provocative way. The book is sometimes polemical and programmatic. We hope to open up debate, to raise issues and to question some current practices – even if in places this means that we have to argue against the grain of some current language teaching orthodoxies. In so doing, we can try only to make our arguments sufficiently precise and explicit in order to allow readers to engage with them and can finally say that we welcome argued responses to the positions adopted in the book.

Michael McCarthy   *Nottingham*
Ronald Carter

Acknowledgements

We wish to acknowledge the following people for kindly providing data and allowing it to be used in this book:
Mark Bishop, Lamees Nuseibeh, Beth Sims and Faye Wadsworth, former students of the University of Nottingham; Rosa Gimenez, of the University of Valencia; Lucy Cruttenden, formerly of the University of Birmingham; Per Olsson, of the University of Uppsala; colleagues in the International Certificate Conference (ICC); advisory teachers and consortium co-ordinators who worked in the Language in the National Curriculum (LINC) project (1989–92), an in-service teacher education project funded by the British Department of Education and Science and the local education authorities of England and Wales. Data drawn from the project are referred to as LINC data.
We wish also to thank Martin Hewings for permission to use some material from a previously published co-authored article (Hewings and McCarthy 1988). Our series editor, Chris Candlin, has once again been an unfailing source of advice, encouragement and perceptive support.

M McCarthy
R Carter

copyright Bureau of Freelance Photographers; Carnell Ltd for an advertisement from *The Observer* newspaper, 22.3.92, copyright © 1992 by Carnell Ltd; the author's agent for extracts from an article by John Collee from *Observer Magazine* 10.5.92; Emap Women's Group for extracts from a horoscope from *More!* magazine, 30th October–12th November 1991; Greenpeace Ltd for extracts from *Greenpeace News* magazine, Spring 1990; Guardian News Service Ltd for the article 'Hunters under fire from two fronts' by Maev Kennedy from *The Guardian* newspaper, 15.12.88, © The Guardian; Longman Group UK Ltd for an extract from *Openings* by Brian Tomlinson (1989); The Observer Ltd for an adapted extract from an article from *The Observer* newspaper, 8.12.85, © copyright The Observer, London, 1985; The Rover group Ltd for a slogan from an advertisement; Syndication International (1986) Ltd for an extract from the article 'Just the job for Shilts' by Matt Hughes from *Daily Mirror* 26.7.90, an extract from the article 'Sam Dies at 109' from *Daily Mirror* 26.7.90, an extract from the article 'Invasion of the Crawlies' from *Daily Mirror* 27.7.90, an extract from the article 'Electricity Chiefs to axe 5,000' from *Daily Mirror* 27.7.90 and an adapted extract from the article 'Workers Sun Peril' from *Daily Mirror* newspaper, 22.6.92; University of Birmingham for an advertisement from *The Guardian* newspaper, 15.9.87; HarperCollins for material from Collins COBUILD English Course Student's Book 2 by Jane & Dave Willis, © William Collins Sons & Co Ltd 1988.

APPLIED LINGUISTICS AND LANGUAGE STUDY

General Editor
Professor Christopher N. Candlin, Macquarie University

Error Analysis
Perspectives on second
language acquisition
JACK C. RICHARDS (ED.)

Stylistics and the Teaching of
Literature
HENRY WIDDOWSON

Language Tests at School
A pragmatic approach
JOHN W. OLLER JNR

Contrastive Analysis
CARL JAMES

Language and Communication
JACK R. RICHARDS AND
RICHARD W. SCHMIDT (EDS)

Learning to Write: First Language/
Second Language
AVIVA FREDMAN, IAN PRINGLE
AND JANIC YALDEN (EDS)

Strategies in Interlanguage
Communication
CLAUS FAERCH AND
GABRIELE KASPER (EDS)

Reading in a Foreign Language
J. CHARLES ALDERSON AND
A.H. URQUHART (EDS)

An Introduction to Discourse
Analysis
New Edition
MALCOLM COULTHARD

Computers in English Language
Teaching and Research
GEOFFREY LEECH AND
CHRISTOPHER N. CANDLIN (EDS)

Language Awareness in the
Classroom
CARL JAMES AND
PETER GARRETT

Bilingualism in Education
Aspects of theory, research and
practice
JIM CUMMINS AND
MERRILL SWAIN

Second Language Grammar:
Learning and Teaching
WILLIAM E. RUTHERFORD

The Classroom and the Language
Learner
Ethnography and second-language
classroom research
LEO VAN LIER

Vocabulary and Language Teaching
RONALD CARTER AND MICHAEL
McCARTHY (EDS)

Observation in the Language
Classroom
DICK ALLWRIGHT

Listening to Spoken English
Second Edition
GILLIAN BROWN

Listening in Language Learning
MICHAEL ROST

An Introduction to Second Language
Acquisition Research
DIANE LARSEN-FREEMAN AND
MICHAEL H. LONG

Language and Discrimination
A study of communication in
multi-ethnic workplaces
CELIA ROBERTS, TOM JUPP AND
EVELYN DAVIES

Translation and Translating:
Theory and Practice
ROGER T. BELL

Process and Experience in the
Language Classroom
MICHAEL LEGUTKE AND
HOWARD THOMAS

Rediscovering Interlanguage
LARRY SELINKER

to Jeanne and Jane

1 Dividing the world of discourse

1.0 Introduction

As we stated in the introduction to this book, our main concern is with the implications for language teaching of a view of language which takes into account the fact that linguistic patterns exist across stretches of text. These patterns of language extend beyond the words, clauses and sentences which have been the traditional concern of much language teaching. The view of language we take is thus one which focuses, where appropriate, on complete spoken and written texts and on the social and cultural contexts in which such language operates. It is a discourse-based view of language. It contrasts markedly with the approach to language which has, until recently, characterized both mother-tongue and second or foreign language teaching.

In order to prepare the ground for our discourse-based orientation we examine here two representative examples of these more traditional approaches: example 1.1 is taken from a book of English Language test papers for mother-tongue junior school students of English; example 1.2 is taken from a book of practice English Language test papers for learners of English as a second or foreign language. In case the focus on examination papers may be thought untypical of language teaching practices, we point out that such examples are of language outcomes for which students will have to be prepared during the course of their language lessons. In case example 1.1 is thought remote in time, it is necessary to point out that many governments around the world either wish to see a return to such language exercises or endorse their continuation.

(1.1)   Make a word ending in **ing** from the word at the beginning of the line. You may need to drop the final **e** or double the last letter. Write the new word in the space.
   9   cut Michael is _____ his birthday cake.
   10   write David is _____ a letter to his friend.
   11   run Caroline is _____ up the garden path.
   12   ride Susan is _____ a donkey on the beach.
   13   put Tony is _____ on his swimming trunks.

1

Put the following words into the order in which you would find them in a dictionary.

cake   apple   orange   bread   fish

14 (1) _____ 15 (2) _____   16 (3) _____

17 (4) _____ 18 (5) _____

In each space write the opposite of the word in heavy type.

19   Mum says I must stay **in**. I want to go _____.

20   First I turned on the **hot** tap and then I turned on the _____ one.

21   Andrea was **first**, but Sally was _____.

Underline the two words in each line which have similar meanings.

22–23   large   small   big

24–25   hard   easy   simple

26–27   weep   shout   sob

(Bond, 1987, p. 32)

(1.2)   Libra   (23 September–22 October)

Family members may grumble _____ a change in routine, but eventually they adjust to liking _____. Try to co-operate more with _____ at work and get better results. Avoid one who is _____ time waster.

Scorpio   (23 October–21 November)

Start early on business matters so _____ have more time for recreation. Be willing to try new procedures. _____ honest with mate, or spouse about expectations and hopes. Avoid unnecessary spending of _____.

(Moller and Whiteson 1981, p. 42)

Both examples here adopt a static view of language. The emphasis is on choosing correct words within a phrase or sentence. The uses of the language are internal to the system of the language; there is accordingly no emphasis on its use in a context. There is no clear purpose to the writing beyond the choice of correct words and there is no audience, other than the 'examiner', to take account of. There are no dynamic, interactive dimensions to the language required. The cloze test in example 1.2 gathers little evidence of the students' ability to use vocabulary appropriately; indeed, most of the gaps have to be filled by grammatical words (prepositions and deictics). The context or style of the text, the functions of particular features of language, the relationship *between* words, the existence of particular patterns are left out of account. The emphasis is on a static, decontextualized view of language as a particular set of forms. Above all, the assumption is that language exists wholly in a written form and not that written and spoken language coexist. Throughout this first chapter we explore and illustrate the relevance to language teaching, both EFL/ESL and

English as a mother tongue, of a discourse-based view of language. We begin with the relationship between spoken and written texts.

1.1 Speech and writing

The first and most immediate problem for a language teacher trying to identify a cross-section of the target language in the form of written texts or spoken material for presentation to learners is just how enormous and all-pervasive everyday language use is. The amount of language produced in one day, whether in written or spoken form, by even a relatively small number of people (for example, the population of one medium-sized town) is vast. It is probably impossible even to estimate the number of words produced by such a population in a twenty-four-hour span, let alone begin to analyse so much language. And yet it is clearly of importance to language teachers to know as much as can be known about people's day-to-day uses of language. Syllabuses and materials are necessarily selective in what they teach and usually classify their content in some way. The problems of how and what to select and how to classify are considerably lessened the more we know about actual language use. For the majority of language teachers, the most important need is a practical framework for exploiting what can be observed of people's day-to-day uses of language. Knowing how language works and how people use it is a first and indispensable step towards deciding what shall be taught, and is one of the components, along with knowledge of the psychology of learning and the social and cultural contexts of learning, which feed in to how we teach languages. We cannot hope to answer basic questions about the form and content of language teaching syllabuses and materials without subjecting their raw material, the target language, to close scrutiny. This chapter will therefore look at how discourse analysis has contributed to formulating ways of dividing up and classifying the everyday manifestations of language in use.

One traditional way of dividing language use which is reflected in practice in the language teaching profession is *spoken* versus *written*. Teachers often find themselves assigned as teachers of 'spoken skills' or teachers of 'writing', and the syllabus may equally have spoken and written language among its major divisions. The following is an extract from the contents page of an adult education foreign language-learning syllabus (ICC, 1986). It is typical of many such syllabuses in the assumptions it makes about dividing the world of discourse:

3.1   Language Skills and Level of Language Proficiency
3.1.1   Listening comprehension
3.1.2   Oral proficiency
3.1.3   Reading comprehension
3.1.4   Written expression

Under 'Written expression', the learner is expected to produce writing 'appropriate in expression', a statement which suggests that recognition of appropriateness in writing is part of linguistic competence. Similarly, publishers often divide their materials up along the written and spoken divide, and course-book titles reflect this. Such a division may serve practical purposes in vocational contexts, but it raises complex questions when looked at from a descriptive viewpoint, when we consider real language data.

For one thing, we have to distinguish between the *medium* that is used to communicate the message (see Crystal and Davy 1969: 68–70) and what we shall here call the *mode* of language which the sender of the message adopts. Medium refers to the overall distinction between linguistic messages transmitted to their receivers via phonic or graphic means, that is by sound or by writing, and is a basic practical division for the assembly of syllabuses and materials. It also involves us in finer distinctions of what Crystal and Davy (1969: 70) refer to as *complex medium*. For instance, a message may be written but intended to be delivered as speech (eg a university lecture), or spoken, but destined to be transmitted to its intended audience in writing (eg a statement at a press conference). Medium as a general heading, alongside the recognition of the existence of complex media, already provides us with quite a variety of categorizations for the world of text and discourse. But medium, as we shall see, needs to be accompanied by consideration of an independent level of choice, that of mode. Mode refers to choices that the sender makes as to whether features normally associated with speech or writing shall be included in the message, regardless of the medium in which it is to be transmitted. For example, a university lecture is usually transmitted to its audience using the medium of speech, but may well have many of the features associated with the mode of a written academic article (carefully planned and structured language, impersonal grammatical forms, etc). However, an advertisement transmitted through the medium of writing may immediately evoke a spoken, conversational mode of language use (direct address to the receiver, ellipted and contracted forms, etc). Other examples of language use may be quite neutral with regard to mode, regardless of the medium through which they are delivered. We use the term *mode* here differently from the way it is used by some linguists, especially Halliday, who, as we shall see in later chapters, uses it more to refer to channels of communication and the textual choices these relate to.

We shall illustrate our view of medium and mode with some samples of language taken out of the contexts in which they were actually used. In other words, you, the reader, will receive them through the written medium (this book). At the same time, you will almost certainly be able to make judgements as to whether a spoken or written mode is suggested by each extract, or whether the extract is neutral with regard to mode. The extracts come from a variety of sources.

(1.3)

A ... no, it'll shut. So, try it now. It's better ...

B ... are erased away. Now, wouldn't you like to change your image? ...

C ... and should be adjusted clockwise to reach the slowest speed while still ...

D ... so, you know, up I get, bad temper ...

E ... well, eventually he came home, and they had ...

F ... our answers to these questions may not be definitive or complete, but even if ...

G ... your worries are over. Far from it. The little so-and-so's will turn up again ...

H ... opportunities in space. Well, not strictly in space, but in space research ...

I ... well, the place is gone now; not a stone remains ...

J ... into my eyes and said nothing. Well, it was a good defence ...

Fifty-five informants (consisting of native- and non-native speakers of English) were asked to tag each extract for mode, whether predominantly 'spoken' or 'written'. Almost everyone agreed that extracts A and D suggested spoken language; a sizeable number also thought that extracts E, G and H evoked speech rather than writing.[1] Extracts C and F were thought by significant majorities to evoke writing, while extracts B, I and J caused more of a division of opinion or were felt to be neutral. Such patterning of response is significant, given the small amount of language in each extract, and suggests that people have as part of their general linguistic competence a very strong sense of what uses of language are appropriate to spoken contexts and what to written. The spoken/written divide seems to be deeply rooted in terms of recognition of modes and their appropriacy to contexts. This broad, intuitive division of modes could form an alternative basis for the classification of the world of discourse separately from the broader division of medium. For the syllabus or materials designer, dividing the raw material solely in terms of medium (put simply, 'tape versus text', or 'speaking versus writing') is too blunt an instrument. A piece of written language may well be ideal for teaching features of spoken mode, just as a piece of recorded spoken language may prove perfectly suitable for extracting features of written mode. We are, though, left first with the question of what the features of different modes are that enable them to be recognized so easily, and second, what the relationships are between modes and their contexts of use, that is to say, their appropriacy for the performing of specific tasks and achieving specific outcomes through language, and for the creation of forms of discourse which can realize those goals in conventionally acceptable ways. Sections 1.1, 1.2, 1.3 and 1.4 deal with the first question, sections 1.5 and 1.6 with the second. Our overriding concern will be to examine in what ways the description of media and modes is relevant to language teaching and we shall be seeking to answer questions such as the following:

1   Can modes be sufficiently differentiated at the very practical levels of grammar and lexis?
2   Can we isolate the key grammatical and lexical features that play a major role in creating larger discourses (eg a news report, a recipe, a lecture)?
3   Can syllabuses and materials incorporate the descriptive statements that we shall be making and meet learners' needs more efficiently?
4   Will the resultant syllabus/materials represent the target language more faithfully?

The informants who judged our ten data extracts in example 1.3 often referred to aspects of language form (rather than content) when asked to justify their decisions. For instance, extract A, as well as containing a free-standing *no*, a form associated with dialogue, also has a direct imperative and two contracted verb forms, part of what we might call 'the grammar of informal speech'. Extract G was felt to contain colloquial lexical expressions (*far from it, little so-and-so's*, etc), and a moodless sentence (ie one not containing a clause in declarative, interrogative or imperative form: again *far from it*) and was therefore, like A, associated with spoken mode for grammatical and lexical reasons. Extracts B, E, H, I and J all contain conjunctive items such as *now*, and *well* (which we shall later call *discourse markers*; see Schiffrin 1987), which are typical of speech, and which Biber (1988: 241) claims to be 'rare outside of the conversational genres'. Extract D contains what was felt to be a resultative *so* and a *you know* (again interpretable as discourse markers), and a very high level of ellipsis in (*I was in a*) *bad temper*, argued to be typical of the grammar of spoken mode. Extract C contains grammatical features felt more likely to occur in written mode: a passive verb and a non-finite *while*-clause, and extract F has what was felt to be 'written' vocabulary (*definitive/complete*). Some informants also felt that extract I had a written 'literary' feel to it because of *not a stone remains*.

Our informants were using grammatical and lexical forms as evidence of mode, a fact which should serve as a constant reminder that, even when we are examining whole texts and discourses and their internal structuring on a large scale (eg what constitutes a 'story' or a 'service encounter'), as we shall do frequently in this book, we should never ignore the significance of grammatical and lexical choice in creating these larger artifacts. Chapter 3 will concentrate on this linking of levels between grammar/lexis and discourse.

Our informants also displayed another type of competence: a willingness to accept that the instances of spoken and written modes that they had identified were no guarantee that the original sources of the extracts were necessarily spoken ones for the extracts with 'spoken mode' or written ones for those with 'written mode'. In other words, they are quite used to elements of one mode commonly occurring in discourses delivered in the opposite medium. No one is surprised that written advertisements for consumer goods (from which extracts B and G are taken) should utilize features of spoken mode. Equally, the informants accepted without any objection that extracts I and J were from a literary source, in which the narrator was 'speaking directly' to the reader. The source for extracts I and J is Sean O'Faoláin's novel *Bird Alone* (1985: pp. 56 and 129), in which the author often uses discourse markers such as *well*, *still*, and *anyway* to evoke a conversational mode of narrative. Advertisements for consumer goods and novels may, conventionally, contain elements of spoken mode. This permissibility or otherwise of particular features is one of the aspects of what we shall term *genre* in section 1.5. However, the informants had far greater difficulty in coming to terms with the source of extract H, which is taken from a British quality newspaper in the section advertising academic posts in colleges and universities. The advertisement was headlined as follows:

(1.4)   UNIVERSITY OF BIRMINGHAM
OPPORTUNITIES IN SPACE
Well, not strictly in space,
but in Space Research

(*Guardian*, 15 September 1987: 20)

After the headline came the usual details of the post advertised. No other academic post advertised in the newspaper on that day (or to the best of our knowledge, before or since) contained an item such as the discourse marker *well*, used here in what Quirk et al (1985: 1313) call a 'claim editing' function, so instantly redolent of spoken mode. This advertisement was, therefore, seen to be breaking the conventions of academic job advertisements, which are clearly different from those of consumer goods advertisements, even though both types of advertisements appear in the written medium, in newspapers or magazines, and may be aimed at the same or similar readers. Our advertisement breaks the conventions to great effect: the space research post stands out in an otherwise uniform, lacklustre broadsheet of job ads all adhering to 'written mode'. Such creativity, where it occurs, is based on a strong sense of what the norm is. Unwitting use of speech markers in writing may be negatively evaluated, as sometimes occurs in student essay-writing (in L1 and L2); *well* as a claim-editing marker in a university essay is likely to be frowned upon.

What we have tried to demonstrate so far is that spoken and written language not only are associated with different media of communication (eg radio versus newspaper) and thereby different linguistic products (eg written essay versus tape-recorded speech), but also have evolved different modes or types of language use which are conventionally related to different contexts and different types of discourse. The emergence of such mode differentiation can be traced historically (see Biber and Finegan 1989), but that is not our main concern here. What is also apparent is that spoken and written modes can be used creatively in untypical contexts, but that it is *typicality* which is the foundation of our linguistic competence in this respect. It is typical, for instance, for written instructions to be expressed as in extract C (which comes from a set of instructions for a door-closing device), just as extract F is typical of written academic text (with its first person pronoun, its modal *may*, and its vocabulary). However, typicality is more restricted in some contexts than others (see Crystal and Davy 1969: 63–6); there is more scope for creativity in advertising text than in the composition of legal statutes, and the text of a church sermon can break its conventions with greater ease than the text of a religious litany. Therefore, on the long cline representing the admixing of modes that will be found in different products of the spoken and written media, products will be archetypically more 'written' or more 'spoken' in their features of mode than others. Archetypical of the written will be legal statutes, business letters and reports, academic texts, reference books, etc. Archetypical of the spoken will be casual conversations and 'language-in-action' (language used in the service of performing some real-world task; such was the case in extract A, where two people are attending to a troublesome door-closing mechanism), real-life dramas such as TV soap operas, and so on. In between, we shall find many products that can hop freely from one mode to another: the personal letter, the poem, the press conference, the sales pitch, and, as we have seen, the literary text or the consumer goods advertisement.

What we find, therefore, when we look at the world of spoken and written language, is a complex of relationships between language forms and contexts of use, certainly not a simple division between written and spoken media. The selection of discourse-types for inclusion in the syllabus or in materials will therefore ideally be done within a framework that enables us first, to present the linguistic features that distinguish spoken from written modes, second to present a range of written texts and spoken material that adequately reflects the broader and narrower restrictions on appropriacy of occurrence of spoken and written modes in particular contexts, and third, to present at least some examples of creativity and norm-breaking to set the norms in relief and to underline their power in creating conventionally acceptable products. Although medium of communication will be a relevant choice in the syllabus or materials design, it will not be the only one, and language courses exclusively concerned with either spoken or written skills will be enriched by encounters with a variety of media of presentation, carefully selected to reflect the sets of features deemed necessary to teach.

1.2 Frameworks for classifying spoken and written modes

Descriptive linguists have devoted much energy to classifying spoken and written modes, and have approached the task from different angles. We have stated that our informants were using the evidence of the presence of certain linguistic forms to assign a mode to any given stretch of language, and the presence or absence of forms has been the basis of classic studies of speech and writing, such as Crystal and Davy (1969). Crystal and Davy offer an inventory of linguistic forms (syntactic, lexical, phonological) and use these to examine, among other types, conversational language, newspaper reports and religious language. The language forms are examined within a framework that isolates relevant features of the situation, such as medium, the relationship between participants, what they call modality (eg the choice between sending a written message as a letter, a postcard or a memo), and so on. Significant correlations between occurrences of forms and situational features enable variations in language use to be mapped systematically. Other linguists have attempted to relate formal differences to broader functional scales and clines in an attempt to establish the basic characteristics that differentiate speech and writing. For instance, Chafe (1982) uses functional categories such as *explicit* versus *implicit*, and *context-free* versus *context-dependent* to describe characteristic aspects of written and spoken modes, respectively. Thus our extract A in example 1.3 contains language which is implicit and heavily context-dependent (eg *try it* and *better*), while extract E (the set of written instructions for the door-closure mechanism being serviced in extract A) comes from a text which can be read and to a great extent interpreted in isolation from the actual context in which it is intended to be used, thanks to its explicit vocabulary. However, terms such as *implicit* and *explicit* are not absolutes, and are to be seen as tendencies rather than as sufficient or necessary conditions for classification. For instance, it could be argued that the passive-voice verb in extract E (often deemed so typical of written mode) leaves its addressee implicit, while extract B, although containing an element of spoken mode (*now*), has quite explicit vocabulary and comes from a text which provides its own context and is 'free-standing'.

Challenges to the dangers of over-simplification of this type of categorization can be found in Tannen (1982a) and Mazzie (1987). Mazzie, for instance, found in her data that *content* rather than what she calls *modality* (which we have referred to as *medium* or channel of communication) was a greater determinant of features such as implicitness: written and spoken data with abstract subject matter contained more 'inferrable' information than narrative data, regardless of whether they were in spoken or written medium. Tannen also notes that contrasts such as *implicit/explicit* depend on higher-order influences such as *register* (the relationship between language forms and features of the context) and *genre* (see section 1.6), rather than merely on medium of communication. Likewise, Ure's (1971) study of lexical density (the relative density in a message between lexical and grammatical items) found that density variation depended on what was being done when language was being used (eg language-in-action), rather than simply on a spoken–written medium division.

The work of Biber and Finegan provides an expanded framework for the study of form and function in spoken and written modes and the classification of discourse types. Biber and Finegan (1989) use three sets of oppositions to distinguish written from spoken features and relate these to how language forms cluster in different spoken and written texts. The written versus spoken oppositions are

1 informational versus involved production
2 elaborated versus situation-dependent reference
3 abstract versus non-abstract style.

These terms are not unlike the sets of oppositions already discussed, and, once again, are best viewed as tendencies rather than absolutes ('abstract style', for instance, includes counts of agentless passive voices). With large-scale computer analyses (see especially Biber 1988), it is possible to see tendencies towards the clustering of certain forms (and their assigned functions) in different discourse types. In their historical study of seventeenth- to twentieth-century fiction, essays and letters, Biber and Finegan (1989) observe a drift towards more 'spoken' characteristics occurring in written texts, underlining the point we have already made about the need to differentiate medium and mode. More interestingly, Biber (1988) shows how the relationship between different discourse types changes depending on what one is measuring. For example, on the scale of *explicit* versus *situation-dependent* reference (*explicit* here meaning references that can be decoded without recourse to the situation), written texts such as official documents and academic prose contain more explicit references than do editorials, biographies and spoken discourses such as spontaneous speeches and prepared speeches (Biber 1988: 143). However, within this particular scale, biographies and spontaneous speeches are not significantly different from each other, and personal letters and adventure fiction score about the same as face-to-face conversation, again making the point that features of mode generate a different classification from that based only on medium. When the same sets of texts are subjected to measurement in terms of the presence or absence of *narrative* elements (see section 2.7), written fiction of various kinds scores most highly, but now spontaneous and prepared speeches move higher up the scale while press editorials move lower down than their previous position (Biber 1988: 136). What Biber calls *popular lore* texts (eg informative texts in popular magazines), although low in narrative concerns, are located towards the *situation dependent* end of the scale of reference, in which respect they are close to spoken discourses, and might thus be considered as a possible source for features of spoken mode in the context of the language teaching syllabus or materials.

Promising though such techniques as Biber and Finegan's cluster analyses might be as a way of dividing up the complex world of discourse, there are problems with the assignment of functional categories, the biggest danger being that the categories are assigned *a priori* to language forms, thereby entrapping the analyst in the circular exercise of proving what one has already decided to be the case from the very beginning. However, our informant test quoted above shows a uniformity of intuition among practising teachers and students of language (which the informants were) that cannot be neglected and which can serve as a reliable, common-sense basis for assigning functional significance to particular language forms. Once intuitive decisions have been made and reaffirmed concerning overall modes, finer classifications must be made through closer scrutiny of what forms occur in particular sets of texts, and it is to such other possible divisions we now turn.

1.3   Applying and refining frameworks

In this section we shall apply some of the principles outlined in the previous sections to real texts and see what adaptations or refinements can be made to existing approaches.

The literary text is often thought of as a prime example of the written medium, and yet, as we have already suggested, literary texts show a remarkable freedom of mixing of modes. Tannen (1989) makes the point that a range of features typical of conversation can be found in literary texts. As well as the obvious techniques of using various ways of expressing the speech of characters (whether as direct, indirect, or 'free-direct' and 'free-indirect' speech), the writer can also vary his or her own relationship with the reader by changing modes. O'Faoláin's novel *Bird Alone*, which we used in our test extracts I and J in example 1.3, shifts from a typical 'written' mode of narration to passages where features strongly associated with conversational speech and oral story-telling are included. Note the contrast between the neutrality and typicality of literary narration in example 1.5 and the spoken-record features of example 1.6, even though both are the narrator's words and both have first-person pronouns.

> (1.5)   When I visited Youghal towards the middle of March I found that Marion had discovered everything except my part in the affair. It had eased Elise a little to share her secret with another woman, but a hunted look caught her when she saw the horror with which Marion heard her confession.
>
> (O'Faoláin 1985: 262)

> (1.6)   Oh, Gilabbey was a good place to live in, all right, the very names a history of Ireland: Saint Finbarr's, Dean Street, Bishop Street, Cat Fort, the South-Gate Bridge a stone's throw away, Wandesford Quay (some Lord Lieutenant or other), Hanover Street across the river, Saint Mary's-of-the-Isle at our back door. As a boy, I need hardly say, we accepted it in the all too easy acceptance, the lovely too-innocent acceptance of childhood.
>
> (O'Faoláin 1985: 12)

The point to be noted here is that example 1.6, no less than example 1.5, contains canonical features of literary style and vocabulary (the dense pre-modification and syntactic parallelism of 'the all too easy acceptance, the lovely too-innocent acceptance'); it is no less 'literary' despite its markers of spoken mode (*Oh, all right, I need hardly say*). Cultures with a long tradition of oral story-telling, such as O'Faoláin's native Ireland, may be expected to reflect the tension between the oral-literary and the written-literary (an argument taken up by Nagy 1989), but the point for our present concerns is that a category heading such as 'literary text' in a syllabus will need careful consideration before it is subdivided. Syllabuses often treat literary text as a separate world from other, more everyday texts, and yet it is in literary text that we can find an extremely wide range of modes of speech and writing, such that many literary texts will display features of spoken mode similar to those found in advertising texts, while others may display the planning and structuring, the detachment and explicitness of technical or academic writing. Short and Candlin (1986) are committed to the view that using a wide variety of different, non-literary texts is an important way to promote a fuller appreciation of literature in the classroom. Once again, what the syllabus and materials choose to bring together under one heading or adjacent to one another in a teaching unit or exercise will vary greatly depending on initial classificational criteria. On a cline of 'features of spokenness', extracts from O'Faoláin's novel may well end up higher than extracts from a party-political broadcast on radio.

But just what might the subdivisions of an alternative framework based on modes of language look like? Our task here is not to compose a complete syllabus, but we can point to the kinds of criteria that might be usable. One such criterion could be to sub-classify texts according to the notion of *reciprocity*, that is the degree of 'presence' or 'absence' of senders and receivers in the text itself and the overt signals that denote awareness of a sender–receiver relationship. For example, the kinds of features we have noted in our test samples may be plotted on scales designed to indicate 'presence or absence of a speaker' and 'presence or absence of a writer'. Smith (1986) provides us with an example of a scale for measuring 'formality' and 'informality' in written texts, where the greater degree of reciprocal marking of the presence of the writer/reader spells the greater informality. The scale offers the potential of adaptation for examining mode variation, and might look something like example 1.7.

As we work down the scale, the more of the centre-column

(1.7)

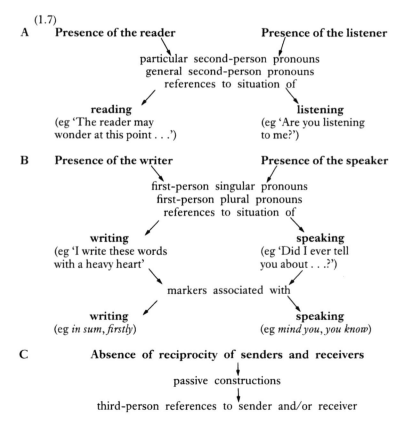

A   **Presence of the reader**   **Presence of the listener**

particular second-person pronouns
general second-person pronouns
references to situation of

reading   **listening**
(eg 'The reader may   (eg 'Are you listening
wonder at this point . . .')   to me?')

B   **Presence of the writer**   **Presence of the speaker**

first-person singular pronouns
first-person plural pronouns
references to situation of

writing   **speaking**
(eg 'I write these words   (eg 'Did I ever tell
with a heavy heart'   you about . . .?')

markers associated with

writing   **speaking**
(eg *in sum, firstly*)   (eg *mind you, you know*)

C   **Absence of reciprocity of senders and receivers**

passive constructions

third-person references to sender and/or receiver

features that accrue for any given text in categories A and B, the more the sender/receiver function is foregrounded, and the more features it displays from either the left-hand forks (written mode features) or the right-hand forks (spoken-mode features), the more achetypical that piece of language becomes of its particular mode. In category C are features that militate against sender/receiver reciprocity. This allows for texts not displaying reciprocal features or displaying 'absence of reciprocity' features (which will then be recorded as neutral) and for mode-mixing, which may display both left-hand and right-hand features. Where features are listed in common, this allows both for neutrality of mode and for the fact that few texts will ever display a total absence or exclusive presence of these particular features (see Crystal and Davy 1969: 63). For example, passive voices have no exclusive privilege of occurrence in written mode. The scale takes only a selection of features considered relevant to the notion of reciprocal foregrounding of sender and receiver and could be expanded or contracted for different practical needs. Other scales might use other features. For instance, we might have a scale measuring 'degree of intimacy', where contracted verb-forms might appear as markers of intimate spoken mode, with the impersonal pronoun *one* as a marker of 'absence of intimacy' in either mode. Contracted verb-forms would cover the many cases where, in written text, intimacy is created by deliberate switching to features strongly associated with spoken mode. Yet another scale might examine degrees of projections of shared knowledge, and distinguish between the kinds of ellipsis common in spoken mode (eg subject ellipsis) from those more common in written (eg subject and verb in certain sub-clauses, as in 'The substance, when mixed with water . . .').

If we apply our scale of reciprocity to a section of a written advertisement text for sun-tan lotion, we see how the relevant features enable us to characterize the text for mode.

(1.8)   **BROWNIES GO AS DEEP AS THEY CAN**
Would you like to tan deeper than you've ever tanned before? And faster?
Well, New Formula Bergasol has been specially formulated to help everyone do just that.
And we do mean everyone.
From the fairest of the fair to those lucky enough to have a head start.
(*Cosmopolitan*, May 1989: 80)

The text contains a particular second person pronoun (*you*), a first-person plural one (*we*), and third-person references to the receiver ('as deep as they can', 'those lucky enough'). It also has a spoken discourse marker (*well*), and a passive (*has been specially formulated*).

Even this small amount of text shows the characteristic mixing of features typical of consumer advertising, with a tendency towards evoking spoken mode (marked especially by *well*), but often resorting to written mode features for technical details of the product advertised.

The possibilities for adaptation of such scales are many, and, as we have stressed, they start from a basis of people's strong intuitive sense of the features of different modes of language use, rather than somewhat arbitrary divisions such as 'literary' versus 'journalistic' text. Whether we start from a randomly chosen corpus of texts and work towards classifying them or start from the other end, as it were, and specify the varieties of language that need to be covered and then go out to look for actual examples, frameworks of the kind we have been considering here for describing language use will be necessary, and will become quite complex as we further subdivide, as we hope our examples show.

1.4   Monologue and dialogue

The sun-tan lotion advertisement (example 1.8) contains another feature that we have not attended to, and that is a direct question to the reader ('Would you like to tan deeper . . .?'), which raises another major dividing criterion for the world of text and discourse, that between *monologue* and *dialogue*. In a sense, of course, the advertisement is a monologue (by the writer or pseudo-speaker, without any overt textual contribution by a second party). However, the question to the reader, and especially the presence of the marker *well*, suggest a possible dialogic structure for the text where the receiver's 'reply' is understood:

(1.9)
SENDER: Would you like to tan deeper than you've ever tanned before?
(RECEIVER: Yes! Who wouldn't?)
SENDER: Well, New Formula Bergasol has been . . . etc.

The question can then be seen as a topic-opener, and the *well* as marking the beginning of the main topic. Such opening sequences are quite common in spoken narratives ('Shall I tell you what happened to me yesterday?' – 'Yes' – 'Well, I was walking along the street, when . . . etc').

The monologue versus dialogue distinction cuts across considerations such as medium and mode, and needs separate consideration. Here we are not simply concerned with whether one person or more than one is represented as speaking *overtly*, that is *on the surface* of the text, but whether there is evidence in the text of the sender taking into account and adjusting the text accordingly, for a (projected or assumed) response by the receiver to the message as a whole and its subcomponents. Of course, in a sense, all linguistic messages must be sensitive to their receivers, as language is rarely, if ever, addressed into empty space with no intention of being received by anyone, but senders can make their receivers' assumed responses more, or less, overt in the text, or not take them into account at all. Texts that show no overt evidence of taking the receiver into account will be considered maximally monologic, and texts which depend crucially on overt receiver response or which explicitly include assumed receiver response, will be considered maximally dialogic. Once again, we are dealing with a scale, rather than absolutes. At the extreme dialogic end of the scale we shall find spoken 'conversations' of various kinds (traditionally understood as virtually synonymous with 'dialogue'). But we shall also find written forms of various kinds, which are incomplete as discourses until they have been filled in by the form-filler, and are thus truly dialogic. At the extreme of monologue, we shall find the internal monologues of 'stream-of-consciousness' writing, personal diaries, reference texts (eg encyclopedia entries) and certain types of 'uninterruptable' speech-forms (eg recitations, formal lectures, judges' summing-up speeches, church sermons). In between, there will be degrees of monologue and dialogue, and mixtures of both.

A typically monologic text is this extract from a book about the Russian language:

> (1.10)   A living language is continually changing, even in a small community. Usually, linguistic changes take place so slowly that it is only by looking back over at least several decades that one can detect changes. The most obvious changes in the language of a large, sophisticated community occur in the field of vocabulary, for in such a community new words are constantly being created and old words discarded.
> (D Ward 1965 *The Russian Language Today*. London: Hutchinson
> University Library, p. 17)

We could say a number of things about this text in terms of mode and register. It contains a conjunctive *for*, typical of written mode, its vocabulary is formal, and it contains an impersonal pronoun *one*. But further to these features we may observe that no overt signs exist of the possible response of the reader to the information being transmitted. In our terms, therefore, this text is highly monologic. Compare this with a typically dialogic advertising text. Example 1.11

is from an advertisement for a whirlpool bath; it constantly adjusts its message for how the copy-writer imagines the reader will be reacting to the information, and what sorts of questions the reader will want answered. This foregrounding of the reader is overtly evidenced in the change from impersonal, passive constructions in the first paragraph of technical description to direct, second-person address, and projected 'modalized' (ie concerned with possibilities) clauses in paragraph-initial positions (here in italics), foregrounding the reader's assumed responses.

> (1.11)   For convenience and safety the control unit should be fixed to the wall and permanently wired. A wall mounting kit and instructions which explain everything clearly are included in the pack.
> However, *if you are worried* about installing the unit yourself, it's a simple task for a competent electrician.
> *You need not have any doubts* about fixing this product in your bathroom. Every part of the Homespa has been put through the most rigorous tests by a government approved testing house. (Even the people who tested it were tested.) Regina is the world's largest whirlpool manufacturer and once the unit has been correctly installed it meets British safety standards.
> *All this may lead you to think* that it will cost a fortune, but at just under £100.00 the Homespa is a great way to enjoy a health spa in the comfort of your own home.
>
> (*Cosmopolitan's Zest*, May 1988: 49)

This text contains strong dialogic elements: both participants, sender and receiver, are considered as having a right to an input into its message, just as would occur in a real conversation. Dialogic elements in texts include projected questions that the receiver might want answered (a common type of 'rhetorical' question), discourse markers that presuppose a contribution by another participant (such as the *well* of the sun tan ad in example 1.8) and actual inclusion of what a second party's contributions might have been. This last type of feature is exemplified in example 1.12, from a British football fan magazine, a type of magazine which characteristically recreates the conversations that fans have among themselves after football matches (see McCarthy 1992b). Here, the author and the reader's 'parts' in the dialogue are represented in the text. The writer is discussing the behaviour of the police at a match and criticizing their decisions:

> (1.12)   So what's the sensible option, obviously number 1, but what do the police do, take number 2 – dead stupid.
>
> (*Ugly Inside*, Southampton, issue no. 10)

Questions and their supposed responses are both present in the text, and the dialogic mode is foregrounded.

Literary narratives are often divided into 'third-person' and 'first-person' narratives. In the third-person narrative, the voice addressing the reader is that of the author, who recounts events as they occurred to fictional or historical characters. In the first-person narrative, the voice that the reader hears is that of the main character, to whom the events of the story happened or are happening. It is this latter type which is often referred to as 'monologue', and yet, as many literary critics have shown, the 'monologue' novel, in our terms, often contains overt references to the presence of the 'listener', and is much more truly 'dialogic' than third-person narration. Clews has made the point that the monologue novel offers 'The stylized presentation of a background which the reader as audience shares with the apparent speaker' (Clews 1985: 13). Monologue narratives are, like dramatic and poetic monologues, 'addressed to a listener whose presence is overtly acknowledged by the speaker' (Clews 1985: 15).

The degree of overt reference to the listener/reader varies, and factors such as the use of questions, projected dialogue and interactive discourse markers will be relevant in literary as much as in other kinds of texts. Therefore, literary texts need not be seen as some peculiar phenomenon difficult to integrate into the textual world of language learning syllabuses and materials. On the monologue–dialogue scale their status will be determined in relation to many other text types, including lectures, sermons, diaries, advertisements, and so on.

So far, we have examined various ways in which texts can be classified as a means of representing a wide range of language in our syllabus. But classifying according to surface textual features ignores the fact that language users create discourses that are appropriate in form and content to whatever activity they are engaged in. It is to the institutionalized aspects of the relationship between textual forms and particular activities that we now turn.

1.5 Text typologies

A separation of texts into broadly spoken and written categories is one way of dividing up the world of language and texts. Language courses also divide up teaching programmes between speaking and writing, between, for example, 'intermediate conversation' and 'advanced writing' classes. Beyond this, teachers and learners are conscious of a whole range of texts – simultaneously exciting and bewildering in their variety – which can enter the classroom in various forms and on which teaching can be based. Making appropriate selections from this rich and diverse textual world requires careful judgement if students are to extract maximum linguistic benefit from their contact with the selected texts. For some teachers the selections can be conveniently constrained. Students may, for example, be specializing in particular fields and may wish to learn English only in order to read material on banking and economics or to understand the language of air-traffic control. By contrast, mother-tongue students of English may be judged to benefit from exposure to as eclectic but balanced a variety of texts as possible. However, most groups of language learners and their teachers do have to make selections. One of the main criteria for selection is that of *usefulness*. In this connection a key question is: will the types of texts presented or studied in class be of maximum benefit to a developing competence in using the language?

As we have seen, two of the main categories into which language may be divided are speech and writing. Another main way in which language may be segmented is according to *subject matter* or *topic*. In educational settings, in particular, a wide range of textbooks exists with titles such as *The Language of Banking, The Language of Motor Engineering, The Language of Biology* – all offering a reassuring promise of demystification of specialized terms.

A further important parameter is the relationship which is constructed between participants. The tone established between a speaker and an audience or a reader and a writer is affected by the different language choices. Thus books on motor engineering will vary in the language used according to audience and purpose. A book for the specialist or specialist in training will involve linguistic choices different from a book on the same topic for the do-it-yourself enthusiast. Similarly an article on economics in a popular newspaper will be different stylistically from one in an academic journal. The different choices in vocabulary, grammar and discourse structure signal a different relationship between sender and receiver for the text. We have noted though that changes in the mode – particularly within the parameters of spoken and written styles – regularly determine the variety of language produced. And closely related to usefulness is a criterion of *relevance*: are the texts sufficiently central to contexts of use likely to be encountered by the learner?

Selecting texts as classroom material according to criteria of relevance and usefulness is a complex undertaking. It is difficult, for example, to gauge relative frequencies of occurrence of different text types; in many domains people will *read* certain types of texts more than they will *write* them or produce them *orally*.

Our main argument in the remainder of this chapter is that insights from discourse analysis can help teachers refine their decision-making processes of text selection and can help them towards a more principled basis on which – in their roles as syllabus/course designers and materials writers – they can organize their textual examples in purposeful and progressive ways.

1.5.1 Theories of language variation

One powerful theory of language variation – which can be of particular use to teachers – has been developed by Michael Halliday (see Halliday 1989 for a restatement of it). It will be seen that Halliday's theory lays great emphasis on categories of language such as spoken and written and on the kinds of parameters of variation outlined above.

Both as underlying concepts and as descriptive categories the main terms used by Halliday are: *field, tenor,* and *mode* of discourse. As concepts they help to explain how language users interpret the social contexts or textual environments in which meanings are made. As descriptive terms, *field* refers broadly to the 'subject matter' or topic of a stretch of language (eg the weather, geography, the local football team's failure). It refers to what is happening in a discourse, what a particular 'text' is about. It also includes what Benson and Greaves (1981) refer to as the *institutional focus* of the discourse, how speakers and writers orient their language towards socially and institutionally accepted norms (for example, the use of particular collocations that identify the text as belonging to a certain field: *'click* the *mouse'*, for instance, suggests the field of computers rather than zoology). *Tenor* refers to the roles of the participants, their respective status and power, within a communicative exchange. In particular, such role relationships will affect the formality of the language used in the text, both in spoken and written contexts. The *mode* refers rather more directly to what the language is doing itself as a channel of communication – that is, is it spoken or written or some combination of the two? This, as we have noted, is a slightly different use of *mode* from our use of the term. Halliday's terms can be summarized as follows:

Field – What is happening? What is the text about?
Tenor– Who are taking part?
Mode – What is the language itself doing?

Halliday's account of language variation is often referred to as a *functional* approach. He is not interested in linguistic features for their own sakes; neither is he primarily interested in sentence or clause level descriptions of linguistic forms. His main interest is in the functions which are realized by such forms in a variety of different kinds of texts. The theory lays an emphasis on language as social semiotic, on language variation in relation to social contexts, on descriptions of language according to the user (dialects) and according to use (diatypes or *registers*). The term 'register' is a widely employed one and we shall continue to refer to it here.

In fact, the notion of register is widely agreed to be a useful way of systematizing the diversity of textual variation in a language. It can certainly help teachers who wish to have broad classifications of texts for teaching purposes. It also offers a clear and accessible framework for students enhancing their language awareness by learning not simply to use language but to learn *about* language and reflect on how it varies in different contexts of use (see section 4.9).

Yet the notion of register is not without its problems; indeed the more it is investigated, the more slippery and difficult to pin down it becomes. One of the main reasons for this is that both dialects and registers (diatypes) form a continuum and may overlap in various areas and in varying degrees. Some registers contain predictable features of language and a one-to-one correspondence between language and situation can be posited. For example, certain lexical items (eg *hereditament, affidavit*) and certain orthographic conventions (eg no punctuation in wills, testaments and contracts) are exclusively associated with the language of law. Some registers such as the language of air-traffic control are even more restricted.

Other registers also appear to be stylistically straightforward. For example, there would seem to be a limited set of features associated with weather-forecasting in a language, namely a set of domain-specific lexical items such as *front, high pressure, trough, ground-frost, depression, anti-cyclone*, etc, together with a set of syntactic structures which enable reference to future time and which allow appropriate prediction. But a little thought will reveal that there are as many weather forecasts as there are situations in which such forecasts are made. A weather forecast in a newspaper will be different from a TV or radio broadcast; there will be differences in formality between newspapers and between different TV and radio channels in that the mode of presentation will presume different audiences. A shipping forecast is likely to be much more specialized, detailed and geographically specific compared with a breakfast television national weather report. It is thus clear, as Wallace (1981) argues, that 'we must be able to talk about how one register fits into the overall pattern of registers in a variety of language' while at the same time being able to 'account for variation in the actual features of more than one occurrence of one register'. Wallace notes additionally that a number of registers can be adequately defined only because they *mix* styles or interweave different registerial features.

Teachers who prepare students for the kinds of transactional writing required of them in the world of work often stress the centrality of *reports* in the domains of discourse they are likely to encounter. In fact, it is difficult to envisage situations of work in which reports would not be quite regularly required of employees at whatever level in an organization they were employed. However, it could be argued that there are as many registers of report as there are people writing or delivering them. Reports might, for example, be required in the following contexts and for the following main purposes:

- A foreman/forewoman reporting on the condition of some machinery or on how a piece of machinery works.
- A nurse reporting on the progress of a patient.
- A sales representative reporting on action undertaken in response to a survey.
- A supervisor completing an annual performance report.
- An interviewer writing up a report of a recently conducted interview.
- A student writing a report of an experiment.
- A student completing a report reviewing a language course he or she has just undergone.

The examples indicate that the writing of the reports is more likely to be the province of first or, occasionally, second language learners but it is a key text-type none the less. Yet the report itself as a type of writing or 'register' is not as homogeneous or as well defined as the singular term 'report' may suggest. Carter (1990a) argues that a 'report' can be institutionally variable, that is different kinds of writing can constitute a report from one company or business organization to another or from one subject domain to another in a school or college. Even within the same company reports can mean different things to different departments.

It is also the case that reports often do more than they are conventionally assumed to do: store or present general facts or information. Much depends on the *purpose* of a report. Reports can be evaluative, can recommend a course of action or can investigate phenomena or events in a highly specific manner. In each case the report will involve different forms of language and will result in texts with contrasting styles.

There is clearly a danger here that the notion of register becomes so slippery as to be impractical for purposes of defining different types of text. However, the very existence of the term *report* as well as other terms such as *narrative* or *argument* or *exposition* indicate a shared intuitive awareness of the existence of such texts and that they differ from one another in recognizable ways.

1.6   Genres

The idea that there may be underlying recurrent features which are prototypically present in particular groups of texts is an important one in language teaching at the present time. Indeed, it complements theories which posit a correlation between language use and specific situations. Such a correlation is assumed in many language courses which stress that they are situational, based on teaching how language is used in a range of communicative contexts such as at the post office; in the bank; shopping in the supermarket; at customs, and so on. Often such courses stress spoken proficiency and are deemed to be of especial value to students living, working or holidaying in a country of the target language. Work on the analysis of spoken genres may be of particular relevance in describing the patterns of communication to be found in such contexts. Functional descriptions of text of the kind undertaken by Ruqaiya Hasan and others are a useful starting-point (eg Hasan 1978).

Following the examples of Mitchell (1957), who studied the language of specific social encounters within Libyan culture, Hasan (1978) has studied service encounters of the kind where someone seeks a service from another, such as in a doctor's surgery or buying and selling within a market. Following Hasan, Ventola (1987) has analysed service encounters within a post office, a small souvenir/gift shop and a travel agency. In example 1.13 the data are drawn from a post-office exchange:

(1.13)
SERVER: Yes please [rising tone]
                    [customer turns to server]
CUSTOMER: Six stamps please
                    [server gets stamps and server hands the stamps over the
                    counter]

SERVER: A dollar twenty
[customer hands over a $20 note to server]
SERVER: Thank you
twenty dollars
[server gets the change]
SERVER: It's a dollar twenty
that's . . . two four five ten and ten is twenty
thank you
CUSTOMER: Thanks very much

(Ventola 1987: 3)

Ventola argues that most encounters in shops in Western culture follow this structure: *an offer of service* → *a request for service* → *a transaction* → *a salutation*. It is this structure which, for example, differentiates the genre of a service encounter from the genre of bidding at an auction. The underlying pattern will, naturally, have different surface realizations which will create different *registers*, but it is the underlying pattern itself which genre analysts are keen to capture. Two real examples of service encounters will illustrate this. The first is a traditional British fish-and-chip shop, the second a shoe shop, also in Britain:

(1.14)
ASSISTANT: Erm . . .?
CUSTOMER: Yeah . . . can I have chips, beans and a battered sausage.
ASSISTANT: Chips, beans and a battered sausage.
CUSTOMER: Yeah.
[assistant makes up customer's order]
ASSISTANT: Wrapped up?
CUSTOMER: Open, please.
ASSISTANT: 91 . . . 1–26. 1–26.
[customer pays, change is given]
ASSISTANT: Goodbye, young man.
CUSTOMER: Ta.
ASSISTANT: Bless you.

(Mark Bishop's unpublished data, 1991)

(1.15)
ASSISTANT: Would you like any help?
CUSTOMER: Can I try these on?
[customer hands assistant a shoe]
ASSISTANT: Is that the right size for you?
CUSTOMER: I think so. Do you have the other one to these as well?
[then follow twenty-five turns of conversation between the assistant and customer before the customer pays for the shoes and leaves the shop]

(Bishop's data, 1991)

In both cases an offer of service is made, though in the fish-and-chip shop it need be no more than a non-verbal acknowledgement by the server that he or she is ready to serve, a request for service and a transaction occur and (though not reproduced here) a salutation closes the encounter. The shoe shop requires more in the way of politeness and interpersonal skills, and much more conversation typically occurs between buyer and seller. Also, service encounters may frequently contain unpredictable *interactive* sequences, where servers and customers simply say things to establish or consolidate purely social relationships, as in this example of natural data (see also Aston 1988a):

(1.16)   [At a coach-station. A coach-driver is loading luggage into the boot of the coach. He picks up one passenger's suitcase; it is very heavy and obviously causes him difficulty in lifting it]

PASSENGER: It rolls actually [referring to the wheels on the suitcase]
DRIVER: You what?
PASSENGER: It rolls
DRIVER: So do I when I've had a few drinks

(authors' data, 1992)

But though features of the register may vary (eg the relationship established), the underlying genre pattern is usually maintained. Observing closely how people orient themselves in their linguistic behaviour towards the social norms that constrain genres is very much the manner in which *ethnomethodological* investigations of discourse are carried out, and we shall consider the implications of such analyses in section 3.5.

Ventola (1987) points out that 'social encounters are systems where social processes, which realize the activity, unfold in stages and, in doing so, achieve a certain goal or purpose'. Within such an account genres are thus staged, goal-directed language events. Genres embrace spoken and written texts. A central feature of Hasan's (1978) theories is the notion of *generic structure potential* (GSP). The GSP of a text is a specific realization of *field*, *tenor*, and *mode* within a particular 'contextual configuration'. The GSP is realized in specific forms of language but is best seen as an abstract category which specifies the total possible range of patterns and structures available for selection within a genre.

Our account of genre thus far may suggest that all the texts in a genre must have a uniform, invariant organization. The term *potential* (in generic structure potential) underlines Hasan's view that there is a combination of obligatory *and* optional elements. It is the existence of fixed, *obligatory* features in a particular sequence which defines the limits of a genre and allows us to identify incomplete or unrepresentative texts and to distinguish between different generic forms. But the existence of *optional* features means that there are a range of available choices which allow language users to vary the form of their language within a generally fixed generic structure.

1.6.1   Genres: two main prototypes

Examples 1.17 and 1.18 are of genres of writing produced by junior school children in Australia. The examples are analysed in detail in Christie (1986). These texts are chosen because they can be identified as belonging to different contrasting genres.

(1.17)   Text A
'Sharks'! When people think of sharks they think of harsh, savage fish that attack at sight as a matter of fact they are completely wrong. Although there has been reports of shark attacks these are very rare. Most sharks won't even come near the shore so people swimming near the shore can consider themselves almost guaranteed safe.
Sharks have special sense organs that can sense things up to 1 mile away. The shark uses fins to balance itself and it has to keep swimming or else it will sink. The shark's teeth are razor blade sharp and although you can only see two layers of teeth there are many in the jaw. Usually smaller fish follow the sharks around in hope of gathering up scraps that the shark may leave.

(1.18)   Text B
A long time ago there was a kangaroo who did not have a tail and all the animals laughed at him and that made him sad. How did he get it back? He got it back by dipping his tail into lolly-pop siarp (syrup). The animals started to like him and then thay played with him. Would you like it? I would not because it wold be most annoing.
The End.

One broad distinction between these two pieces of writing is that text A is organized non-chronologically and text B is organized chronologically. Text B is narrated in the past tense, whereas text A is presented largely in a simple present tense (in main clauses). Text B is more person-centred. It involves personal pronouns (*he, they, I*) and the writer engages the reader directly ('*would you like it?*'). This is not the case with text A. The references to the kangaroo in text B are personalized and individualized (*a kangaroo* specifies unique entities compared with references to *the shark*, or *sharks* which serve to generalize). In fact, if *a* shark had occurred in text A it would have signalled generic rather than individual properties; equally, the simple present tense conveys here not so much presentness as unchanging general characteristics. One further point of contrast between the two texts is in the kinds of linkages between clauses and sentences. Text B is marked by a predominantly temporal sequence of *and* or *and then*; text A structures information differently and offers to the reader a number of reasons, elaborations or explanations in support of the general truths concerning the shark's behaviour. These are conveyed by conjunctions such as *in hope of*; *as a matter of fact*; *so*; *although*. Related to this is a strategy – common in texts similar to text A – which modifies propositions and, through words like *most* or *usually*, converts them into generalized statements rather than unsupported assertions. Text B dealing as it does in unique events and specific, individualized participants, has no need of such strategies.

1.6.2   Genres and teaching genres

The previous discussion, as well as the analysis which supports Activity 2 (see pp. 44–5), illustrates that it can be an advantage to teachers to see how particular forms of language function in the creation of different types of texts. The discussion also underlines that analysis of language can reveal patterns which enable different key genres to be identified. It is clear that narratives are organized in markedly different ways from expositions. Competence in both these contrasting genres is one sign of writing development in both a first and a second language and the more teachers know about such genres the better equipped they can be to support students systematically in that development.

Section 1.6.1 does, however, raise important questions for the teaching of genres as well as (a key question for this book) for the relationship between analysis of texts and the teaching of texts. These questions include the following:

1   If teachers are given classifications of texts might they not teach them transmissively, according to a kind of formulaic grid? Should teachers *teach* 'models'? Does this militate against inventiveness and flexibility in the creation of texts?
2   If teachers teach only language-intrinsic, text-internal features of genres does this not produce a static, decontextualized pedagogy? Should genres not be taught in relation to the audience and purpose of the genre as well as to the contexts in and for which it is produced?
3   In teaching English language is the teaching primarily for

instrumental purposes or for purposes which allow scope for the shaping of experience by the individual writer? Should teachers teach more reports than narratives because society and the world of work requires *reports* as a *core* genre? What are the ideological implications of such choices on the part of teachers?

It is, of course, impossible to answer all these questions in an introductory chapter. In the remainder of this chapter the main aim is to explore theoretical and practical points which bear directly on the ways in which the world of discourse is divided. A further aim is the examination of a number of pedagogic and ideological issues connected with genre theory. A number of these issues are returned to in chapter 4.

1.6.3   Genres, ideologies and theories of teaching

Much of the descriptive work in defining generic types has been undertaken by linguists in Australia. The Australian 'genre school' has produced a highly significant body of work during the 1980s; much of it heavily influenced by the systemic-functional theories of language developed by Michael Halliday (1978 and 1985). The main publications specifically concerned with classifying genres are: Martin and Rothery (1981), Kress (1982), Christie and Rothery (1989) and Martin (1989). One of the central statements from Australian genre theorists is as follows:

> Ours is a systemic linguistic theory which holds that language is a resource people use for the construction and negotiation of meaning. The theory holds further that because language is used to build meaning the people in any given culture develop characteristically patterned ways of using language in order to serve the complex set of functions humans have. Such characteristic patterns, then, are social constructs, fashioned out of the constant and ongoing need of people to organise, control and hence make sense of their world.
>
> (Christie and Rothery 1989)

As we can see, of great importance to Australian genre theory is the principle of choice. The principle operates at two main levels: the textual and the ideological. Different choices from within the lexico-grammatical system realize different meanings. For example, to choose a simple past tense in preference to a simple present tense or to choose a particular range of temporal conjunctions rather than a set of non-temporal conjunctions is to make choices which result in different types of texts. This is the level of textual choice. The level of ideological choice involves broader social meanings. For example, Australian genre theorists such as Kress and Christie point to the restricted generic diet traditionally provided in Australian schools because of an emphasis on narrative genres to the exclusion of an equivalent focus on, for example, report or expository genres. Both Christie and Kress criticize the 'intellectual' legacy of influential figures in English language education such as John Dixon (see Dixon 1975) and James Moffett (see Moffett 1968) who stress the primacy of narrative and the liberal-humanist, 'romantic' view of language education which prioritizes personal experience and person-centred writing. The following quotations outline the main parameters of their position.

> In my view the intellectual legacy which lies behind the work of both John Dixon and James Moffett (quoted at one point by Dixon), is of quite another kind. It is a legacy well entrenched in much western thought, for it is the one which prizes persons first, conceived of in some ways apart from social processes. It explains human behaviour less in terms of social experience, and very much more in terms of innate or inner capacities which are to be brought forth in some way.
>
> It is no accident that Dixon quotes Blake, for Blake is one of English literature's great exponents of the individual. It is Blake's sense of the individual, I believe, which lies in Dixon's work.
>
> To turn to the second of the two questions I posed above, concerning the kinds of educational processes to which my theory of the individual disposes us, I should note that I have already partly answered it. An education process in an important sense is a process of initiation: an initiation that is, into the ways of working, or of behaving, or of thinking (the terms all mean similar things to me) particular to one's cultural traditions. Mastery of these ways of working, which are necessarily encoded very heavily in linguistic patternings, represents mastery of the capacity to exercise choice: choice, that is to say, in that one is empowered to make many kinds of meanings, enabled to operate with confidence in one's world. And, let there be no doubt about this, without capacity to exercise choice in this sense, one cannot change one's world. Learning the genres of one's culture is both part of entering into it with understanding, and part of developing the necessary ability to change it.
>
> (Christie 1985: 22)

> The question for me is, at one level, about what actually *is*. In my view there are genres: they, and access to them, are unevenly distributed in society, along the lines of social structuring. Some genres – and the possibility of their use – convey more power than other genres. As a minimal goal I would wish every writer to have access to all powerful genres. That is not the position in society now. Once that position had been achieved the possibilities of challenge to generic boundaries and

limitations could be put on the agenda. Beyond this, I worry that overly strong emphasis on individual creativity quite overlooks the fact that children come to school with very different linguistic/generic preparation from home. To the child from the literate middle-class home the teacher's exhortation to express her-himself is no threat – she or he will implement the generic forms acquired at home. A child from the inner-city slums of Sydney cannot respond in the same way. If the possibility of generic creativity is thought to reside in individuals, then success or failure equally can be laid at the door of the individual – entirely inappropriately. Our society already produces too many instances of 'blaming the victim for the crime' for me to feel comfortable with that possibility here.

(Kress 1987: 43)

These statements and others like them go to the heart of a number of the pedagogic and descriptive questions raised above about text typologies and the place of genres and teaching about genres in classrooms. A counter-example may help further demarcate and clarify these issues. The example is quoted by Dixon (1987) as part of his main argument against what he feels to be the excessively 'linguistic', text-intrinsic approach to genre of many of the Australian genre theorists. The example is drawn from a book read with a class of 6 year olds and is argued by Christie (1985) to be an example of a scientific genre.

(1.19)   The blood [in the egg] is full of food from the yolk. The tiny chick begins to grow. It is called an embryo. All animals are called embryos when they first begin to grow.

Christie (1985) specifies the following characteristic linguistic features of the scientific genre:

1   the universal present tense
2   the impersonal passive
3   the verbs identify experiential processes
4   the sentences are asserted (rather than framed as questions) and contain verifiable propositions.

However, Dixon (1987) argues that the above features are not unique to 'scientific discourse' and could appear in

a composition about Law, or History, or even cricket. . . . Aspects of discourse about History, the Law courts or games can all fit these criteria . . . and so could many more social practices, I imagine. . . . Without any difficulty, I believe, I could quote examples of scientific prose – in which each of the criteria forming this so-called genre were not met, whether severally or collectively.

(Dixon 1987: 11)

Dixon is concerned that identification of formal features may draw teachers' and pupils' attention to the rhetorical surface of texts and, as a result, insufficiently highlight the social contexts in which texts are produced. Even the notion of the different language choices available to writers is too behaviouristic or merely empiricist, too restrictively routine and formulaic for Dixon. Instead, helping writers to be sensitive to reader and writer purposes, to participants' goals, to the finer features of the writing process should be a main objective. For Dixon such attention to context is more appropriate to a process-based writing pedagogy which stresses what students can do and does not enforce a deficit view of learning which, by following a predetermined set of steps, stresses only what you cannot do. Dixon concedes that there *are* language-specific generic choices but rather than a 'once and for all set' it is preferable, he argues, for them to be construed as a provisional set to be revised according to the meanings and purposes the writer wants to achieve. Activity 6 (pp. 48–51) illustrates many aspects of a process-based approach to the teaching of writing.

1.6.4   How many genres?

Implicit in Dixon's reservations about work on generic organization is a concern that the descriptions and categorizations of different genres may not be as clear cut as is sometimes claimed. Is there, for example, a limited finite set of genres or is the world of discourse characterized by infinite textual variety? There is some uncertainty among the main proponents. For example, in 1982 Gunter Kress wrote:

> Just as there is a small and fixed number of sentence types, so there exists a small and fixed number of genres in any written tradition. The individual can no more create a new genre type than he or she can create a new sentence type.
>
> (Kress 1982: 98)

In 1987 this assertion has been modified in the following ways:

> Genres are dynamic, responding to the dynamics of other parts of social systems. Hence genres change historically; hence new genres emerge over time and hence, too, what appears as 'the same' generic form at one level has recognizable distinct forms in differing social groups.
>
> (Kress 1987:42)

If Dixon is right, there may be many different genres of scientific writing depending on the purposes of the writer. There may also be an endless continuum of genres with some genres mixing with one another to form generic blends. It may be that there are too many exceptions for the rules to be proved with the result that the notion of genre becomes as slippery as the notion of register. (In fact, how might one differentiate between a genre and a register, if it is necessary to distinguish between a register and a genre at all?) Thus, instead of talking about the genre of report it may be more appropriate to talk about reports (plural) or the activity of reporting. Instead of talking about the genre of science it may be more appropriate to talk about scientific genres or about the activities of hypothesizing or generalizing. This conclusion has important implications if discussion of text typologies and of dividing up the world of discourse is not to become so diffuse as to be unmotivated and unhelpful to teachers dealing with language variation.

1.6.5 Staging

The piece of writing about sharks (example 1.17) can be classified as an information report – a type of expository writing often required of children in schools and often found in language course books. The piece of writing about the kangaroo (example 1.18) is in the form of a narrative – one of the most extensive of genres and considered by many to be *the* prototypical or *core* genre.

Different genres are differently 'staged'. As we have seen, chronological and non-chronological forms are structured according to the nature of the information they convey. Report genres and the information report in particular are relatively simply constructed. For example, there is a 'stage' in which the phenomenon is generally defined, and a stage in which information about the specific characteristics of the phenomenon is given.

The narrative genre has been extensively analysed (see Longacre 1976). One of the most widely employed analytical models – that developed by Labov (1972) – divides the main stages of the narrative genre as follows:

Abstract	–	What is the story going to be about?
Orientation	–	Who are the participants? When and where did the action take place? In which circumstances?
Complicating action	–	Then what happened? What problems occurred?
Evaluation	–	What is the point of the story? So what?
Resolution	–	How did events sort themselves out? What finally happened?

Coda   – What is the bridge between the events in the story and the present situation of the narration?

Of course, not all stories have these ingredients and many storytellers dispense with a formal abstract and coda. However, a story cannot normally be considered to be a well-formed narrative if it lacks any of the other main constituents. Genre theorists underline the importance of teachers knowing about such structure and staging and that such knowledge can help them support pupils' writing development by encouraging children to move from less complete narratives (a lot of stories by younger children contain mainly orientations and resolutions) to more complete narratives.

For example, in the 'kangaroo' text (example 1.18) it can be seen that the first sentence embraces both an 'orientation' and a 'complicating action'. The second, third and fourth sentences produce a resolution and the final two sentences a coda. In the process of developing the story further the teacher might encourage the pupil to elaborate more details at the complicating action stage, to make other stages more explicit and to insert more elements at the evaluation stage.

These categories are neither discrete nor sequential. As we can see, there is a fair amount of embedding of one category within another; any one stage is not necessarily compatible with a single sentence since a category can overlap with anything from a single phrase to a stretch of several clauses. Although the sequencing of stages listed above is the expected one, a story can involve, in particular, more than one layer of orientation and complicating action. Evaluation is a further key ingredient which can be threaded through the whole narrative, its main purpose being to draw constant attention to the very reliability of the narrative. This can be done either by direct contact with a supposed audience (eg *you'll love this one*; *it's one of the strangest incidents I've ever heard of*) or by means of a number of devices internal to the story such as repetition, recreation of sound effects, deliberate use of imagery and so on, including quite explicit evaluation of events (*what really amazed me was . . .*)

It should also be remembered that Labov's model is derived from a study of spoken narratives and should be applied with some caution to written narratives. For example, sequencing in spoken narratives, which do not allow for retrospective reshaping, will tend to be more linear, with less embedding and may tend to have more explicit markers of particular categories. For example, markers such as '*and then suddenly/right before our eyes/next thing we knew/then guess what happened*' mark complicating events while markers such as '*makes you think doesn't it*' or '*looking back it all meant . . .*' or '*so that was the end of it . . .*' tend to introduce codas. It is less likely that written narratives will draw on these explicit interactive devices, leaving readers to construe and construct such categories largely for themselves. The existence at all of these markers in narrative does, however, raise the question of if, when and how they might be taught, particularly to non-native learners. We can note that they are not normally present in course-books or dictionaries. A number of these questions, with their specific implications for teaching, are taken up at the end of this chapter; further analysis of narrative genres and of relevant literary and cultural issues is undertaken in section 4.4.

1.6.6 Prototypes

The conclusion reached in section 1.6.5 suggests that definitions of genre wholly based on text-internal linguistic criteria may be limited and that assumptions that genres are either fixed, unchanging, discrete or singular may obscure the reality of the textual world. The suggestion of textual continua, rather in the manner of continua between spoken and written text types, is a potentially powerful one. As long as points along a continuum can be broadly defined and in terms accessible to teachers, then generic variation does not have to be a fuzzy and indeterminate concept. In fact, this position suggests that underlying different genres, registers or text-types there are textual *prototypes*.

In recommendations for the National Curriculum in England and Wales the following range of functions are stipulated in the context of attainment targets for writing performance at the age of 16 (cf. Cox Report, DES 1989: 38):

> reporting, narrating, persuading, arguing, describing, instructing, explaining . . .
>
> recollecting, organizing thoughts, reconstructing, reviewing, hypothesizing . . .

There is a clear recognition of generic structuring here. The statements of attainment also indirectly propose that there are certain types of generic activity which are sufficiently central or core for competence in such genres to need to be assessed. There is a further possibility here for clear lines to be drawn, within theory and practice, between the notions of register and genre. If we again take the report genre, for example, these distinctions may be represented diagrammatically, as in Figure 1.1.

Figure 1.1 represents a provisional relationship between major textual categories such as speech and writing and the notions of genre and register. It is designed, however, to provide both a summary to

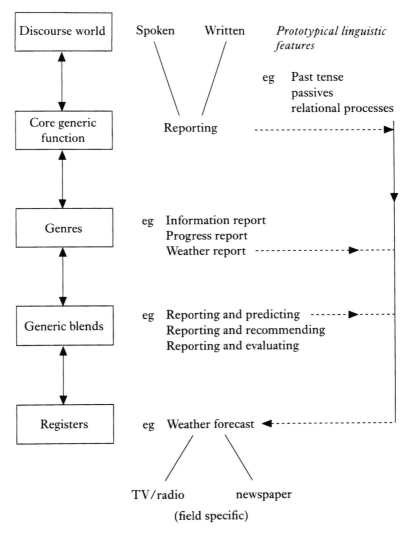

Figure 1.1   Reporting genres

this chapter and a heuristic model to assist teachers in work with students which requires recognition of some ways in which the textual world is divided up.

Continuing with the example of reports we posit, first, that reporting is a core or prototype generic activity, central to language competence, second, that reports can be either spoken or written and that they are characterized by certain key prototypical linguistic features, not all of which need be present in any one text, third, that there are a number of different genres of report which will differ according to the parameters of field, tenor and mode. Some genres are also likely to be marked by a blending of different generic activities. Fourth, that different text types which are marked by different lexico-grammatical patterns and different choices in schematic structure are most conveniently described as *registers*. Registers vary in relation to social contexts of use but are most markedly field-specific. For example, weather reports are field-specific, that is they are most clearly identified with reference to a set of lexical items (*front, high pressure, depression, ground frost, isobars*). But there are different registers of weather report according to *medium* (spoken or written; written to be spoken; spoken but rehearsed), and *tenor* (TV or radio; popular radio or highbrow radio channel; meteorological report for professionals, etc).

Figure 1.1 allows us to conclude the following main points from our investigations so far in this chapter:

1 Speech and writing are major categories with recognizably different characteristics. Language learning can be more effectively supported if teachers know more about these differences and distinctions. Additionally, learners need to know that, according to context, speech can be writerly and writing speechlike, that texts can be more or less monologic or more or less dialogic.

2 It is unhelpful for teachers to assume that different varieties of language can be categorized in monolithic terms. Some categories are more determinate and clear cut than others. It is difficult, for example, to see speech and writing as wholly discrete.

3 There are characteristic text-types or genres with identifiable linguistic features. Some genres like narrative, report, or argument are *core* cultural activities and shape the ways in which we see the world and organize our language within it. Competence in core generic activities is a mark of competence in a language. But that competence is also marked by an ability to

adjust, modify and blend language choices according to field, tenor and mode.

4 For teachers, knowing about the prototypical language of core genres or the language organization of different registers is important but it is not the same thing as knowing how to teach students how to read, write, speak or listen to such registers and genres. Language is not neutral and decisions to teach certain types of language use rather than others often involves ideologies. Ideologies inhere in social contexts within and beyond the classroom. Ideologies inform and even determine methodologies of language teaching.

1.7 Conclusion

A discourse-based view of language involves us in looking not just at isolated, decontextualized bits of language. It involves examining how bits of language contribute to the making of complete texts. It involves exploring the relationship between the linguistic patterns of complete texts and the social contexts in which they function. It involves considering the higher-order operations of language at the interface of cultural and ideological meanings and returning to the lower-order forms of language which are often crucial to the patterning of such meanings. A discourse-based view of language also prioritizes an interactive approach to analysis of texts which takes proper account of the dynamism inherent in linguistic contexts. Language learning is also a dynamic process in which learning how to produce and understand texts and their variation is crucial. In the remaining chapters of this book we shall continue to demonstrate the relevance of a discourse-based view of language to language teaching.

Reader activities

Activity 1

Judge whether you feel the following decontextualized extracts are predominantly in spoken mode or written mode, or whether you feel they are neutral for mode. Consider the reasons for making your choice in terms of particular language features. You may also like to use the extracts with your own group of informants, or on a group of language learners. If you use them

continued

Activity 1 *continued*

with learners, how good are they at recognizing the different modes? Do they use mostly lexical criteria, and, if so, are they missing grammatical cues, or vice versa? What are the pedagogical implications for you as a teacher of their degree of success or otherwise in performing the task?

A . . . Not everybody knew about the lake, for to reach it, you had to find your way down a long, dark walk . . .

B . . . In concept, the sole of an energy-return shoe stores energy when it is compressed by the foot . . .

C . . . but then there's a lot of people got a cat and a dog and they never go to the vet's you know . . .

D . . . You won't of course forget to pop down to your local showroom and have a good look though, will you? . . .

E . . . I think we must establish that we do not cure people and we do not train people and we do not rehabilitate in the . . .

F . . . Lexical density is a statistical measure; it does not tell us how difficult or obscure the words in a text are . . .

Activity 2

Look at these two short literary excerpts, both 'monologues' in the traditional sense, in that they are first-person narratives. Which of them seems to you more overtly dialogic, and why?

A I was set down from the carrier's cart at the age of three; and there with a sense of bewilderment and terror my life in the village began.

The June grass, amongst which I stood, was taller than I was, and I wept. I had never been so close to grass before. It towered above me and all round me, each blade tattooed with tiger-skins of sunlight. It was knife-edged, dark, and a wicked green, thick as a forest and alive with grasshoppers that chirped and chattered and leapt through the air like monkeys.

I was lost and didn't know where to move. A tropic heat oozed up from the ground, rank with sharp odours of roots and nettles. (Laurie Lee, 1962, *Cider with Rosie.* Harmondsworth: Penguin, p. 9)

B If I were a child again and both schools stood, to which would I go? If not to some sterner, more ambitious school than either of

continued

Activity 2 continued

them? Certainly, if it is a matter of getting on in the world, to neither. For though that old ruin kept up by the cobwebs is a joke by comparison with the modern place, where there is no atmosphere, but where they have real equipment – real Bunsens and real gas where we had a painter's blowlamp that went on fire at every experiment and smashed every retort it tried to heat so that Magnus would say, 'Well, that's burst again, but I'll tell ye what would have happened if we could have done it . . .' – still, both of them are very simple preparations for the business of 'getting on in the world'.

(Sean O'Faoláin, 1985, *Bird Alone*, Oxford: OUP, p. 56)

Activity 3

The following piece of writing was produced by a 10-year-old girl in a junior school in England. To which 'genre' of writing might it be assigned? What particular features of language use support your decision? Does the writing have identifiable 'stages' of generic structure?

Snakes

Snakes are reptiles. They belong to the lizards family. Snakes have no legs but for a long time ago they had claws to help them slitter along. Snakes are not slimy. they are covered in scales. The scales are just bumps on the skin. Their skin is hard and glossy. Snakes often sunbathe on rocks. This is because snakes are cold-blooded and they need the warm sun in order to heat their body up. Most snakes live in the county. Some types of snakes live in trees, some live in water but most live on land in thick long grass.

A snake will usually eat frogs, lizards, mice and even small crocodiles.

(LINC Project Data 1989–1992)

Activity 4

The following list gives TV programme names and descriptive labels. How much do the words in bold type predict the content and type of language that might be found in each programme? Under 'types of language' you might include uses such as

continued

Activity **4** *continued*

'narrative', 'interviews', 'jokes', as well as more specific descriptions such as 'technical language', 'colloquial language', 'persuasive language' and so on. To what extent are you using your knowledge of *genres* to make your predictions?

9.25 am	Snowbound: **Thriller** starring Robert Newton, Denis Price
2.50 pm	All Clued Up: **Word Quiz** for couples
10.30 pm	A **Party Political Broadcast** by the Conservative Party
12.10 am	Special Report: A **fly-on-the-wall documentary**
11.05 am	Our House: American **family drama**
8.00 pm	East: The **magazine programme** covering Asian affairs

---

Activity **5**

The following paragraphs are taken from a non-native speaker's university essay on the problem of Evil. Bearing in mind our discussion on modes, how might you explain how *well* is most appropriately used in English?

But what is evil? Couldn't it be that evil is relative, following Protagoras' most famous maxim, 'Man is the measure of all things'?
Well, I think that even if evil were but a spark, this spark is capable of producing a great incendiary.
Evil is a disease and good is its remedy. But what is good? Couldn't it be that good is relative too?
Well, even if good were but an atom, its great value is endless.

(authors' data, 1991)

Activity **6**

The following two drafts are written by a 12-year-old girl, Rachel, in connection with a class project to devise an anti-smoking campaign. This writing was to form part of a class

continued

Activity 6 *continued*

news-sheet on the dangers of smoking. Rachel undertook to write an article for the news-sheet.

Compare the two drafts and make notes on the changes made between the drafts, both linguistic changes and changes in the organization of ideas.

What further support would you provide for Rachel?

Why people shouldn't smoke

Draft 1
There are many reasons why people should not smoke.

I think people often smoke because it makes them look cool, as in an advertisement or because they feel insecure at parties and in places like that. They don't think of other people only of themselves because they can damage their health.

Smoking can damage your health. I read in the newspaper that there are a lot of deaths in Britain (not just lung cancer) because people smoke too much. I would ban it in all public places because children get influenced. Teachers should not smoke in school. Some of our teachers do.

Research demonstrates that smoking can cut your life expectation quite dramatically. Your lungs clog up and breathing problems occur.

These are some of the reasons why people shouldn't smoke.

Draft 2

Until recently, smoking was more normal in public places. Now there is public awareness that smoking can damage your health and other's health. It is dangerous and anti-social.

Research demonstrates that a number of diseases are caused by smoking. It is thought that smoking results in lung cancer but other serious illnesses including heart attacks are caused by smoking as well. Great Britain has one of the highest death rates anywhere in the world for smoking.

Advertisers must be blamed. I think people often smoke because it makes them look like actors in television or newspapers advertisements. Those people that smoke at parties because they feel nervous must also realise how much they damage others. I would also question whether people take notice of the warnings advertisers put on cigarette packets and advertisements. In colour advertisements advertisers are too clever and find ways of drawing our attention. I also feel strongly that teachers must set a good example in schools. They should not smoke in front of the pupils.

These are some reasons why people shouldn't smoke.

(LINC Project Data 1989–1992)

Activity 7

With reference to analyses of narrative in section 1.6.5 identify a range of activities and tasks, both for mother-tongue and second/ foreign language learners of English, which will promote awareness of the organization of narrative genres.

Notes on activities

Activity 1

Origins of the extracts

A   From a short story by Graham Greene, 1963, *Under the Garden* (in *A Sense of Reality*. London: Bodley Head). *For* suggests a written (literary) mode, but the writer does use *you* (rather than the impersonal 'one'), which is more typical of spoken narrative style. As with many literary texts, there is a mixing of modes here.

B   From an article in a news magazine (*Newsweek*, 17 October 1988: 3, author John Wojno) about a new kind of running shoe. The grammar is in fact fairly neutral; it is probably vocabulary, more than anything, that evokes 'technical writing', though it could just as well be a lecture. The more formal lectures are, the more they tend to be associated with features of written mode.

C   From a tape-recorded natural conversation between two men talking about a leaflet advertising a vet's services (data kindly supplied by Jim Lawley of Madrid). Here we have ellipsis in the verb phrase (*have*) *got* and of the relative particle (*who*) *have got*, both common in informal speech, as well as the discourse marker *you know*. Making no distinction between *there is* (singular) and *there are* (plural) is also typical of speech rather than writing. Using *and* as a wide-ranging conjunction, to express adversative (*but*-type) relations as well as the adding relation usually associated with *and*, is also common in informal speech (see McCarthy 1991: 48).

D   From a written advertisement for a gas cooker in a popular women's magazine (British Gas advertisement, *Cosmopolitan*, June 1987: 197). As we have seen, consumer goods advertisements of this kind frequently evoke spoken mode and create a chatty, conversational relationship with the reader. Note the direct address (*you*), the informal vocabulary (*pop down*, *have a good look*), the clause-final *though* and the tag *will you?*, all typical of conversational mode. Elsewhere in the ad, we see the typical mixing of modes: for instance, technical details are often presented in a more 'written' mode, as in: 'It also *features* a *toughened glass* lid which *when closed* cuts out gas to the hotplates, *should you* forget'.

E   From a tape-recorded interview with the late Michael Griffiths, Senior Prison Officer at Cardiff Gaol, Britain, at the time, talking about his work (authors' own data). He treated the interview with great formality, and there are features typical of written mode: syntactic parallelism, prefacing the message with a modal expression and a metastatement of purpose (*I think we must establish*), and full rather than contracted verb-forms. The extract also serves as an example of complex medium: the speaker was told that the interview would be written up and used in a forthcoming book; his choice of mode was probably influenced, therefore, by what he felt were the requirements of the ultimate medium and the context in which the interview would appear.

F   From an academic book (McCarthy 1990: 72). There is no direct address to the reader, verb-forms are not contracted, and the vocabulary is rather technical. Much the same can be said here as for extract B.

If you use these extracts with a group of learners, it may be useful to follow up with some sort of explicit test of their awareness of the kinds of grammatical features highlighted in them. Some aspects of grammar (eg ellipsis) are under-represented in syllabuses and materials, and may need explicit intervention by the teacher (see McCarthy 1991: ch. 2).

Activity 2

According to our criteria, text B is more dialogic. It starts with a question, as though the reader might share the narrator's pondering on what he might have done. It is not a genuine question by the narrator to himself, since he already has the answer in his mind. We also have two very interactive words, the modal disjunct *certainly* and the discourse marker *still*. Both these words represent the speaker/

writer adjusting the message with the listener/reader in mind, and are very common in spoken dialogue.

Activity 3

There are two main 'stages' to the 'schematic structure' or to what might be termed the global patterning of this piece of writing. (For a 10-year old the writing demonstrates an impressive control of the language.) The first stage classifies the phenomenon; the second provides further information, usually descriptive, about the phenomenon. The existence of such stages helps to differentiate this genre of writing from other genres of writing. It has been categorized as an *information report*. (See Derewianka 1990 for discussion of schematic structural differences between this report and 'procedural' and 'explanatory' reports – all of which are common genres of writing required of children in upper junior and secondary schools.)

This information report is also characterized by the following linguistic features which are prevalent in most report genres. First, the main tense is a timeless, simple present (*live, sunbathe, have*). It serves to generalize and to convey general truths about the phenomenon – almost a sequence of scientifically verifiable facts. The iterative *will* (A snake *will* usually eat) conveys a general action not a future prediction. Second, nouns are more common than pronouns. There are no personal pronouns. The nouns serve to generalize: either they are preceded by an indefinite article (*a snake*) or they are in plural form (*snakes*). The strategy is to describe and classify snakes not as individualized entities but as general phenomena. Third, the vocabulary is mainly neutral and not attitudinal. (Although there are no technical words, they would not be out of place.) This is an impersonal classification, not a record of personal observation. Fourth, passive forms (eg They *are covered* in scales) presuppose the same impersonal presentation. Fifth, many of the verbs encode 'relational' processes (Halliday 1985: 112 ff.) (eg *have, is, belong to, consist of*). Relational processes underlie a defining style – this is the way things are and what are the relevant properties. Sixth, there are a number of moderating words (eg *usually*, *some/most*) which are necessary to a process of classifying, comparing and contrasting. Finally, nominalizations (Halliday 1985: 329) are also frequent in information reports, though there are no examples here. Nominalizations give a text a marked writerly style and are far removed from most styles of spoken language. If used here, a sentence like

Snakes need the warm sun

would be nominalized by changing an adjective into a noun:

Snakes need the warmth of the sun

or a sentence like

A snake will usually eat . . .

would be nominalized by changing the verb eat into an appropriate noun:

A snake's diet usually consists of . . .

The general style of the information report is *impersonal, formal,* and *writerly.* (It would be difficult to envisage contexts in which spoken information reports would be appropriate.) We should note, however, that the linguistic features of such texts are not fixed and immutable. Instead, it may be preferable to speak of prototypical features of language in different genres. These prototypical features are not permanent unchanging linguistic codes. They are tendencies which occur probabilistically rather than absolutely in particular genres. This same important point is developed in section 1.6, where relevant implications for teaching are also considered.

Activity 4

Most people have very clear ideas of what labels such as *thriller* suggest, and that is precisely why the magazine uses them. Television has created its own genres, which viewers have become used to. Viewers use their genre knowledge (not necessarily consciously) to know what to expect when they look at the TV magazine and decide what to watch.

A *thriller* will be narrative in structure, with the emphasis on a mystery to be solved. There will be much dialogue, two-party and probably multi-party. Levels of formality will probably vary (there may be police or court-room interviews as well as informal and very intimate dialogue). The conclusion of the narrative (the solution of the mystery) will preferably be left as late as possible. Somewhere in the earlier stages of the narrative there may be vital clues in the language or setting which could help us solve the mystery.

A *word quiz* will have quite a different structure. The interaction will be governed by the questioner, who will ask questions and evaluate the answers given. There will be frequent interrogative structures. There will probably also be personal details about contestants, which may be given as a monologue or may be extracted through 'conversation' between questioner and contestant. Some sort of final score and possibly a prize will form the closure of the event.

Party political broadcasts are often monologues, delivered by one or more voices, directly to the viewer, though in Britain, nowadays, they may also include interviews with people in the street and inserted clips of formal speeches from different occasions in time. The discourse will project into the future, as well as reporting past successes. Persuasive language will be all-important, and a direct form of address to the viewer will probably be apparent.

A *fly-on-the-wall documentary* will investigate important events at close range. It will probably contain interviews of a fairly formal nature, but may also contain more informal, surreptitiously recorded speech. Written documents may be quoted or projected directly on to the screen with a voice-over. The programme may be narrative in structure, though not necessarily, and the events may not be reported strictly chronologically. There will almost certainly be a main commentator whose job it will be to organize and structure the diverse material into a coherent account.

A *family drama* will have a narrative structure and may well take place in settings focused around the domestic one. There will be an attempt to re-create casual conversation, though topics will include highly emotionally charged ones as well as mundane ones. A wide variety of discourse types may be represented (doctor–patient interviews, domestic arguments, work-related talk among colleagues, formal interviews with police, speech-styles of different generations, and so on).

A *magazine programme* will contain a wide variety of discourse-types. Formal and informal interviews will co-occur with documentary-narratives, monologues by the presenter(s), settings will vary widely within and without the studio. Some instructional discourse may be included (recipes, how to make things, etc), there may be book and film reviews, as well as purely informative, news-type reports. There could be songs and viewers' letters. In fact, it would be just like a printed magazine.

Activity 5

There are two problems here. One is that university tutors (at least in Britain) do not often tolerate contracted verb-forms (here *couldn't* is used twice), which they associate with spoken mode, or simply with 'sloppy' writing. The other problem is the repeated use of *well*, which, as we have seen, is strongly associated with spoken mode.

The problem of contractions can simply be resolved by telling the learner that they are used only in spoken mode and very informal written texts (especially those trying to re-create spoken mode). The problem of *well* may not be so simple. We could tell the learner that *well* belongs to speech, as a marker of response, but in both cases here, the learner has used it to signal the 'response' to two rhetorical questions. It may be that he or she wishes to use a marker to signal the response. In formal written texts, *in fact* and *indeed* are often used in this way, and it does seem that *in fact* could substitute for the first use of *well*, and *indeed* would make a suitable substitute if the writer did not want to repeat *in fact*. Repetition here would have its own significance, as we shall argue in Chapter 4.

Activity 6

Writing arguments is a complex undertaking. Points need to be ordered, theses and antitheses established and arguments and examples interrelated. Writing arguments is an activity close to speech and is at its best when the writer's personal voice is clear; but in many examples impersonal advocacy is also necessary and a case needs to be made as objectively as possible. Many teachers comment on the difficulties that pupils have in writing scientific discourse; writing arguments embracing a mixed personal/impersonal mode can create greater difficulties. Arguments do involve writers, however, and the shaping and re-shaping of ideas and language choices can make drafting a process which pupils will readily see as supportive.

There are several main changes that Rachel makes between Drafts 1 and 2. First, Draft 2 has a greater balance between personal and impersonal language use. Draft 1 contains a lot of personal pronouns; in Draft 2 personal statements are combined with passives (eg 'heart attacks are caused by smoking; it is thought that . . .').

Second, in addition to passives there are other impersonal uses of language in Draft 2: non-animate agents (eg 'Research demonstrates', also in Draft 1) and nominalizations (eg 'there is public awareness that . . .') in place of more straightforward verbal structures (such as 'People are aware that . . .')

Third, Draft 2 has a discursive style which is closer to the conventions of written argument. For example, there are a number of expanded noun phrases, which are extended by qualifying elements which are positioned after the main noun. One example is:

> Those people that smoke at parties because they feel nervous must also . . .

Here the main noun is 'people', and everything which appears before the verb 'must' is an expanded noun phrase. Another example is: '. . . the warnings [that] advertisers put on cigarette packets and advertisements', where all the elements after the noun 'warnings' qualify that noun in an extended structure. Such structures show a considerable control on Rachel's part of both sense and structure and of more 'writerly' presentation. Related to this, Rachel's use of grammatical structures is more varied in Draft 2. Draft 1 relies on a pattern of main clause followed by subordinate clause, usually a subordinate clause of reason (linked by 'because'). The pattern of, for example, 'People often smoke because . . .' tends to be over-repeated.

Fourth, some potential ambiguities (eg pronouns at the end of Draft 1, para 2) have been clarified. Yet Draft 2 may be even more powerful as a result of the strong personal statement being placed in a single paragraph after a more impersonal and factual case has been established. The changes do not cause Rachel to lose her personal voice.

Finally, Draft 2 also improves on Draft 1 in the organization and sequencing of ideas. The first paragraph presents contextualities; the second paragraph presents a series of general facts or truths; the third paragraph presents a personal viewpoint organized mainly around the 'theme' of smoking and advertising.

There is, of course, no correct way to present an argument, nor any set of linguistic structures which automatically correlate with such a type of writing. Rachel has, however, successfully begun to use some of the main conventions of argumentative discourse and could be supported further in the following ways. First, further drafting could involve reflecting more explicitly on the generic structure of persuasive/argumentative writing. Second, she could be helped to embed narratives within arguments in order to reinforce examples. Third, her teacher could 'model' arguments by writing alongside pupils, and giving good examples for pupils to read, discuss and reflect on. Work on conclusions could help Rachel in further drafts. Finally, Rachel could be introduced to lists of linking words and phrases (see Table 1.1): they are particularly associated with

Table 1.1   Linking Words and Phrases

Linking Words and Phrases

1 Time
At first
Next
Later
In the end
Eventually

2 Comparison
In comparison
In contrast
Similarly

3 Contrast
But
Still
However
Yet
Nevertheless (after a negative idea)
On the other hand (sometimes preceded by On the one hand)
On the contrary (after a negative)
In spite of this

4 Addition
Moreover
Furthermore
What is more
In addition
. . . also . . .
Nor
Not only . . . but also

5 Reason
For this reason
Owing to this
. . . therefore . . .

6 Result
As a result
Consequently
So

Therefore
Thus
Accordingly

7 Order
First
In the first place
Firstly
To begin with
Second
Secondly
Lastly
Finally

8 Example
For example
For instance
Thus

9 Explanation
In other words
That is to say

10 Attitude
Naturally
Of course
Certainly
Strangely enough
Oddly enough
Luckily
Fortunately
Unfortunately
Admittedly
Undoubtedly

11 Summary
Finally
In conclusion
In short
To sum up

Source: LINC Project Data 1989–92.

processes of argumentation and would be used to signal connections, attitudes and emphases more explicitly. The teacher could discuss with the whole class examples of the uses of such words and phrases, encouraging students to insert them at appropriate points in their own writing. Discussion could also centre on the connection between these phrases and particular genres. For example, written narratives generally employ fewer such explicit markers, preferring to leave readers to discern relations by more implicit means.

Activity 7

As guidance for this activity we would suggest consulting some sources of classroom-based work on the generic structure of narrative, for example Harris and Wilkinson (1986), Toolan (1988: ch. 6) and Carter and Long (1991: ch. 8).

Further reading

Biber (1988: 47–58) provides a useful summary of some of the main contributions to the study of differences between speech and writing. Biber's own work involves large-scale computer counts which plot the occurrences of an inventory of linguistic features on different dimensional scales. There are problems, though, in the relationship between the functions assigned to forms and the various scales. Biber's work includes a study of primary school reading materials (Biber 1991). Ure's (1971) study of lexical density has recently been taken up and challenged by Stubbs (1986a). Stubbs (1986b) is also relevant to the arguments we have put forward in this chapter. Murry (1988) is an excellent paper on the relationship of medium and mode in different socio-linguistic contexts.

On issues such as structural complexity and planning as differentiating features, Niyi Akinnaso (1982) should be consulted. Brown and Yule (1983: 4–19) also offer comments on organizational and structural differences. Niyi Akinnaso (1982) takes to task the quantifying/statistical approach to analysis and argues for closer qualitative analysis. Tannen (1982b) includes not only Chafe (1982) but also Rader (1982), who offers further evidence against the context-free/context-dependent equation with writing and speech, respectively. Chafe (1982) is central to the study of speech and writing, and Chafe (1986) adds further to the 1982 paper. Ferrara, Brunner and Whittemore (1991) show how electronic communications are influencing the mixing of modes. Fairclough (1988) is a fascinating study of the relationship between mixed registers and ideology in a credit card advertisement.

An interesting view of the different types of rhetorical patterning found in speech and writing and how these are manifested in patterns of pronoun reference may be found in Fox (1987a). Halliday (1989) is a good general source for the study of speech and writing as phonic and graphic substance and for the emergence of different modes. Brimley Norris (1991) shows how control of medium and mode can be used practically in the EFL classroom in 'writing-as-if-speaking' activities.

On the monologic–dialogic distinction, a further dimension to the argument, concerning the formalist position (where meaning is held to inhere in properties of the text itself) and the dialogical position (where meaning inheres in the interactive processes of reading and writing), and the reciprocity between writers and readers, is presented in Nystrand and Wiemelt (1991).

A traditional but very clearly expounded approach to basic text-types and their realizations may be found in Werlich (1976). Creating text typologies on the basis of discourse frameworks (underlying macro-purposes) rather than surface linguistic realizations is the subject of Smith (1985). Smith's classification owes much to Longacre (1983), whose typology for texts rests on two major parameters: agent orientation and temporal succession (chronology).

On register, as well as the works already referred to, papers by Haegeman (1987; 1990) should be consulted. Ventola (1989) gives an excellent summary of developments in genre theory and argues for its relevance in foreign language teaching. Samraj (1989) looks at the genre of 'picture-talk lessons' and puts the case for more emphasis on variation in the realizations of genres. Wolf and Hicks (1989) is interesting for its claim that children develop early in life an awareness of intertextuality in story-telling as a feature of their burgeoning awareness of genre and register.

Studies in genre theory, description and genre-based pedagogies abound, particularly since the late 1980s. For useful bibliographies of relevant items see Stainton (1989; 1992) and Christie and Rothery (1989). Reid (1987), Littlefair (1991), and especially Hasan and Martin (1989) give useful overviews of the main issues. For a coherent collection of materials, originally written for purposes of correspondence courses for teachers in Australia, see the books published by OUP in the Language Education series and edited by Frances Christie. Christie (1990) also explores the overlap of spoken and written genres with particular reference to educational contexts. Swales (1990) is a recent study of genre with reference to second and foreign language teaching and English for Special Purposes (ESP), in particular. See also Bhatia (1993) for a valuable contribution to genre study along similar lines. For studies critical of the genre theory enterprise see Barrs (1987) and Rosen (1988).

On the relationship between narrative and argument see Dixon and Stratta (1986), papers collected in Andrews (1989) and Wilkinson (1986). Threadgold (1988; 1989) mounts powerful arguments against the reification of texts into rigid generic categories and for the flexibility and social sensitivity of mixed genres and blendings of categories. Recent work in genre theory stresses the development in learners not simply of literacy but of *critical* literacy, the aim being to promote awareness of the social relationships which inhere in all language choices. This is an empowering literacy and is a sharply political issue. The literacy projects such as the Disadvantaged Schools Program in Sydney (eg Macken and Rotherey 1991) do not endorse a purely functional or vocational literacy designed only to support the requirements of a market economy; rather they want to equip learners with an additional set of critical skills which will enable them to criticize and, if necessary, redirect the discourses of the societies in which they live. Such materials also develop a range of methodologies for teaching generic structure which go beyond teacher-centred transmission to strategies such as 'joint construction' in which pupils and teachers work collaboratively to model particular genres. Such procedures combine process-centred and product-based approaches to the teaching of writing.

Note

1   The results of the informant test were as follows (fifty-five informants):

Number of informants assigning extract to

Extract	Spoken	Written	Either/undecided
A	55	0	0
B	36	8	11
C	0	54	1
D	54	0	1
E	30	16	9
F	2	34	19
G	29	14	12
H	41	6	8
I	19	16	20
J	6	16	33

2 Observing and exploiting patterns

2.0 Introduction

In Chapter 1 we devoted much space to language variation across texts. We have given attention to traditional areas of language teaching such as grammar and vocabulary; but the focus on grammar and vocabulary has not been a traditional focus on the place of such elements within a single sentence. The impetus for grammatical and lexical analysis has always been to unravel the patterns which make up larger stretches of text and ultimately different text-types or genres.

We continue such an orientation in this chapter by exploring further the relationship between micro-structural properties of texts (grammar, vocabulary, cohesive relations between sentences) and macro-structural organization of texts. Our goal will be not so much to show how discourse varies, but to discover some of the underlying patterns that different texts can have in common. In other words, after dividing the world of discourse in Chapter 1, we shall now bring things together more to see what implications common patterns have for syllabuses, materials and classroom activities.

To make sense of a text, one of the tasks facing the reader is to comprehend the connections between its various elements. Consider the following example:

Joe was desperate, for everything he had tried had failed miserably.

Here 'for' clearly signals that what follows is to be interpreted as a reason for Joe's desperation referred to in the first clause. If we rewrite the example as

Joe was desperate. Everything he had tried had failed miserably.

even with no overt signalling, the reader infers the nature of the connection. These connections, either signalled or inferred are called **clause relations** by Winter (1977):

A clause relation is the cognitive process whereby the reader interprets the meaning of a clause, sentence, or groups of sentences in the context of one or more preceding clauses, sentences, or groups of sentences in the same text.

(Winter 1977)

Clause relations may combine in text to form recognizable patterns. These are the 'macro' patterns of text organization referred to above. In section 2.1 we shall consider some of these commonly occurring patterns of text organization.

2.1   Common core patterns of clause relations

In this section we shall discuss three patterns of text organization that have been identified by, among others, Winter (1977; 1978) and Hoey (1983). They label them *problem-solution*, *hypothetical-real* and *general-particular*.

The problem-solution pattern occurs frequently, but not exclusively, in expository text. To illustrate this, let us consider the following advertising text:

> (2.1)   (1) One of the irritations for joggers is having to stop every five or ten minutes and retie their shoe laces. (2) A new device – the Lacelock – puts an end to those involuntary pauses. (3) The laces are threaded through the ends of a simple plastic barrel. (4) This is pushed down on the tongue of the shoe and locked into place. (5a) The tie is then completed and (5b) the shoes will stay done up, throughout a bout of running, cycling or squash playing.
>
> (*The Observer*, 8 December 1985: 40)

Sentence (1) presents a situation and a problem associated with it. Sentence (2) introduces a *response* to the problem. Sentences (3) to (5a) give details of how the device works, while (5b) gives a positive *evaluation* of the effectiveness of the device, in other words, evaluates it as a solution to the problem. That a positive evaluation is to be given is also indicated in sentence (2) by 'puts an end to'. We thus have a pattern: *situation-problem-response-evaluation of response*.

It is worth noting that the sentence and clauses marked (2) to (5a) are all covered by one label: *response*. Text segments such as response, evaluation, and so on, do not necessarily coincide with sentences. They may contain less than a sentence, one sentence, or several sentences. In the problem-solution pattern, the key element that marks the completion of the pattern is a positive evaluation of at least one of the possible solutions offered. If positive evaluation for any particular solution is withheld, the writer normally turns to consider other possible solutions. A text which ends with no positive solution offered leaves the reader with a feeling of unease; no one likes to think problems are insoluble. Leaving the reader in a state of unease is, of course, a legitimate device of some styles of writing (eg campaigning journalism, literary writing). Most problem-solution patterns will end with a preferred solution, but may have stages in between where solutions are rejected, or partially accepted, creating more complex patterns. This text on global warming is an example of what happens when a possible solution is rejected:

> (2.2)   What will it take to stop global warming? Or, more practically, what is needed to stabilize global warming?
>
> Even if the world stopped emitting all greenhouse gases today, the atmosphere would still be fated to warm by a degree or so because of past emissions.
>
> But we are destined to keep pumping greenhouse gases, like carbon dioxide (CO_2), into the air for the foreseeable future. If we can't stop the warming, we can at least stabilise it. But we must minimise the warming to the lowest 'tolerable' amount. And that is why it is imperative that action starts now.
>
> Greenpeace has published a study of how a disastrous greenhouse warming could be averted. It is a study presenting what the environment needs; not what politicians and governments think they need. As such it is a benchmark, against which all anti-greenhouse actions can be judged [then follow further details of the Greenpeace study].
>
> (*Greenpeace News*, spring 1990: 4)

First, we see that the initial solution (the world stopping emitting all greenhouse gases at once) is considered insufficient. Second, it will not happen anyway, and so the potential solution is rejected. The alternative solution (Greenpeace's own study) is then proposed and positively evaluated in the final paragraph. The text can be schematized thus:

PROBLEM
↓
POTENTIAL SOLUTION(S)
↓
REJECT
↓
POSITIVE EVALUATION

In complex texts, the loop back to potential solutions can be repeated many times, until the final positive evaluation. The diagram shows how crucial evaluation is to the pattern; students often have difficulty with precisely this element, and it may need special attention in the syllabus or course materials.

The second pattern we shall consider is termed a hypothetical-real structure. In the *hypothetical* element the writer reports what has been said or written but does not accede to its truth: the statement to be affirmed or denied is presented. In the *real* element the writer gives what he or she considers to be the truth: the statement is affirmed or denied. This can be illustrated in the following extract:

> (2.3)   (1) Every other critic has said that *On Food and Cooking* is brilliant, a revelation, and a unique combination of scientific insight and literacy which sweeps aside all myth and jargon as none have done before.
> (2) McGee's book is indeed well written, is full of good things and is good to have on the shelves as a continuing source of reference and quotes.
> (3) But it also has its fair share of mistakes, omissions and misalignments of emphasis.
> (C Tudge, Review of H McGee 1986 *On Food and Cooking*, London: Allen & Unwin, in *New Scientist* 6 November 1986, **112** (1533): 56)

Sentence (1) is the hypothetical element in the structure, reporting the widely held opinion of the writer of the book. By the end of (1) the reader does not yet know whether the writer intends to support this view or refute it in some way. Sentences (2) and (3), the real element, establish the writer's own view, first outlining positive aspects of the book, but going on in (3) to give reasons why the writer does not find the book 'brilliant'. In this way the writer prepares the ground for a generally unfavourable review to follow.

The third common pattern to be presented is a general-particular structure, where a *generalization* is followed by more specific statements, perhaps exemplifying the generalization. Generalization followed by example or examples is one type of general-particular structure. Another type is what Hoey (1983) calls a preview-detail relation in which the *detail* element provides information about what is referred to in the preview element, as in example 2.4.

> (2.4)   (1) A poem differs from most prose in several ways. (2) For one, both writer and reader tend to regard it differently. (3) The poet's attitude is as if, sticking his neck out, he were to say: I offer this piece of writing to be read not as prose but as a poem – that is, more perceptively, thoughtfully, and considerately, with more attention to sounds and connotations. (4) This is a great deal to expect, but in return, the reader has a right to his own expectations. (5) He approaches the poem in the anticipation of out-of-the-ordinary knowledge and pleasure . . .
> (X J Kennedy 'Literature'. In F Schmidt, T L Wullen (eds) 1985 *Discoveries: Working with Texts*. Munich: Hueber, p. 218)

Here we can see a kind of embedded general-particular structure. Sentence (1) provides a generalization. Anticipation of examples of the differences referred to is given by 'in several ways'. Sentence (2) gives the first difference and functions as a preview which is then detailed in sentences (3) to (5).

2.2   Teaching suggestions

2.2.1   *Text frames*

One of the skills of efficient readers of English is the ability to recognize typical patterns of organization in texts. So, for example, if we read of a problem we look for some response to it; if we read a generalization we anticipate some support for it. Once a pattern is recognized, the reader's task in inferring connections between the elements is largely done. As teachers, then, one of our tasks is to develop the necessary linguistic skills in our students so that they can recognize these typical patterns, make the appropriate anticipations and comprehend the implications of a writer's choosing *not* to adhere to the pattern once it is begun.

A useful approach to this task is the preparation of what Hewings and McCarthy (1988) call a *text frame*. This is a diagrammatic representation of the organization or macro-structure of a particular text. We suggest that once a text frame is prepared it gives us a useful pedagogical tool not only enabling us to draw attention to macro-structure but also providing a systematic way of approaching other aspects of teaching with text. We present example 2.5 as an illustration.

(2.5)   (1) 'In only six days I lost four inches off my waist and seven
                pounds of weight.'
          (2) 'In only five weeks I added two inches to my bust line.'
          (3) 'Two full inches in the first three days!'
     (4) These are the kinds of testimonials used in magazines, newspaper,
radio and television ads, promising new shapes, new looks, and new
happiness to those who buy the preparation, the device, or the prescribed
program of action. (5) The promoters of such products claim they can
develop the bust, shape the legs, wipe out double chins, build muscles,
eradicate wrinkles, or in some other way enhance beauty or desirability.
     (6) Often such devices or treatments are nothing more than money
making schemes for their promoters. (7) The results they produce are
questionable, and some are hazardous to health.
     (8) To understand how these products can be legally promoted to the
public, it is necessary to understand something of the laws covering their
regulation. (9) If the product is a drug, FDA (Food and Drug
Administration) can require proof under the Food, Drug, and Cosmetic
(FD & C) Act that it is safe and effective before it is put on the market.
(10) But if the product is a device, FDA has no authority to require
premarketing proof of safety or effectiveness. (11) If a product already on
the market is a hazard to health, FDA can request the manufacturer or
distributor to remove it from the market voluntarily, or the Agency can
resort to legal actions, including seizure of the product. (12) In such cases
FDA must prove that the device is adulterated or misbranded if the

directions for use on the label are inadequate, or if the product is dangerous to health when used in the dosage or manner or with the frequency or duration prescribed, recommended, or suggested in the labelling. (13) Obviously, most of the devices on the market have never been the subject of courtroom proceedings, and new devices appear on the scene continually. (14) Before buying, it is up to the consumer to judge the safety or effectiveness of such items. (15) It may be useful to consumers to know about some of the cases in which FDA has taken legal action.

(16) One notable case a few years ago involved an electrical device called the Relaxacisor, which had been sold for reducing the waistline. (17) The Relaxacisor produced electrical shocks to the body through contact pads. (18) FAD brought suit against the distributor in 1970 to halt the sale of the device on the grounds that (18a) it was dangerous to health and life.

(19) During the five-month trial, about 40 witnesses testified that they had suffered varying degrees of injury while using the machine, and U.S. District Court Judge William P. Gray issued a permanent injunction prohibiting the sale of the device to the general public. (20) It is to be hoped that all owners of Relaxacisors have destroyed the device so there is no longer a possibility of harm to a user who might not be aware of the danger . . .

(HEW No. 76-4001 June 1975. © FDA Consumer)

We now give a suggested analysis for the text structure; the extract exemplifies all three of the text patterns we have noted. In sentences 1–7 we find a *hypothetical-real* structure: sentences 1–5 present the hypothetical element and 6–7 the real. The remainder of the extract provides bases for the counter claim proposed therein in the form of two *general-particular* structures (sentences 8–14 and 15–20). The detail element (sentences 16–20) is itself organized in a *problem-solution* pattern. The intention that sentences 8–20 should be interpreted as bases for the counter claim is signalled in sentence 8 by 'it is necessary to understand' and in sentence 15 by 'it may be useful . . . to know about' (see Figure 2.1).

Once such a text frame has been prepared it can provide the basis for a number of classroom activities. Suggestions are now given for the development of understanding of text organization, comprehension and style.

2.2.2 Text organization

The ultimate aim might be for students to construct their own text frames for complete texts or for chosen extracts. A careful build-up of the complexity of activities is, of course, necessary for this to be achieved. Activities might include the following suggestions.

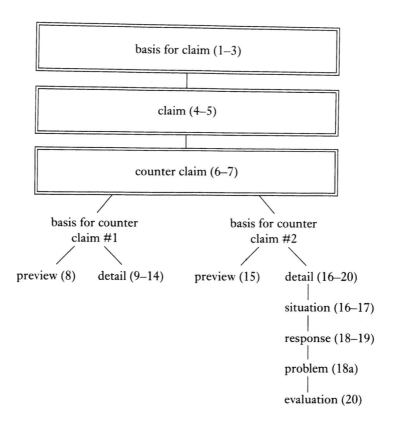

Figure 2.1   Text Frame

First, students are given the text, the text frame (as in Figure 2.1) and a 'blank frame', that is a copy of the text frame *without* any entries (labels and line numbers). They can be asked to make brief notes in the blank frame that will answer questions such as 'What is the basis for the claim in sentences 1–3?' (the note might simply read '3 testimonials'), 'What claim is made in sentences 4–6?' ('Products and devices can improve beauty'), and so on.

Second, students are given the text, a frame completed with notes and a blank frame. They can be asked to produce a labelled text frame in the blank frame.

Third, students are given the text, a blank frame and a text frame with labels removed but sentence numbers remaining. Students can be asked to provide labels.

Eventually students can be asked to construct their own text frames for parts of or for whole texts, with labels and sentence numbers. If groups of students are asked to work together on this activity the results can then be compared across groups. In our experience this generates lively discussion leading to a better understanding of text organization.

2.2.3 Comprehension

The construction of a text frame provides the teacher with a structured approach to the setting of comprehension questions. This was touched upon in the first suggestion in section 2.2.2. If we consider sentences 16–20, our text frame provides the following possible series of questions:

- What device is given as an example?   (*situation*)
- What did the device aim to do?   (*situation*)
- What was wrong with the device?   (*problem*)
- What did the FDA do about it?   (*response*)
- What was the result of this?   (*response*)
- What is the author's opinion of the device? (*evaluation*)

2.2.4 Style

The text frame allows us to note and to draw students' attention to parts of the text that, for certain stylistic reasons, deviate from the typical or 'unmarked' pattern of text organization. In example 2.5 we find the order 'basis for claim', 'claim', 'counter claim'. More typically, perhaps, 'basis for claim' would follow 'claim'. Consideration can be given to why the writer has chosen this order and what stylistic effect it has. Another stylistic aspect might be the way that authors regularly use the same types of text patterns in their writings.

Three comments need to be made at this point. First, the activities we have outlined represent a very limited selection from a large number that, with a little imagination, it is possible to devise based on a text frame. Second, *all* texts have organization, which means that a text frame can be constructed for all texts. With a little practice it becomes a relatively straightforward matter to prepare a text frame on which to base activities to complement normal teaching procedures. Third, we consider the *accuracy* of the analysis of a given text to be of secondary importance to the preparation of a text frame providing pedagogical potential. There will always be disagreement over how a text should be analysed and any lack of confidence in ability to analyse texts accurately should not discourage teachers from attempting to employ the procedures that we have suggested in their own teaching.

2.3   Embedded patterns

'The Relaxacisor' text (example 2.5) illustrated that different kinds of patterns may comprise a text and that these patterns can be embedded within one another. Some text types are discrete, consisting of a core generic pattern; others are necessarily not wholly pure. Some genres are even sufficiently core *and* pure also to function in text types which have another main generic label. Example 2.6 is another instance of a 'mixed genre'. The basic function is that of an argument but, as is often the case with arguments, the argument is supported by examples which in turn depend on narrative patterns (for their particular point).

This text, written by an 11-year-old native speaker of English, has an identifiable structure.

> (2.6)   It would be wonderful if the IRA [Irish Republican Army] would stop bombing homes and other people's property and to stop killings and kidnapping like the two year old girl who was kidnapped from her home on Friday night. She was in her cot sleeping. She was found some miles away from her home dead and that's why I would like Ireland to be peaceful then more people would come to Ireland. Then there would be no villains to fear.
>
> (LINC Project Data 1989–1992)

Thesis	– statement of issue and preview ('It would be wonderful if . . .')
Supporting argument	– with elaboration and illustration ('. . . like the two year old girl . . .')
Recommendations	– with appropriate summary ('. . . and that's why I would like . . .')

In the central portion of this text, signalled by the illustrative phrase 'like the two year old girl', the use of language has a quite marked character. One instance of everyday violence is recounted. There is a specific orientation which leads into a narrative style which is also quite speech-like in organization. The tense switches to the simple past; the chronological reporting of time is altered to put the fact of the kidnapping before the circumstance of the girl sleeping. Personal pronouns and specific participants sit alongside more impersonal passive structures. Narrative pattern is embedded within and supports an overall pattern of advocacy and argument. In teaching writing it is vital for the teacher to recognize the existence of both pure and discrete generic types. Narrative structures are one of the most common ways in which arguments are exemplified.

2.4 Openings and closings

To say that discourses have beginnings, middles and ends may seem a rather otiose statement, but it is the complexity and variety of such phenomena that interests us here, and their often culturally motivated features which make them relevant to the language teaching enterprise. We saw in Chapter 1 how service encounters in shops required openings of some sort. The fish-and-chip shop example (p. 25) seemed to require no more than a grunt of recognition by the server that the next transaction could begin; the same level of acknowledgement in the shoe shop (p. 25) would almost certainly have been considered rude and out of order. Purchases of much larger items (cars, houses) require an even longer courtship dance between buyer and vendor, such that the following two (invented) examples are ill formed as discourses:

(2.7) [in a fish and chip shop]
CUSTOMER: I'm interested in looking at a piece of cod, please.
SERVER: Yes, madam, would you like to come and sit down.

(2.8) [in a new car salesroom]
CUSTOMER: A Ford Escort 1.6L, please, blue.
SERVER: Right, £10,760, please.

The crucial point about such openings is that they serve to signal and establish for the participants the kind of activity which is about to take place. They represent an orientation (or refusal to orientate) towards the features of genres that are socially and culturally instituted. The orientation works at three levels: the ideational or topical (what are the participants going to talk about), interpersonal (what kind of relationship is being established between participants, whether informal, distant, etc), and the enabling or textual level (how are we going to communicate about the matter in hand, is it a business letter, a telephone call, a face-to-face talk, how does one typically go about buying a car? and so on). Genres thus become quickly established in their opening phases, even though individual features of register (eg just how formal or informal the communication will be) may vary.

Casual conversations usually have recognizable beginnings when people come face-to-face. A greeting (even if only a paralinguistic one such as a wave or a smile) signals the opening of an encounter, and may, in most cultures, be followed by exchanges which establish and/or confirm social relations. These often formulaic, *phatic* utterances (see Laver 1975) can vary from culture to culture. On the lexical level, speakers from some cultures may enquire of the person they meet where that person is going and whether they have eaten, even if the person is a stranger (see Hong 1985 for examples from Chinese). These utterances can sound too direct and intrusive to the Western European ear, but are a matter of formulaic phrases quickly learnable and no more intended as genuine enquiries than the English 'How-do-you-do'.

Perhaps more subtly interesting are those cases where it seems the distribution of phatic formulae varies in quantity as well as lexical realization across cultures. Discourse analysts set out to observe and describe such significant differences and it is these which may need special attention in teaching programmes. Our argument is that viewing language as discourse enables us often to unlock cultural differences which might otherwise go unnoticed or detected only via a sense of unease that learners are not quite performing in the way we (and they) should like.

An example of the kind of insight that discourse analysis can offer is Jaworski's (1990) investigation of conversational openings among Polish native speakers and American English speakers learning Polish. Jaworski looked at the distribution of greetings, health enquiries and statements of pleasure at meeting (eg 'nice to see you') in data from the two different groups. The American subjects, on the whole, used more formulae at the beginning of the conversation. The Polish native speakers, on the other hand, used some types that the Americans did not (eg commenting on someone being late, commenting on elapsed time since last meeting). Expression of surprise at meeting someone varied greatly, there being eight Polish examples in the data and only one American. Clearly, the more studies of this kind that are available to language practitioners, the better we will be able to specify in syllabuses and materials the normal and natural language behaviour pertaining to target cultures. A language-as-discourse approach, with its principled scrutiny of discrete phases of discourses can give structure and rigour to cross-cultural observation of this type.

The same principles applying to spoken language openings apply to written texts. The newspaper headline, with its special grammar and lexis, signals the opening of a particular genre (see Iarovici and Amel 1989), but other headlines, headings and titles do so too, though often in less obvious ways. Swales (1988) makes fascinating observations on the correlation between certain grammatical types and activity types (or genres) in the titles of academic papers at conferences. Titles of conference papers beginning with *Verb* + -*ing* (eg 'Developing Listening Comprehension in the Beginning Learner') tended to be practically oriented, while such things as titles consisting solely of one noun-phrase, and the distribution of hedges and other linguistic devices, also had significance in interpreting the up-coming genre. Swales suggests that such 'mini-texts' are a useful classroom resource at the advanced level for training the discourse awareness of learners. As well as titles, one might look at abstracts, and, as section 2.1 implies, the opening textual segments of patterns such as *preview-detail* and *hypothetical-real* will contain significant grammatical and lexical signals of the unfolding genre. In Chapter 3 we shall see how certain kinds of newspaper reports and scientific articles have regularly patterned openings in terms of tense and aspect choices. The approach in either case, spoken or written, is the same: the observation and exploitation of patterns above and beyond the sentence, but signalled and realized with the lexico-grammatical resources of the language, mediated through cultural and social norms.

Closings may be just as elaborate as openings. In casual conversation, the social bonds effected or reinforced by the discourse as it has developed must be temporarily severed without hurt to any party involved. Thus, characteristically, speakers signal to one another that they think things ought to come to an end. The discourse marker *anyway* has this as one of its regular functions in English, both in speech and in spoken-mode written texts, such as personal letters, whose last paragraphs often use it to signal closure:

> (2.9) [the writer has been giving personal news]
> Anyway, Mick, I must go and plant some spinach, make some bread, complain to an estate agency office and post this letter. Look after yourself.
> Love,
> Grace
>
> (authors' data, 1992)

In British English, telephone-closing routines can be quite elaborate, as this real example shows:

> (2.10) [conclusion of a business call]
> A: I'll be here at this number anyway, most of the time.
> B: Yes, right.
> A: Right, well, good to talk to you.

B: Yes, right, thanks for calling.
A: Yes, okay, bye.
B: Thanks, bye.

                                            (authors' data, 1992)

We note here the very heavy marking that takes place on both sides to indicate mutual consent that the call has reached its closure. The usual combination of elements (here projecting to future contact, thanking the caller, saying goodbye) and signals provide us with a potential for description; to do the job properly, of course, we should need much more than one piece of datum.

Conclusions in spoken narrative data (resolutions and codas) are well documented, and share with ordinary conversational encounters in English a tendency to prefer some sort of summary of gist (see Heritage and Watson 1979), often a saying or formula of some kind ('Oh well, that's life', 'Well, there you go', etc), which are items often ignored in teaching materials and very hard indeed to locate in dictionaries, if they are there at all. Learners are usually left to pick them up in a haphazard way. Conclusions in more formal kinds of texts (eg academic essays) are even more poorly researched, but are equally important as objects of study if the discourse-based approach to language and language teaching is to be anything more than a tacking-on of a few features connected with cohesion, a tendency that we criticize in Chapter 5.

2.5   The developing discourse

After beginnings, discourses develop and conduct their main business. Main business need be no more than casually meandering through day-to-day topics, where coherence is created by often quite tenuous associative links. At the other end of the scale, highly formulaic genres (eg narrative sub-types such as joke-telling, or written academic genres such as scientific research reports) will have clearly identifiable stages. In Chapter 3 we shall look at some of the grammatical and lexical patterns that signal the development of discourses in greater detail, but here we shall simply look at two extracts of spoken English, one narrative and one non-narrative, and observe some of the significant surface features.

(2.11) [five friends, three women, two men, 19–20 year olds, round dinner table]

AMANDA: Well, I've got the other camera, so, . . . if Dave . . . then we can

	load that and have lots of jolly photographs in the pub.
BOB:	Mm
CATHY:	Mm
BOB:	Mm
DAVE:	[to Bob] It won't rewind.
BOB:	What . . . the batteries are flat.
DAVE:	They're not, they're brand new. I put them in the other day. Maybe it's just the way it rewinds . . .
BOB:	That's the film speed type.
DAVE:	I may have over taken one.
BOB:	Well, it should have recovered by now.
EVE:	Oh, he's licking my feet.
BOB:	What? [laughs] It's only a dog.
EVE:	It's a dog.
AMANDA:	Woof.
DAVE:	Right, that should be it, well, Amanda.
AMANDA:	Yeah?
DAVE:	Why don't I put your film in here?
AMANDA:	Okay, and I can
DAVE:	└Or put those batteries in the other camera?
AMANDA:	I can't take it out half way through though and
DAVE:	└Well, have you started it? What is it then, a thirty-six? . . . Well, why don't I put my batteries in your camera?
AMANDA:	Yeah . . . I don't . . . I mean I don't mind putting my film in there.
DAVE:	No, well, yeah, if you want to use the film at some other time.
BOB:	I'm sure it's got no batteries in. It feels extremely light to me. [to Dave] Just put the batteries in that camera.
DAVE:	Yes, that's what I'm doing.
BOB:	Yeah

(Faye Wadsworth's unpublished data, 1990)

What we note immediately here is that the language produced is mainly in the service of a series of actions connected with solving a problem with a camera, which the participants have in front of them. The extract is what we might call a 'language-in-action' text. A number of the words in the text are of the type that need an understanding of the entities and locations in the immediate environment (*that, here, there,* the *other* camera, *he's* licking my feet, as well as the frequent use of *it* to refer to the camera, the problem, the dog, etc). In terms of the categories that we examined in Chapter 1, this would be classed as a heavily context-dependent text; its coherent development depends on a common understanding of the entities and events in the environment where the speakers are. Such texts are extremely useful in language teaching for raising awareness of differences in usage of pronouns and demonstratives, especially for speakers of languages where the distinctions are not the same as those in the target language.

Another thing we may note in example 2.11 is the way that speakers use discourse markers. *Well* occurs six times, *so*, *right*, *oh* and *I mean* also occur, and there are several uses of *yeah* and *no* which are not answers to polar questions but which serve more as markers. It seems that speakers, when speaking naturally, use markers quite a lot. They themselves may not even be aware of this (see Watts 1989a), but the markers have been shown by discourse analysts (especially Schiffrin 1987) to perform important interpersonal and text-building functions. In terms of our present discussion, the coherent development of the central segments of discourse, *so* and *right*, for example, have segmenting functions; *well*, as is typical of that marker, represents respondents' signals of divergence from most-preferred next utterance:

(2.12)
DAVE: I may have over taken one.
BOB: [preferred response] Yeah, perhaps.
         [divergent response] *Well*, it should have recovered by now.

One of the difficulties that language teachers face with features such as discourse markers is how does one 'teach' such features in a natural way, not only given that they are almost subconscious items for speakers, but also given that they seem to be so central to natural discourse? Throughout this book we shall argue for the importance of learning about language as a component of the syllabus (see especially section 4.9), and one of the ways such language awareness components can differ crucially from direct input language 'teaching' is that learning about language need not be 'presentational' in style. That is to say, the normal *presentation-practice-production* cycle should not be seen as binding for all features of discourse, and in the case of markers, these would seem to be a feature best handled by other types of activity: language-observation activities, problem-solving, perhaps cross-linguistic comparisons. The main point is that the syllabus and the types of activities that it generates should be seen as inextricably linked and tailored one to the other, some syllabus items generating one type of activity, others another. As always, proper analysis of a variety of discourse-types and their characteristic features is the precursor to such decisions. Example 2.13 is a naturally occurring narrative.

(2.13)   [the speaker is telling how he had to leave his car at an airport in a place where he feared he might get wheel-clamped because he didn't have time before his flight to sort the matter out]

A: Nothing at Luton⌐

B: ⌊Yeah⌐

A: ⌊so I scooted down to the car park
I'd always used before, number two, the one on the left. . . .
Now the trouble with these things is you have to get off the
main road going through the airport on to a special road which
then goes round a bend and you're faced with the fact that
you've come up the wrong way, you see . . .

B/C: [laugh]

A: And you can't get back because there's cars behind you, you
see.

B: Yeah, yeah, yeah.

A: So you've gotta go through and it's automatic and you pull out
this red ticket that says '24 hours duration, any further than
this you will be clamped'

B: ⌊Yeah

A: or towed away . . . an explosive charge will
be fitted to your car and a penalty charge, you see . . . yeah . . .
sort of depressing.

(authors' data, 1990)

Here we note that the talk is structured according to the features described by Labov (1972), which we discussed in Chapter 1. The speaker (male) orients his listeners to the point where he comes to car park number two, then clearly signals a complication with the discourse marker *now* and the lexical phrases 'the trouble with these things' and 'you're faced with the fact that . . .'. *So* signals the resolution of the difficulty (in this case not a very satisfactory resolution, hence his worry), and the story ends with a general evaluation: 'sort of depressing'. Again, we have the developing discourse marked by conventional means. Additionally, the speaker seeks to confirm understanding and coherence by three times using the marker 'you see'.

We shall say more concerning narrative in Chapter 4, but suffice it to say here that narrative is an all-pervasive genre in speech and writing and is one of the best examples of how the main section of a discourse can be seen to be internally structured and, on the surface, managed and signalled by the producer, and participated in by the listener(s). The issues of this kind of discourse signalling and management in relation to the syllabus and teaching–learning activities are similar to those raised by the camera-loading text, (example 2.11) but here we might argue that narrative *is* something that can be practised naturally. However, judging what a successful narrative is will go far beyond simply judging whether the necessary information has been conveyed, and will involve grammatical and lexical resources which regularly constitute narrative patterns. These we shall look more closely at in Chapter 3.

But what of the notion of 'main business' in other kinds of discourse? A large and increasing body of research is now providing us with more accurate descriptions of the internal patterns typically found in different discourse-types, and space precludes dealing with all of them here. But the general principles still apply: speakers and writers orient themselves to conventional patterns and they engage in some kind of discourse management and signalling of the development and direction of the discourse. We could mention, for example, the considerable literature on direction-giving (eg Psathas and Kozloff 1976; Psathas 1986), where regular sequences of elements occur, or the work on interviews of more and less formal kinds as reported by researchers such as Blum-Kulka (1983) and Jucker (1986), where again, development of main business takes regular, patterned forms. In written text, the genre-analytical work done on scientific text (eg Dudley-Evans 1987; Swales 1990) all offer the language teacher access to detailed description which might form the basis of activity design or input into the syllabus.

2.6   Thematic development

The limited scope of this book does not allow us a detailed treatment of theme. There is an extensive literature on theme (see the further reading section of this chapter for a selection), and it is a rapidly developing area of description within different domains of linguistics, particularly within text-linguistics and functional grammar. A main aim is to use thematic analysis to establish the relative coherence of a text and to show how paragraphs can be organized across sentence boundaries by means of patterns of theme (and rheme) development. For a detailed description of theme see Fries (1983) and Halliday (1985), and for theme in relation to topic see Brown and Yule (1983: ch. 4).

In keeping with the orientation of this chapter our purpose in highlighting thematic development is to allow us to make further distinctions between various kinds of texts, to help further in establishing differences between spoken and written discourse and to lay the foundations for a principled approach to the discourse-based syllabus. Thematic analysis can be of use to teachers to this end and awareness of thematic organization can be of value to learners in helping them to shape and pattern their writing. Throughout the extensive literature on theme, researchers equate theme with first position in a clause or sentence, underlining that this position is not automatically identifiable with the grammatical subject of a sentence. Brown and Yule (1983: ch. 4) underline how certain types of information can be foregrounded or 'thematized' in this way and that different varieties of English can use first position in different ways. For example interactional thematization – in which items such as *I* and *you* are placed in first position – is more usually associated with conversational speech; topic-based thematization – in which pieces of information are ordered – is more usually associated with written text. As an example of topic-based thematization we may consider the items in theme (main-clause-initial) position in this extract from an article about sleep disorders:

(2.14)   This said, *insufficient or unsatisfactory sleep* is a common problem, seriously affecting over 20% of the population. *Poor sleep per se* won't damage you physically, but *the daytime tiredness caused by insomnia* is reckoned to cause a significant proportion of accidents and injuries. *The most spectacular recent example of this* was the Exxon Valdez disaster in which a tanker captain fell asleep at the wheel and ran into Alaska.
    Some sleep disorders are due to a very short-term problem like jet-lag, or a passing crisis like a bereavement. *In these circumstances, sleeping pills* are absolutely justifiable.
                    (John Collee, *Observer Magazine*, 10 May 1992: 62)

In example 2.14 the themes are the main topics that structure the embedded problem-solution pattern, and neither the writer nor the reader is foregrounded. Readers can sometimes skim texts like this and by isolating topic-based themes may be able to say what a text is about after only an initial reading.

As a general rule, a theme is interactional if it contains words or phrases which specifically refer to the sender or receiver(s) of the message; a theme is topic-based if it contains words or phrases which refer to some aspect of the topic (including pronouns or deictics which allow a continuation of the topic).

Oral narratives of personal experience tend to thematize the teller, not only as a participant in events but also as the main evaluator (in Labov's sense) of them. Note how the teller (female) in example 2.15 thematizes herself (*I* and *we*) both in narrative clauses (ie the actual sequential events) and in evaluative ones (where she is reporting her thoughts, feelings and reactions).

(2.15)   [the teller is a student recounting a drinking story]
    A: *Anyway*, *we* went off to the nightclub and *we* had an absolutely brilliant

time there, and erm, *he* was drinking a lot more. *Then they* took him into the blokes' loos, with this pint of stuff. *It* tasted of Pernod, but *it* looked like lager.

B: Was it really spiked?

A: *It* was half a pint of lager and half a pint of shorts. *Cost* them eleven quid in 'happy hour'! *Horrible pint of disgusting whisky, vodka, everything, Pernod, everything.*

B: Wasn't he sick?

A: *Well, I* was expecting him to be. *Now, I* tasted it before they gave it to him and *I* said: '*You*'re going to kill him if you give him that, make him drink that down in one.' *And they* said: '*No we* won't.' *I* just said: '*Look, if you* kill him, *I*'m gonna kill you.' *I* was really cross.

(Rosa Gimenez's unpublished data, 1991)

Though much of the work on theme and rheme has been carried out in relation to written text, the oral narrative shows its potential relevance to spoken data too. Maynard (1986), in one of the few examples of thematic analysis of spoken data, argues that a balance of theme and rheme between speakers in ordinary conversation is a sign of a truly equal encounter. If one speaker constantly inserts new themes, he or she may be heard as dominant or aggressive. Maynard suggests that theme–rheme interplay is crucial to the creation of cohesion, fluidity, conversational well-being and interactivity in conversational encounters.

It is clear that whatever we decide to bring to the front of a clause is a signal of what is to be taken as the framework within which what we want to say is to be understood. This includes the particular attitudes or point of view which we wish to communicate. For example, words such as *surprisingly*, *undoubtedly*, *obviously* reveal attitudes on the part of the speaker or writer about the truth or validity of the propositions which will follow. It also includes words and phrases which provide explicit organizational signals of how the text is to be read. Items such as *for example, to sum up, then, in the previous chapter, similarly*, provide important clues as to the functions of the discourse at any one point in its reading. Halliday (1985) refers to the attitudinal markers as interpersonal theme and to the organizational markers as textual theme. It will be clear that many more subdivisions and fine classifications of types of themes are possible. For our purposes we believe that the broad distinction between topic-based and interactional themes is a useful starting-point for distinguishing different textual varieties. In this respect we follow Berry (1989), who uses these categories to distinguish different degrees of success in writing by junior school children. We also follow Berry in extending the definition of theme to include everything in first position that precedes the main verb of the main clause.

As an example of thematic analysis and of its potential usefulness in developing genre awareness we undertake an analysis of an advertisement for timeshare properties (Figure 2.2). The text is characteristic of its type in that it may be divided into two parts: the main text and the sub-text (in small print). To this extent the whole text is a kind of mixed genre. The themes are listed below:

5 Star Holidays	*Claiming Your Holiday Voucher*
You	To qualify you
You	Present owners
Flights	These conditions
They	You and your partner
You	You
All we	Each couple
There, you	It
At Barratt we	Whilst every endeavour
You	All flight arrangements
To make your appointment for a	If you
presentation at your nearest	Some specific flight dates
Barratt International Holiday	This offer
Resort in the UK you . . .	We

It will be seen that we follow Berry in analysing only declarative main clauses (ignoring in this text imperative and non-finite clauses). We also do not pay close attention to items which either continue or develop the thematic elements. In the further reading section of this chapter we suggest ways in which readers can follow up aspects of theme not covered here. We argue, however, that this fairly straightforward analysis of theme is revealing.

The first text aims to persuade the reader of the advantages of timeshare properties, offering in the process extra inducements such as 'free' holidays; the second text is a little more coercive and aims to control the terms on which the free holiday is offered. It is an example of what Fairclough (1989) has termed a 'mixed register', that is the language, multifunctional and multivalent, communicates with the reader on different planes simultaneously. The mixed textual functions are produced by contrasting linguistic choices. It is revealing, for example, to note contrasts in items placed in the theme position. In the first text a majority of themes are plural personal pronouns (what Berry terms collective interactional themes) or include such pronouns in a phrase (eg *you; they; all we; at Barratt we*);

THE HOLIDAY OF A LIFETIME

5 STAR HOLIDAYS – SPAIN £119 PER PERSON, UK £59 PER PERSON.

You could soon be enjoying a 5 star holiday – one of 1500 available at a very special price from Barratt International Resorts.

You can choose a week at our Doña Lola resort near Marbella in Southern Spain, for just £119 per person, inclusive of accommodation, flights from Gatwick and airport transfer. Flights are also available from Birmingham and Glasgow.

Or a week at one of five of our UK resorts, for just £59 per person. They're located in the New Forest, Scotland and Wales. You can take your holiday any time between March 1st and December 22nd, 1990. But you must book it by the end of March.

All we ask is that you spend two hours of your time attending a Barratt sales presentation. There, you'll discover the benefits of timeshare. At Barratt we call it Holiday Ownership because that's what it really is. You'll be under no obligation to purchase, but we think you may be tempted!

To make your appointment for a presentation at your nearest Barratt International Holiday resort in the UK or at our new Sales Centre in Birmingham, you must call us within the next two weeks.

But please remember that there are a limited amount of holidays available – so call us early to avoid disappointment. Then start looking forward to your 5 star holiday.

Call us now, free, on

0800 39 31 39

Monday–Friday 9am–7pm
Weekends 10am–4pm

B A R R A T T
International
R E S O R T S

CLAIMING YOUR HOLIDAY VOUCHER.

To qualify you must be over 21, in full-time employment unless retired. Present owners are not eligible. These conditions can only be varied by special arrangement. You and your partner must attend for the full length of the presentation. You must bring this advertisement with you.

Each couple will receive a voucher entitling them to this offer. It is not transferable. Whilst every endeavour will be made to offer you the resort and holiday week of your choice this cannot be guaranteed.

All flight arrangements are made by the Barratt Travel Club Ltd acting as agents for Owners Abroad Plc, ATOL 230. If you choose to fly from either Birmingham or Glasgow a supplement must be paid. Birmingham £20 per person. Glasgow £30 per person. Some specific flight dates may not be available. This offer is valid only on the day of your first visit and cannot be used in conjunction with any other Barratt offer.

We apologise to those who do not meet our conditions of eligibility.

A COMPANY OF BARRATT DEVELOPMENTS PLC   DMI

Figure 2.2   Advertisement for timeshare properties

in the second text these are replaced by nouns and noun phrases, usually of an abstract nature (eg *All flight arrangements*; *these conditions*; *present owners*). These topic-based themes make the text more impersonal and distance the reader from the text. Aided by the smaller typeface the aim is to discourage the reader from any sustained reading of this section of the text. It contrasts clearly with the more dialogic style of the first part of the text, with its interactional themes serving to involve the reader more directly during the process of reading.

Although having nothing directly to do with theme, we might also note that a further significant contrast in the two texts is the presence in the second text of different modal verb choices. Here the greater sense of obligation, conveyed by *must* and *should*, can be compared with the greater sense of promise and potential, conveyed by *can*, necessary to the act of persuasion central to the first text. The different modalities of the two texts, together with the different thematic choices, position the reader differently, expressing on the part of the writer a contrasting point of view of the propositions advanced. Buying a timeshare property is made to sound attractive but there are 'hidden' restrictions, embedded in language choices, for the target audience desired by the company. Readers who are encouraged to recognize such strategies are also beginning to 'see through language' (Carter and Nash 1990) to the ideologies which underlie choices of language and patterns of language. They begin to develop skills and insights which are part of a critical literacy in addition to those which are of direct use to them for purposes of functional literacy (see further reading section in Chapter 1). The relationships between language, point of view and ideology are taken up in greater detail in Chapter 4.

In terms of distinctions between different genres a focus on theme can be a useful aid to description. Texts with a more dialogic, interpersonal orientation and spoken discourse markers are likely to thematize a range of more 'personal' features of language, whereas more writerly texts will foreground items more specifically to do with the topic and the development of the topic under consideration. Within these broad distinctions we might say that narratives, in addition to what we said about the timeshare advertisement, are more likely to involve some thematization of temporal and orientational sequence (time and place markers) whereas arguments are likely to involve some thematization of logical or attitudinal connectives. Different registers will likewise display specific thematic tendencies. For example, descriptions of places (in encyclopedias, travel brochures, tourist guides) are likely to have regular front-placing of adverbials of location. As we have seen, promotional literature such as advertisements or travel brochures are likely to thematize collective interactional themes.

Throughout this chapter we have stressed the advantages of seeking connections between choices of language patterns and types of variation in language. Throughout the chapter we have also stressed the dangers of positing too rigid a correlation between language forms and contexts, preferring instead to talk of tendencies and to recognise the existence of mixed modes. For example, brochures and promotional literature for companies or for institutions are less likely than travel brochures to thematize interaction with the reader, though they still remain brochures. Martin (1986), in an analysis of letters written in the workplace, points out that letters replying to customer complaints may be more successful if there is interactional thematization at the beginning ('to put a human face on the organization') and more topic-based thematization for apology to the customer which must not assume too direct and personal a responsibility for the original error.

Language course-books and materials only very rarely pay attention to thematic patterning or to assisting learners to pattern the texts they produce according to thematic choices. The teaching possibilities are many and varied but one will be explored here since it returns us both to the text discussed in our introduction to Chapter 1 and to the strategy of cloze procedure, in particular. One conclusion may be drawn from this chapter concerning the use of cloze techniques. Instead of targeting words at essentially random intervals throughout a text and instead of deleting every *n*th word or instead of using the exercise to test grammatical knowledge, it may be more productive to draw attention to the specifically discourse properties of the text. This can be brought about in several ways. Connecting words can be targeted; or lexical signals which realize different aspects of textual structure such as problem/solution or hypothetical/real can be deleted; or thematizations can be deleted and learners invited to insert appropriate items either entirely from their own linguistic resources or, more probably, from a list of items supplied by the teacher. Cloze deletions which draw attention to the different thematic patterns appropriate to different varieties of language can do much to sensitize students to the relationship between text and discourse patterns. A relatively arbitrary focus on grammatical words does little to generate awareness of the key words in the realization of textual meanings.

2.7 Conclusion

This Chapter has tried to bring together a number of different ways of looking at how patterns are formed in discourse. Just as Chapter 1 concentrated on variation and dividing up the world of discourse, Chapter 2 has emphasized regularity across a wide range of discourse-types. That regularity is observable in patterns of clause-relations and patterns created by thematic choices. But just as at least one of our textual examples (the sleep disorders text: example 2.14) showed that theme choices were utilized to foreground elements of the problem-solution clause-relation pattern, and thereby that the different discourse options complemented and interacted with each other, we should not like to suggest that variation of the kind illustrated in Chapter 1 is independent of the regularities displayed in Chapter 2. The bridge between the two chapters is the notion of genre, which is the over-arching orientation to which both variation and pattern are subservient. All the various linguistic options interweave in the discourse processes that realize genres and the final product, the text (whether spoken or written) is a complex balance of many diverse elements. Those elements are, themselves, ultimately, realized in the lexical and grammatical choices of the unfolding discourse, and it is to these we turn to pay more detailed attention in Chapter 3.

Reader activities

Activity 1

In this reordering task, try to order the paragraphs in terms of a preview-detail pattern, that is to say, look for a statement or statements which provide a general summary of what is to come, then order the rest of the paragraphs in terms of specific detail. Is there only one order for the remaining paragraphs? What criteria do you use to decide this last question? The text is a newspaper report.

WORKERS' SUN PERIL

A 'The types of skin cancer outdoor workers are prone to are rarely fatal but they can be disfiguring.'

continued

Activity 1 *continued*

B   Labourers were warned to keep covered up while toiling on road repairs, buildings or gardens.
C   Dr Julia Newton explained: 'Doctors are seeing more and more outdoor workers who have developed skin cancer because they didn't know that they should cut their sun exposure. This cancer is easily prevented, which is why we need to get the message across to people.'
D   Outdoor workers who strip off in the sunshine risk getting skin cancer, it was claimed yesterday.
E   More than 33,000 people are treated for skin cancer each year. Men who think it is macho to peel off their shirts and not use sunscreen creams are among the most vulnerable, said the Imperial Cancer Research Fund.

(*Daily Mirror*, 22 June 1992: 7)

Activity 2

Which of the three clause-relational patterns discussed in this chapter is realized in this short extract, and how would you label the function of each sentence as contributing to the pattern? The extract is taken from the same sleep disorders text that we used to illustrate topical themes (example 2.14). A paragraph that appeared between the first and second one in the original has been left out here, in order to make the text a more usable length for classroom use. It is a good example of how longer texts can be edited and chopped up in a systematic way for classroom use into extracts containing complete embedded patterns with the essential elements still present even if some material has been omitted.

Several words and phrases in the text *signal* the elements of the pattern. What sorts of classroom activities could be devised to concentrate on those signals using this text?

They say Margaret Thatcher only required three hours sleep a night. They said the same of Winston Churchill. It may be true of both of them, but I'm not convinced. We still tend to mythologise political leaders, and reported sleep patterns are notoriously unreliable, even when the sleeping pattern in question is your own. There was a study 10 years ago in America which showed that the average person who declared themselves an insomniac could be shown on objective testing to be getting more than six hours sleep a night.

continued

Activity 2 *continued*

Anyway, the amount of time other people claim to spend under the duvet is not only unreliable but also irrelevant. The correct amount of sleep for you is a personal thing which depends entirely on how you feel the next morning. Sleeping ten hours is fine if it doesn't make you feel fuddled afterwards (oversleeping causes 'sleep inertia' which can last four to six hours the next day). Sleeping for four hours a night is not a problem if you wake up feeling rested.

(John Collee, *Observer Magazine*, 10 May 1992: 62)

Activity 3

Openings, main business, closings.
Look at this naturally occurring oral narrative and do the following activities.

1 Segment the text into the main narrative elements as described by Labov (1972): (orientation – complicating events – resolution – evaluation)
2 Does the story have (a) an *abstract* (summary of what the story is going to be) and/or (b) a *coda* (a 'bridge' between the story time and the real time of the speakers)?
3 How does the teller *signal* to her listeners that different segments of the story are beginning (eg use of markers, lexical phrases)?
4 Do a topping-and-tailing activity of the type you could do with a group of learners, that is write what you think the participants might have said just *before* we come in on the extract and just *after* the end of it.

[A is telling a story about a conference she attended]

A: Well, the conference theme was the 1990s and they did this talk and there was this amphitheatre that seats 2,000. They started off this sort of slide and sound sequence.
B: Ah 'Son et Lumière'.
A: 'Son et Lumière'.
B: I see, and they zapped it to you.
A: It starts off with this tiny black, we're all in the dark you see and tiny little . . . and we hear this 'click-click' and you see this little

continued

Activity 3 *continued*

> coloured pattern and this coloured pattern gets bigger and bigger.
>
> B: What was this projected by, a movie projector or video or what?
> A: No, it was ... erm ... a slide sequence, but it was one after another ... anyway, the very funny bit was that the sound went.
> B: [laughs] That's the trouble when you rely on technology.
> A: Yeah, and that was very very funny and we're all sitting there in the dark and this picture thing going on you see, obviously going ahead of the sound and him saying 'Why can't we hear any sound? Why is there no sound, technician?' You know, chaos, and a great big smile on everybody's face.
> B: Especially the other companies.
> A: And, anyway, they got it going again and you heard this 'click-click' again and this coloured thing suddenly reveals itself to be the Berlin Wall, with people on the top of it.
> B: That's a novel idea. Was Pavarotti singing as well?
> A: Oh yeah, yeah.
>
> (authors' data, 1990)

Activity 4

Language-in-action

Here is an extract of conversation. It is clearly dependent very much on the immediate environment for its development and interpretation.

1 Where do you think these people are?
2 What, exactly, is going on?
3 Recalling what we said about discourse markers, is any character 'organizing' the discourse more than others?
4 How could you use this script in class?

> WENDY: Where are you going, David? You'll have to take your napkin with you.
> DAVID: I'll have to go to one end then, won't I? Right.
> HEATHER: Where would you like to be, Wendy?
> WENDY: Erm, where did you put Heather?
> DAVID: You're there, right there.
> HEATHER: Here?
> DAVID: Right. You can sit there if you behave yourself.
> ALL: [laugh]

continued

Activity **4** *continued*

SUZANNE:	[indistinct utterance]
SARAH:	It's a secret, I'm not going to tell you.
DAVID:	Right. Yes.
WENDY:	Here?
DAVID:	You go there, yes.
SARAH:	Oh, I want the green cracker.
SUZANNE:	I'm orange.
DAVID:	Sarah, you sit there.
SARAH:	Oh, I'm there.
DAVID:	Right. Move down a bit.
SARAH:	Oh, no, I'm next to Duncan.
DAVID:	That's right.

(Lamees Nuseibeh's unpublished data, 1992)

Notes on activities

Activity 1

The original order of the paragraphs was as follows.

WORKERS' SUN PERIL

Outdoor workers who strip off in the sunshine risk getting skin cancer, it was claimed yesterday.

Labourers were warned to keep covered up while toiling on road repairs, buildings or gardens.

More than 33,000 people are treated for skin cancer each year. Men who think it is macho to peel off their shirts and not use sunscreen creams are among the most vulnerable, said the Imperial Cancer Research Fund.

Dr Julia Newton explained: 'Doctors are seeing more and more outdoor workers who have developed skin cancer because they didn't know that they should cut their sun exposure. This cancer is easily prevented, which is why we need to get the message across to people.'

'The types of skin cancer outdoor workers are prone to are rarely fatal but they can be disfiguring.'

(*Daily Mirror*, 22 June 1992: 7)

The headline is a very general statement, which is followed by the first two paragraphs, which preview what will be elaborated in the remaining paragraphs. It is difficult to imagine any other ordering for the remaining paragraphs, since the mention of the Imperial Cancer Research Fund provides the context for identifying who Dr Newton is (it would be rather odd to introduce her without saying who she is or what her affiliation was). Similarly, the last paragraph of all must come after Dr Newton's name, otherwise we have no idea who the quotation is to be attributed to.

This is a typical pattern of news report texts which report some piece of public information. It can be schematized thus:

General statement of fact or assertion
↓
Support: eg statistics/background facts
↓
Quotation(s) from authorities in the field

As such it makes a neat pattern for the type of essay that students are often asked to write evaluating some assertion (eg 'The world is in danger from the Greenhouse Effect'). In this case, though, we might add that we expect the student to add his or her own final evaluation of the situation, with perhaps some recommendations. This text could be used in class for a tailing activity where students are asked to do just that. Such partial writing exercises take the stress and strain of having to write whole essays away from the learner and could be seen as useful activities in themselves or as way-stage activities in writing programmes. The main point is to encourage the creation of culturally appropriate patterns in writing.

Activity 2

The pattern here is clearly a hypothetical-real one, where the writer is concerned to correct what is in his opinion a mistaken set of beliefs about sleep. Our analysis of the text would be as follows (but remember what was said in this chapter about 'right' analyses; there may often be other possible ones – we are concerned here with a pedagogically useful analysis).

They say Margaret Thatcher only required three hours sleep a night. They said the same of Winston Churchill. (REPORTED CLAIMS)

It may be true of both of them, but I'm not convinced. (DENIAL/ REJECTION OF CLAIMS)

We still tend to mythologise political leaders, and reported sleep patterns are notoriously unreliable, even when the sleeping pattern in question is your own. (REASON FOR DENIAL/REJECTION)

There was a study 10 years ago in America which showed that the average person who declared themselves an insomniac could be shown on objective testing to be getting more than six hours sleep a night. (SUPPORT/EVIDENCE FOR THE DENIAL)

Anyway, the amount of time other people claim to spend under the duvet is not only unreliable but also irrelevant. (FURTHER REASON FOR DENIAL/REJECTION)

The correct amount of sleep for you is a personal thing which depends entirely on how you feel the next morning. (CORRECTION/AUTHOR'S OWN VIEW)

Sleeping ten hours is fine if it doesn't make you feel fuddled afterwards (oversleeping causes 'sleep inertia' which can last four to six hours the next day). Sleeping for four hours a night is not a problem if you wake up feeling rested. (BASIS/JUSTIFICATION OF AUTHOR'S VIEW)

Signalling words and phrases

They say/said: attributes a claim to a third party.

It may be true . . . but I'm not convinced: seems initially to accept the claim, but then denies it personally. This is an example of the 'agreement-before-disagreement' convention common in speech and writing which is one of the basic politeness strategies of English-speaking culture (see Chapter 3).

We still tend to mythologise: *mythologise* suggests something is not founded in fact or reason. Note again the politeness strategy of the collective interactional theme, *we*.

Reported (sleep patterns): *reported* attributes the claim to a third party and distances the author from commitment to the reliability of such reports. This is confirmed in *notoriously unreliable*.

In question: suggests that the 'facts' are open to debate/discussion/disagreement.

There was a study . . . which showed: signals the presentation of supporting evidence; note the choice of *showed* (cf *claimed*, *suggested*, which would have weakened the writer's own position). This is further strengthened by *could be shown on objective testing*.

Unreliable . . . irrelevant: signals of rejection of the claims.

Correct: signals the writer's strong commitment to his position.

Fine . . . not a problem: evaluate positively his own claim.

As we can see, quite a lot of the vocabulary in the text is concerned with signalling the pattern (for further examples of this, see McCarthy 1991: 74–84).

Classroom activities to concentrate on these items could include rewrites *strengthening* the denial phrases, *softening* the supporting evidence phrases or transferring the phrases to another, specially prepared or edited text which has a similar argument structure but which does not have much overt signalling, or from which the signals have been removed. Textually synonymic phrases can also be explored (eg *not a problem* = *perfectly acceptable*) in pair-group work at the advanced level.

Activity 3

The suggested segmentation of the text is as follows:

A: //(ORIENTATION) Well, the conference theme was the 1990s and they did this talk and there was this amphitheatre that seats 2,000. They started off this sort of slide and sound sequence. //

B: (EVALUATION) Ah 'Son et Lumière'.

A: Son et Lumière.

B: I see, and they zapped it to you. //

A: (COMPLICATING ACTIONS) It starts off with this tiny black, we're all in the dark you see and tiny little . . . and we hear this 'click-click' and you see this little coloured pattern and this coloured pattern gets bigger and bigger.

B: What was this projected by, a movie projector or video or what?

A: No, it was . . . erm . . . a slide sequence, but it was one after another . . . anyway, // (PEAK OF COMPLICATING ACTIONS) the very funny bit was that the sound went. //

B: (EVALUATION) [laughs] That's the trouble when you rely on technology.

A: Yeah, and that was very very funny // (ORIENTATION) and we're all sitting there in the dark and this picture thing going on you see, // (COMPLICATING ACTION) obviously going ahead of the sound and him saying 'Why can't we hear any sound? Why is there no sound, technician?' // (EVALUATION) You know, chaos, and a great big smile on everybody's face.

B: Especially the other companies. //

A: (RESOLUTION) And, anyway, they got it going again and you heard this 'click-click' again and this coloured thing suddenly reveals itself to be the Berlin Wall, with people on the top of it. //

B: (EVALUATION) That's a novel idea. // (CODA) Was Pavarotti singing as well?

A: Oh yeah, yeah. //

Notable here is the way that evaluation weaves its way in and out of the main narrative, and how the listener contributes frequently to it. In informal story-telling of this kind, it is one of the listener's roles to evaluate the story, thus strengthening the conversational bond and providing important feedback to the teller.

There is no abstract reproduced here. Stories often arise simply out of association with something already in the conversation. In this case the speakers were already talking about conferences, and another speaker, C, who is A's spouse, said 'tell them about that conference you went to in Italy'; so other participants in the conversation can in fact provide the abstract, which C in fact did. The labelling of the utterance 'Was Pavarotti singing as well?' as the coda needs some explanation. The anecdote was recorded in 1990, just around the time of the World Cup football championship, when the voice of the Italian opera singer Luciano Pavarotti was on British television almost daily singing the theme song of the championship. Thus Pavarotti provides a bridge between the story time and the real time in which the speakers are conversing. Note again, though, that it is the listener who provides it. Listeners are by no means inactive during story-tellings, and learning to be a responsive listener, using appropriate strategies which do not constitute interruptions (eg checking on orientational details, evaluating, offering a coda, as B does) is something that may need to be practised in the language class just as much as being the actual teller, which activities tend to concentrate on. The discourse syllabus should, therefore, not underestimate the active role of the listener.

The teller signals the story's opening with *well*. *Well* frequently opens the main business of stories in English, when the ground has been laid, the abstract (if any) given, and everyone is ready for the orientation. *Anyway* is twice used to signal new segments, once for the beginning of the peak or main complicating action and once for the resolution. Segmenting narratives is an important function of *anyway* in English. This activity and what we have said about discourse markers in Chapters 1 and 2 underline just how ubiquitous they are in talk and how the discourse syllabus must seek ways of tackling them. First and foremost, an understanding of their functions is important, and this is where discourse analysts such as Schiffrin (1987) have provided such useful information. The speaker also marks the important bits of the story with the remarks 'the very funny bit was . . .', and 'that was very very funny', evaluating them as peaks of the narrative, its justification as a humorous story.

There are many possible openings and continuations. Possible openings could have been:

> 'I must tell you about the funny thing that happened at this conference I went to'
> 'Did I ever tell you what happened at that conference in Italy?'

In either case, what the teller is doing is providing an abstract, as well as signalling a desire to tell an anecdote.

Possible continuations may have included remarks about the story such as

> 'Yes, you can never trust high technology, it always lets you down'
> 'I expect that's the last time they'll ever use a light show!'

which are codas, or perhaps an invitation to another participant to tell a further anecdote may occur:

> 'Have you got any funny conference stories?'

The activity, whichever way it goes, enables the teacher and learners to concentrate on conversational boundaries, which are often neglected in teaching.

Activity 4

1   They are in fact around a dinner table at home; references to sitting positions might have helped. Possibly also a restaurant.
2   This is sitting down to a traditional British Christmas dinner. The cultural clue of fighting over which colour cracker to have may have helped you if you knew that percussion crackers with paper hats and small gifts hidden inside them are usually pulled at table during Christmas dinner. The main business of the discourse is organizing who sits where.
3   David seems to be the dominant organizer here (he is in fact the father of the family). He thrice uses the marker *right*, characteristic of teachers in classrooms and anyone organizing things to segment each organizational operation.
4   One way of getting learners to concentrate on the sorts of immediate references created by words such as *here, there, right there, next to, down a bit, to one end* is to simply present them with this script and ask them, in groups of five, to act out the script, with movements, using the classroom furniture, as a piece of drama. Any 'spare' students can be employed as 'directors'. This is one of the ways that such real spoken data can be brought straight into the classroom. The vocabulary is not difficult, which is typical of language-in-action texts; they tend to have a low lexical density and to contain a lot of deictic words and pro-forms.

Further reading

There have been several studies exploring patterns of language in text, drawing on and extending the work of Hoey and Winter, especially Winter (1977) and Hoey (1983). Van Dijk (1985) is a comprehensive survey; Carter (1990c) explores the relationship between cloze procedures and discourse patterns. Hewings and McCarthy (1988) explore the relationship between textual patterns and language teaching strategies. Allison (1991) looks at hypothetical-real patterns in written instructional scientific texts, while Ghadessy (1983) examines them in 'letters to the editor' texts in newspapers. Problem-recounting in therapeutic discourse is taken up by Wodak (1981). Francis (1986) focuses specifically on lexical signalling involving nouns; Fries (1986) also looks at lexis. Crismore (1984) and Vande Kopple (1985a; 1985b) discuss the part played by metadiscoursal elements in the signalling process between writers and readers. Kurzon (1985) looks at what he calls 'text deixis', the kind of overt signalling whereby authors of written texts direct the reader around the text with phrases such as 'in the next section', 'below', and so on, which is useful material for teachers of English for academic purposes. Hoey (1991a) is a detailed study of the part played by lexical networks across paragraphs and a valuable elaboration of his earlier work. Hamp-Lyons and Heasley (1987) is a textbook which involves specific application to the teaching of writing to second and foreign language learners.

For studies of openings, closings and topic with particular attention to possibilities for language teaching see Nolasco and Arthur (1987), Cook (1989), Hoey (1991b) and McCarthy (1991). Schegloff (1979) looks more specifically at openings in telephone calls. American news interview openings are analysed by Clayman (1991), who establishes clear segmental patterns such as 'pre-headline', 'headline', 'story', etc, within the opening phase. Schegloff and Sacks (1973) is the classic study of sequential organization in conversational closings, and Button (1987) takes their work further and underlines the sensitive, delicate nature of the closing operation. The best study of leave-taking is by Knapp et al (1973), who identify fourteen possible key language features that occur in the leave-taking phase of conversations. On discourse markers, apart from Schiffrin (1987), other good sources include Schourup (1985), the papers in Tottie and Bäcklund (1986), Fraser (1990) and Redeker (1990).

Further sources on narrative include the special issue of *Journal of Pragmatics* (1982) on stories, and a paper by Duranti (1991), which is relevant to the discussion of the role of the listener in story-telling in the notes on activity 3.

Brown and Yule (1983: 126–33) provide useful overviews of relevant research and theory as well as coverage of germane work on thematic development. Other sources include Cook (1989: 64–7) and McCarthy (1991: 51–9). Halliday (1985) is essential for the detailed description of theme and rheme. Key sources for the study of theme as it originated in the Prague School of linguists are Firbas (1972) and Daneš (1974). Papers on theme include Dubois (1987), who reformulates the notion of theme as expounded by Daneš and the Prague School using real data, and Downing (1991), who takes a systemic-functional perspective. Fries (1991) is a useful addition to studies of information structure in clause-initial position in English.

Hakulinen (1989) is an interesting paper, for it warns of the dangers of applying English-based criteria to the analysis of theme in other languages, in this case Finnish. Giora (1983a) takes the theme-rheme structure and looks at its implications for the study of larger segments of the text and the creation of cohesion, thus linking different discourse features in the way that we advocate in this book.

3 Linking the levels: grammar, lexis and discourse

3.0 Introduction

Chapters 1 and 2 have been very much concerned with the larger-scale phenomena of discourse: genres, registers, patterns, modes and theme-rheme structures across texts. Throughout both chapters, we constantly implied that such phenomena cannot be properly understood without examining the effects of lexical and grammatical choices at a very delicate level. In this chapter, we turn to look in greater detail at some aspects of grammatical and lexical choice which we feel illustrate particularly well that the lexico-grammatical system and the discourse patterns of a language are not two separate things, but that, rather, we should think of all language as discourse. This may involve rethinking our attitudes to traditional lexico-grammatical approaches, but the result is an integrated view of discourse. The grammatical and lexical categories we have chosen to look at in this chapter are not comprehensive; they are just taken as examples of an approach which, we feel, could be applied to any lexical or grammatical feature. But we accept that a comprehensive discourse-grammar of English and a convincing discourse-based description of lexical structure for English remain to be written.

3.1 Grammar and discourse management

The description of cohesion in English, associated with Halliday and Hasan (1976), with revisions by Hasan (1984) and further expansion by Halliday (1985) is well established in text analysis as an account of one of the principal ways in which sentences are linked coherently to one another. In applied linguistics and language teaching, cohesion has become one of the elements deemed to be central to the discoursal components of the syllabus, which we discuss further in Chapter 5. How pronouns and articles refer within and without the text, how ellipsis and substitution carry understood information over from previous utterances and signal shared knowledge, how conjunctions create coherent relations between segments of the text, and how lexical items relate to one another across textual boundaries have all been studied and applied (for a discussion of applications, see McCarthy (1991: chs 2 and 3). But cohesion does more than just link sentences and utterances on the surface of the text; it also plays its part in creating genres and registers, and is one of the 'discourse management' features that the lexico-grammatical system offers. By 'management', we mean speaker/writer decisions as to how entities may be made prominent or left as background, how discourses will be segmented and how parts of the discourse may be weighted against one another in terms of importance and textual hierarchy. Cohesive links of the kind described by Halliday and Hasan are among a battery of choices within the grammar that relate to the creation of staged discourses. Here we shall not make a sharp distinction between what is, strictly speaking, cohesive and what devices partake of foregrounding functions, for it is the concern of this chapter to examine the significance of as many choices as possible at the lexico-grammatical level which seem to have implications for the creation of the macro-level features we are interested in as the foundation of a discourse-based view of language and of language teaching. Some of the choices in the grammar that we shall look at will fall within the description of cohesion, others overlap with the notion of theme and topical development and the prominence attaching to particular word-orders.

We can begin by looking at how different distributions of reference-types characterize particular contexts. In Chapter 2 we noted how language-in-action data typically contained a significant number of deictic ('pointing') references to entities and locations in the environment. Face-to-face talk in general need not repeatedly name obvious entities but can simply refer to them in the shorthand of pronouns and deictic words such as *that, there, those ones*, etc. But words like pronouns have to be anchored to some entity which all participants in the conversation can orient too. Entities thus come in and out of 'current focus', and participants do not often have difficulty in knowing what a pronoun refers to. Note in this conversational extract how the pronoun *it* has three referents in a very short span of time: (1) a perfume, (2) a hair-drier and (3) a document:

(3.1)

CLARE:	It's not	dewberry.	
SAM:		Urgh, it's horrible.	
CLARE:	It's not dewberry.	It's white musk.	
SAM:			So, it doesn't mean to say it can't be

horrible, does it? Huh. Don't spray it on my face.

CLARE: I'm not. I'm spraying it on my hand so you can smell it . . .

SAM: It smells of . . .

CLARE: It's quite nice.

SAM: Hang on, let's smell. Mm. I can smell something funny now.

CLARE: I think I've broken Mum's hair-drier.

SAM: How?

CLARE: Don't know. It doesn't work any more.

SAM: What's this? Is – is this the travel soc thing?

CLARE: Ahh. It's awful. Don't have a look?

SAM: Is it the travel soc thing?

CLARE: No, it's not the travel soc.

(Beth Sims's unpublished data, 1992)

Notable here are the way that new topics are brought into being: the hair-drier is introduced as a full noun phrase, and the document is introduced as *this*. Both entities are thereafter referred to simply as *it*. Full noun phrases and demonstratives *topicalize* entities; pronouns simply continue topics already raised to the status of current focus. The pronouns therefore stand in a direct relationship with noun phrases and the demonstratives at the discourse level. In a conventional grammar, pronouns and demonstratives partake of different systems; in a discourse grammar, there is every reason to bring them together. In the discourse-based syllabus, *it* will be studied not only alongside *he* and *she*, but also alongside *this* and *that*, in terms of the basic functions of topic focus that operate in all discourses (see McCarthy 1991: 36–9). Equally, in constructing extended texts, the learner will have to be sensitive to the constraints that require a return to a full noun phrase when topicalization changes, or when new discourse segments begin. There is some evidence in data (eg written English texts produced by Malay speakers) that the patterns of distribution of full noun phrases and pronouns is different from natural English text, and that differences may be cross-linguistically motivated.

The point about discourse segments is relevant to research done into paragraph structure. Hofmann (1989) argues that a pronoun cannot be used to refer across a paragraph boundary except when its referent is the topic of the preceding paragraph. He is supported by Fox's work (1987a; 1987b), which demonstrates the relationship between pronoun- and full noun phrase-selection in terms of 'discourse segments'; Fox claims that the beginning of a new segment (eg a new rhetorical element of a text pattern, a new topical focus) is a more powerful barrier to the use of a pronoun than actual distance in the text from its referent. Hofmann also points out that such 'anaphora barriers' are sensitive to genre, so that narrative can tolerate exceptions to the barrier more easily than other genres. Nor does Fox discount the importance of distance from pronoun to referent: she shows how conversational data, popular written narrative and written expository texts are respectively less tolerant of long-range anaphora (Fox 1986). All this work further underlines the need to look at well-worn traditional categories from a new perspective and suggests powerful links between the higher order choices (such as paragraphing and realizing elements of textual patterns) and the lower order features such as pronoun and demonstrative reference. This is what we mean by a discourse grammar, and this is how the grammatical inventory of the discourse syllabus would differ from the conventional, sentence-based grammatical inventory.

An example of how genre can influence a cohesive feature such as reference is displayed in the football fan magazine data analysed by McCarthy (1992a). British football fan magazines ('fanzines') are written texts with extremely strong spoken mode features. They assume an audience with a high level of shared knowledge with the fanzine writers. Not surprisingly then, McCarthy found that the 'unmarked' topic structure of

full, identifying noun phrase – TOPICALIZATION

$\downarrow$ $\downarrow$

pronoun reference   – TOPIC CONTINUATION

was often disturbed. Initial noun phrases often seemed oblique and minimal in their identifying function, and the full, identifying noun phrase (sufficient to contextualize the participant for the non-group-membershipped reader) often came later. Typical participant reference chains were

1st mention	The boy Sharpe	(group-membershipped noun phrase)
Other mentions (in sequence)	he – him (×3) – he (×2) – him – he –	(topic continuing, pronoun references)
	Lee Sharpe –	(full identifying noun phrase)
	he – [etc]	(topic continuing, prounoun references)

McCarthy found that this type of reference chain did not occur in parallel mainstream newspaper texts reporting the same football matches. The football fanzine genre is partly typified by this sort of grammatical patterning, along with other features. The point here is that the more we know about the kinds of reference chaining that occur in different genres and/or text types, the more accurate our descriptions will be as a basis for teaching models, especially for writing courses, where (it seems) problems do crop up in the creation of appropriate reference chains.

Cleft constructions are another of the discourse management features that should interest us in a discourse grammar. Not only do they represent a particular type of thematizing strategy, but also, it seems, they have longer-range influence well beyond the sentence they occur in, within their textual environment. Johns and Johns (1977) observe how pseudo-clefts such as 'what *is* interesting is that it works' have both a retrospective and prospective function in the text to create patterns of contrast (in this case between something that did not work and this entity, which does). Other researchers have also pointed to the discourse functions of cleft structures: Jones and Jones (1985) suggest that clefts are important in signalling paragraph topic, and Hudson (1990) shows how clefts are central to advice-giving patterns, for example in utterances of the kind: '*what I would do* is wait until . . .'. In this last example we are moving into the territory of interpersonal management, and there we find that not only themes but also *tails* (final-positioned elements) have significant discourse roles. Aijmer (1989) in fact argues for a distinction between the more information-staging function of the theme compared with the more phatic, interpersonal functions of tails, which are more common in contexts of attitudes and evaluations (eg 'they very often are good, *these French ones*'). Once again, studies of real data reveal that grammar choices are directly related to the larger issues of how the discourse is shaped and staged, and offer the possibility of a discourse-related grammatical inventory in the syllabus.

3.2 Tense, aspect and voice

In section 3.1 we considered grammatical cohesion and discourse management devices as examples of how text analysis has extended grammar beyond the bounds of the full stop. We suggested that a discourse-oriented syllabus would need to reinterpret the significance of categories such as *pronoun reference* and *cleft structures* in view of the findings of data analysis, and that we might rethink what we teach with regard to those categories. But another question arises: if things such as demonstratives and pronouns appear in an enhanced light when we consider language beyond the sentence, what of the rest of the stock-in-trade of grammar teaching? What, for example, of verb tense and aspect? Can these too be rethought and approached with a different emphasis?

In the study of English, tense and aspect are basically conceived of as creating the temporal framework within which actions, events and processes are to be interpreted. Thus labels commonly used in teaching, for example *present continuous* and *past perfect*, serve to capture notions such as 'events happening now' or 'actions occurring in a past prior to another past'. These labels are useful mnemonics and, if taken as basic rules of thumb, give the learner a systematic resource with which to communicate effectively. However, the commonly used labels are very much oriented towards the 'objective' representation of time, of time as an *ideational* element of the message, whereas we have argued consistently that language as discourse involves participants whose linguistic choices also reflect their relationships with one another (interpersonal functions) as well as the overriding concern of using the language to create messages in conventionalized forms that are appropriate to the participants' communicative goals (textual functions). How then do choices of tense and aspect reflect these inherent qualities of all language in use?

If we consider a very common textual form, narrative, we get a glimpse of how speakers and writers use tense and aspect to realize narrative structure and to position themselves in relation to the receiver. Conventional grammars have long acknowledged the existence of a *historical present* used by narrators to dramatize the events of a story (eg Quirk et al. 1985: 181 and 183); the historical present uses the present tense to recount past events. Recently, discourse analysts have tried to observe correlations between the use of devices such as historical present and the unfolding and signalling of narrative structures such as we met in the discussion of Labov's (1972) model of narrative in section 1.6.5.

Schiffrin's (1981) study of tense in narrative is a good example of the approach that combines grammar and discourse. She compares the use of past tenses and historical present tenses in spoken narrative data, and finds that historical presents tend to cluster in the *complicating event* segments of narratives (see section 1.6.5.), and even more markedly, in the middle of those segments. The historical present operates as one of Labov's 'internal evaluation' devices, heightening the drama of events and focusing on particularly significant points in the story. It is a perfectly coherent choice of tense, even though the events that it recounts occurred in the past. It brings the listener directly into the action with the teller, and is thus a signal of interpersonal intimacy from the teller. Jokes are a particularly intimate and informal speech event and it is therefore not surprising that the use of historical present has become a highly conventionalized feature of *genre* (see section 1.6) in joke-telling in English and many other languages. In English, for instance, a joke-telling session will often switch from past to present once the discourse form is successfully established as a conversational topic and then continue in present till the end of the joke:

(3.2)
A: Have you heard the one about the vicar who bought a parrot?
B: No, go on.
A: Well, there was this vicar, and he goes into a pet shop and says he's looking for . . .

It is not only verb tense that realizes the elements of discourse structure in narratives; choice of aspect in the verb phrase is also relevant. Schiffrin (1981) notes that speakers will often change from the simple form of historical present tense to continuous aspect to give particular focus to selected actions and events. This sort of super-heightening of attention to stages in the narrative is again an interpersonal as well as textual device, involving the receiver even more directly.

The following data illustrate the points we have been making concerning tense and aspect. The speaker, a tutor at a university hall of residence, is describing the problems caused by students visiting his flat, which has two entrances, a front and a rear one. The speaker recounts a particular episode:

(3.3)
A: So I've got two doors.
B: Yeah.
A: Front and back and they usually never know that but one day I was in bed and this student came and knocked on the door so, you know, up I get, you know, bad temper, 'what the hell now?' you know, and of course I went to the front door, nobody there – ah – so, round to the back door. No one there. But someone was still knocking. Back to the front door. Nobody. Of course, what I don't know is he's knocking at the front door, getting no answer, going round to the back 'cos he *knows* about the two doors, and I'm traipsing back and forth always in the opposite direction. He got me after about the fourth try, by which time I was even more ratty!

(authors' data, 1989)

Significant points in the story (the speaker having to get up in the middle of the night, the explanation of what the problem was) jump into present tense, while the central actions that make the story amusing (the knocking and going back and forth) additionally have continuous aspect. Jokes and stories are not the only example of this close relationship between discourse genre and grammatical features.

Schiffrin (1981) makes the point that the present tense is found recurrently in sports commentaries, in recipe commentaries, and in magicians' commentaries. Fleischman (1985), on the other hand, observes the fact that plot synopses of films, plays, operas, and so on, are in present tense, making them somewhat different from true 'experiential' narratives. Thus the question 'What is *Back to the Future* about?' would yield a present-tense synopsis, whereas 'What happened in last night's episode of *Dallas*?' would likely yield a past-tense narrative. What both analysts are doing is suggesting a close relationship between patterns of grammatical choice and contextual features relating to types of discourse.

The reason for taking narrative as our prime example of grammar and discourse is not only because it is one of the most frequent discourse forms in daily life, but also because it illustrates two important things. First, choice of tense and aspect can be seen to have a discourse dimension, in that the choices are not determined purely by semantic factors relating to 'objective' time. Second, tense and aspect choices have become part of the conventions of the genre; in English, among other things, we recognize the genre of *joke* by its use of certain regular patterns of tense and aspect. These genre-related choices reflect the fact that speakers and writers convey interpersonal and textual meanings as well as the ideational account of actions and events. As Fleischman (1985) puts it:

> A narrative is not simply a linear sequence of events, ordered
> chronologically, but a configuration of events that has 'texture' or 'focus',
> an institution in which all events are NOT created equal!
> (Fleischman 1985, her emphasis)

But what of other types of texts that teachers commonly use in the language classroom? Are there regularities of tense and aspect that signal discourse structure and genre? We shall take three common text-types used in classrooms, newspaper reports, literary narratives and, for the teacher of languages for specific purposes (LSP), scientific articles, to see if such regularities are apparent.

One very common type of news report, which has been referred to as the 'hot news' text (Zydatiss 1986), is the short news story which begins with a preview or summary of the story, followed by the details (in other words, a *preview-detail* pattern such as was mentioned in section 2.1). These texts are very frequent in British English newspapers and radio and TV news bulletins; they are frequently used in class by teachers because of their shortness and (usually) human interest. The convention of this particular genre is that the preview is signalled by the use of present perfect tense, while the details change to past tense. The preview therefore stresses the 'now-relevance' of the events and, once again, is receiver-involving; the details are then related as a regular, past-tense narrative of events. Some examples follow from a British popular newspaper.

(3.4)   INVASION OF THE CRAWLIES
Poisonous black widow spiders have invaded Britain by plane.
They stowed away in crates of ammunition flown from America to RAF Welford, Berks.
   A US airman at the base near Newbury captured one of the spiders in a jar after it crawled out of a crate.
(Daily Mirror, 27 July 1990: 19)

(3.5)   SAM DIES AT 109
The oldest man in Britain has died aged 109 – six weeks after taking the title.
   Sam Crabbe, a former sugar broker, from Cadgwith, Cornwall, did not give up smoking until he was 98 and enjoyed a nightly tot of whisky. He was taken ill just hours before his death.
   Sprightly Sam became Britain's longest living man when 112-year-old Welshman John Evans died last month.
(Daily Mirror, 26 July 1990: 8)

These simple text patterns are highly predictable, and provide, in the form of interesting and sometimes amusing stories, a natural context for the contrast *past-simple* versus *present perfect*, a recurring item in many English language teaching syllabuses, and one that is often handled only in the form of concocted sentences. Concocted, simple sentences may be a useful, first stage in presenting the tense contrast in a context uncluttered by difficult vocabulary, but natural texts can be used as a follow-on at the earlier stages of learning. At more advanced levels, when the desire may be to recycle the tense contrast in order precisely to focus on the interpersonal and textual functions of tense choice, natural texts from a well-defined genre would seem to be preferable to sentences. The intermediate and advanced level syllabus should, therefore, wherever possible, as well as listing the grammatical contrasts to be covered, provide guidance as to the discourse genres which will yield the most fruitful data for materials and activities. Syllabuses often fail lamentably to do this.

Zydattis (1986) identifies the present-perfect/simple past pattern as a characteristic of other genres as well, for instance letters to agony columns of magazines. Knowing the most likely sources of a particular type of grammatical patterning is a very useful short-cut for the teacher, materials writer and syllabus designer, who often choose texts on a rather ad-hoc basis. The work of discourse analysts who have studied large amounts of data can be a good starting-point in the quest for natural resources for language teaching.

The existence of grammatical patterns of the type that we are looking at is not exclusive to English. Many languages will have evolved similar conventions of use for, say, news reports, but what is likely to vary from language to language are actual realizations. The French *passé simple*, for example, has been studied in its discourse function in newpaper writing by Waugh and Monville-Burston (1986); similar types of stories reported in different languages would undoubtedly make interesting data for contrastive analysis at the discourse level. Within the mother-tongue teaching context, sub-genres can be compared and contrasted for their grammatical patterning as a component of language awareness and within the socio-linguistic contexts that generate different varieties of news reporting. For example 'popular' versus 'quality' journalism could be an interesting comparison. Our newspaper texts above are all from a British popular paper; would quality papers as readily yield the same data? Section 4.8 recommends a contrastive principle as one basis for generating greater 'learning about language'.

Literary text offers greater complexity and less regular and predictable patterning in terms of such features as tense and aspect choice. However, when we do find tenses and aspects in contrast with one another, we can observe the same interpersonal and textual mechanisms at work. The writer has the freedom to segment the text into temporal frameworks of great subtlety and complexity, to foreground certain events as a matter of textual organization, and to involve or 'detach' the reader to greater or lesser degrees. Bearing in mind what we have said about tense changes in genres such as jokes and news reports, consider this short passage from the Irish classic, Maurice O'Sullivan's *Twenty Years a-Growing*. The book is a past tense narrative; in this extract, the central character, a young man from a remote island, is taking his first ever trip on a bus:

(3.6)   I felt a prod on my shoulder. 'The bus is coming,' said George.
   She comes across with a loud grating noise. The crowd moves towards her, myself and my companion among them. She moves away rapidly.
Soon motors and cars of all sorts are passing each other like ants, the bus

turning the corners like the wind and a tumult in my head from the horns
blowing to let others know they are coming.
(M O'Sullivan 1953 *Twenty Years a-Growing*. Oxford: OUP World
Classics Edition p. 275)

This extract, being one of the rare present-tense passages of the
book, is a clear example of narrative foregrounding and reader-
involvement, just like the spoken narrative data that we considered
above. Sometimes the literary text can be much more complex in its
changes of tense and aspect, as in this extract from F. Scott
Fitzgerald's *The Great Gatsby*, where the narrator shifts from past
simple tense to present perfect, to present continuous, to present
simple (historical present), all within a relatively short space. The
narrator is describing the grand parties that used to take place at the
house of his neighbour, Gatsby:

(3.7)   In the main hall a bar with a real brass rail was set up, and stocked
with gins and liquors and with cordials so long forgotten that most of his
female guests were too young to know one from another.
    By seven o'clock the orchestra has arrived, no thin five-piece affair, but
a whole pitful of oboes and trombones and saxophones and viols and
cornets and piccolos, and low and high drums. The last swimmers have
come in from the beach now and are dressing upstairs; the cars from New
York are parked five deep in the drive, and already the halls and salons
and verandas are gaudy with primary colours, and hair bobbed in strange
new ways, and shawls beyond the dreams of Castile. The bar is in full
swing, and floating rounds of cocktails permeate the garden outside, until
the air is alive with chatter and laughter, and casual innuendo and
introductions forgotten on the spot, and enthusiastic meetings between
women who never knew each other's names.
    The lights grow brighter as the earth lurches away from the sun, and
now the orchestra is playing yellow cocktail music, and the opera of voices
pitches a key higher.

After four further sentences of present-tense narration, the text
changes back again, via present perfect, to past simple:

The party has begun.
    I believe that on the first night I went to Gatsby's house I was one of the
few guests who had actually been invited.
(F Scott Fitzgerald 1968 *The Great Gatsby* London: The Folio Society
pp. 45–7)

The grammatical segments of the extract, that is sequences of
sentences dominated by particular tenses or aspects, correlate to a
certain extent with the orthographic segmentation of the text into
paragraphs: a new paragraph begins when past changes to present
perfect, then a new one when that changes to present simple, and

there is a paragraph change when the text reverts to past simple. But the correlation is not complete: the segment dominated by present simple is two orthographic paragraphs, and the reversion to present perfect is not accompanied by a new paragraph. For language or literary-stylistic teaching purposes, it is the grammatical segmentation of the text which yields more clues to the narrative structure and to the textual and interpersonal functions realized than does the orthographic structure. The textual function of foregrounding the noisy, colourful description of the party is paralleled by an interpersonal structure that takes the reader over a bridge or transition from the past (the 'now-relevant' present perfects) to the historical present, and back again. Thus the impact of the text is as much at the interpersonal level as at the level of the ideational account of events (see Smith 1986).

The literary texts offer the same language teaching potential as our non-literary extracts: they are examples of creative manipulation of genre-bound expectations and show the tense and aspect contrasts in a naturally occurring context, where the linguistic functions of the grammatical choices can be matched to subjective responses to the text. Simple classroom activities where learners segment texts according to their grammatical patterning can often yield immediate and invaluable insights into structure and literary message.

With our final text-type which language teachers often have occasion to use, the scientific article, we return to closer and more predictable relationships between grammar and genre. In the LSP context, the problem often arises that learners have a command of the lexis of their specialized field but lack knowledge of the 'rules of the game' of academic writing, that is the highly conventionalized forms that accompany particular genres. Swales (1981; 1985; 1990) has shown how many academic texts have regular patterns at the level of discourse in their introductory sections; the segments that form such patterns he labels as *moves* (cf the use of the term in exchange-structure analysis; see Sinclair and Coulthard, 1975), and these segments correlate with grammatical patterning of various kinds. Our concern here is patterns of tense and aspect; these can indeed be observed to match the textual organization of scientific genres in statistically significant ways. In example 3.8 we note even more: not only do tense and aspect choices correlate with the segmentation of the text into *Abstract* and *Introduction*, and a subdivision within the latter, but also *voice* in the verb (ie the choice of active or passive) is highly patterned. All but two clauses of the abstract contain passive voice verbs, the two exceptions having an active verb *be*. In the introduction, passive voice is again prevalent, but with the exception of the very first sentence and the first sentence of the second paragraph. Passive voice has been seen as a marker of informality at the interpersonal level (eg Smith 1986), but again, it is not only its interpersonal function, but also its possible correlation with textual organization which interests us here: it is by no means certain that the distribution of passives in the rest of the article will be as tightly packed as in the Abstract and Introduction. With regard to tense and aspect, the notable features of the extract are as follows.

1   All verbs in the Abstract are simple past tense, except the concluding sentence, which projects forward to 'future research'.
2   All verbs in the first paragraph of the Introduction are present perfect, except for the final sentence, which refers to the present article as opposed to others' work.
3   There is a switch to past simple as the Introduction moves from reviewing past research to detailing the present paper.
4   No verbs anywhere have continuous aspect.

(3.8)   Abstract
Factors contributing to differences in the prevalences of respiratory symptoms and diseases among ethnic groups were studied in primary schoolchildren living in 20 inner city areas of England in 1983. The raised prevalences of respiratory symptoms in these groups were compared with results from a national representative sample of children studied in 1982. Data on age, sex, respiratory illness, and social and environmental variables were obtained by questionnaire for 4815 children living in inner cities. The children were classified as white, Afro–Caribbean, Urdu, Gujarati, Punjabi, other Asian, or 'other'. Significant differences in the prevalence of respiratory conditions were found among the ethnic groups after allowance was made for the effects of interfering variables. Except for asthma all conditions were most prevalent in Afro–Caribbeans and whites. In these two ethnic groups respiratory illness was significantly associated with belonging to a one parent family and the combined use of gas cookers and paraffin heaters at home.

Respiratory illness was found to vary in prevalence among ethnic groups but may be perceived differently by different groups. Further studies, measuring lung function, are necessary.

Introduction
The health of ethnic minority groups in the United Kingdom has been the subject of considerable discussion and concern during the past two decades. Inherited disorders such as sickle cell anaemia and illnesses such as rickets have been highlighted. Respiratory health has not been studied thoroughly, though a higher prevalence of respiratory illness has been reported in West Indians and respiratory illness in infants was reported to be more common among Bengalis than the indigenous population of an inner city area. The cause of these differences has not been studied in

detail, although poor social circumstances are probably a factor in some ethnic groups. As respiratory disease in childhood has been linked with susceptibility to respiratory disease in later life it is important to investigate the causes of variation in respiratory health between children of different ethnic groups to identify preventive measures.

This study of primary schoolchildren investigated the prevalence of respiratory illness in ethnic groups in inner city areas and factors that contribute to differences in prevalence among the ethnic groups and between the groups from inner cities and a national sample of children.

This article, with its conventionalized patterns of tense, voice and aspect, is absolutely typical of hundreds of such papers in the *British Medical Journal*. The shifts in grammatical choice are a fundamental feature of the genre, adhered to by all contributors. As before with our other text-types, such grammatical regularities can be used in language teaching either to illustrate important genre features that may not have been acquired, or as a natural context for illustration of the interpersonal and textual functions of tense, voice and aspect (eg the 'now-relevance' of the review of previous research, or the distancing effected by the passive voice in the 'objective' survey of the review, or the 'report' function of the past tenses in the Abstract).

Indeed, the teacher of LSP is often fortunate in having a rich resource for targeting particular grammatical points and a natural, learner-specialized context simultaneously to hand in these highly conventionalized text forms.

In this section, we have outlined how discourse-level features can be combined with the traditional concerns of the language teacher in terms of tense and aspect, and, in passing, voice. We have suggested that textual resources for grammar teaching may be chosen on a systematic rather than an ad-hoc basis using as a guiding framework the insights of text and discourse analysts. Conversely, we have also demonstrated how genres can be (partly) identified through grammatical regularities. We have also indicated that this combination of grammar and discourse in the syllabus is one useful way forward for constructing syllabuses that truly reflect language in use.

3.3 Modality

Modality, understood in its broadest sense as the speaker/writer's stance towards the message communicated, is an all pervasive feature of most discourses. The traditional syntactico-semantic approach to modality which concentrates on the forms and meanings of the modal verbs is undoubtedly important in any language course, but at the discourse level, a broader view of the devices available for expressing the modal functions of certainty, doubt, commitment, detachment, necessity, obligatoriness, etc, is necessary, along with a consideration of how modality relates to genres and patterns. Various studies (Hermerén 1978; Holmes 1983; Stubbs 1986b) have encouraged us to make a broader sweep in the kinds of items that we include under the general umbrella of modality: lexical modals such as the various forms of words such as *possible, probable, likely, certain*, and so on, along with certain discourse markers (*sort of, like,* etc) should take their place alongside the modal verbs in performing the functions of modality. This raises interesting questions of distribution and functions across genres and registers. Watts (1984) makes the point that the popular horoscope is a good source of modal items in natural contexts; we shall see in section 3.4.2 that horoscopes are an extraordinarily rich textual source for language teachers, not just of modal features. A good example of the mix of modal-verb and lexical modals is this horoscope text (relevant items are in italics):

(3.9)   **Capricorn   22 December–20 January**
Try to keep your distance or distance yourself from trouble-spots this week. For whatever you say or do *will undoubtedly* be taken the wrong way. What's more, both personal and joint financial problems *are liable to* go from bad to worse if you continue to use your usual methods, approach or tactics.

(Patric Walker, *Radio Times*, 24–30 August 1991: 89)

Alongside the definiteness of *will undoubtedly* is the more 'hedged' prediction of *are liable to*. Simple texts like these not only provide natural contexts for a variety of modal types condensed in a short textual space, but also present the opportunity for interesting discussion on the contrast of functions. (Which predictions are the firmest? What is the implication of *liable*? Is it the same as *likely, bound, could*?) Knowing where to find rich textual sources for teaching grammar points is one of the main headaches that teachers face, and often it is easier to resort to made-up examples. Data studies, however, can provide just the sort of information needed concerning the best sources; this is one of the most useful contributions that discourse analysis makes to applied linguistics.

In terms of functions of modality, we can also see correlations with certain textual patterns and genres. Narratives contain evaluations; evaluations are often statements of what could, might, or should have happened, and it is in the evaluative segments of narratives that we often find modal items playing key roles, as in example 3.10.

(3.10)   [A has just finished telling of a problem that he had finding a car-parking space at an airport]

B: So you didn't have time to get back?
A: No, if I'd had, say, an hour to wait I *would* then have said to the parking people
B: Yeah
A: and said, 'look, *shall* I leave the car there⌐
B: └Yeah⌐
A: └or
do you want it moving to a proper park?'
B: Yeah
A: It *would* have meant coming back through the barrier then scooting off to the other end of the airfield.

(authors' data, 1990)

It is a natural feature of narrative to talk of worlds that might have been to evaluate the world as it was.

Speculating and exchanging opinions is another natural context for modal items, as in example 3.11. Note again how the opinions are asserted and hedged both with modal verbs and lexical modals.

(3.11) [students are discussing how they've changed since coming to university]
A: But you don't notice so much in yourself, do you? *I don't think so, on the whole.*
B: *I don't know*, I *definitely* feel different from the first year. *I don't think* I look any different or anything.
A: You're *bound to* keep changing, *really*, all your whole life *hopefully*.
B: *I don't know, I think* it's *probably* a change coming away, *I suppose* . . .

(Lucy Cruttenden's unpublished data, 1988)

Our data here, and the research reported, suggest that modality in the discourse syllabus will be related to its discoursal functions, will be broad enough to include a wide range of hedging and asserting phenomena and will be appropriately contextualized so that the learner can observe its naturally occurring roles in different text-types. As with all the other grammar categories that we have looked at, we may need to rethink the kinds of activities we use in class to raise awareness of the discourse functions and distributions of those categories and to focus on appropriate use.

3.4   Patterns of vocabulary

3.4.1   *Micro-signals and macro patterns*

In written text analysis and more especially in spoken discourse analysis, vocabulary has often been relegated to a minor role in the features that combine to create the higher-order patterns of text-types and genres, but here we shall attempt to demonstrate that vocabulary choice is just as discourse-sensitive as the grammatical choices that we looked at in sections 3.2 and 3.3. If we are to consider language *as* discourse, rather than just thinking of discourse as a 'layer' or 'level' of language, then vocabulary must be a concern as much as any other aspect of language form.

Among work already accomplished in this field which has direct relevance for language teaching is the study of the way certain lexical items are strongly associated with identifiable textual patterns. Winter (1977; 1978) and Hoey (1983) have provoked interest in the existence of lexical fields associated with *problem-solution* patterns and *hypothetical-real* patterns (see section 2.1). Thus a text such as example 3.12 *signals* its structure in advance and as it unfolds, by the use of certain key items (here in italics):

(3.12)   Sleeping for four hours a night is not a *problem* if you wake up feeling rested.
    This said, insufficient or unsatisfactory sleep is a common *problem*, seriously affecting over 20 per cent of the population. . . .
    Some sleep disorders are due to a very short-term *problem* like jet-lag, or a passing *crisis* like a bereavement. In these *circumstances*, sleeping pills are absolutely *justifiable*. But there's a risk of dependency in people who have a longer-term *problem*.
    A lot of the longer-term *problems* are psychological. Depression causes *difficulty* in getting off to sleep and early morning wakening. The best treatment, obviously is not sleeping pills, but to *address* the underlying *issue*.

(John Collee, *Observer Magazine*, 10 May 1992: 62)

The key-words, not tied to any particular ideational domain but occurring across a wide range of possible topics, have an important role at the level of textual organization. Their organizational power is in part due to the linguistic properties of their nominal forms which place them in a half-way house between grammaticality and lexicality (see Francis 1986; Ivanič 1991). Like grammar items such as pronouns, signalling nouns require co-textual words to give them their full meaning and can be read as substitutes for relevant segments of co-text (see McCarthy 1991: 74–5), but like lexical words they represent choices from lexical fields in which nuances of meaning are crucial: whether a writer/speaker refers to an entity in the discourse as a *problem*, an *issue*, a *dilemma*, a *crisis* or a *slight hitch* is a lexical choice constrained by register and, at bottom, by ideological stance, the most obvious examples of which might be found in the evaluation of social and political problems and how they are labelled in genres such as newspaper editorials. As *slight hitch* also shows, like lexical words and unlike pronouns, the signalling headwords can be modified by modalizing and/or attitudinal adjectives (see Carter and McCarthy 1988: ch. 5). In other words, our key items play a major role in realizing the textual and interpersonal meanings of the unfolding discourse.

The relevance to language pedagogy of work done on vocabulary signals of this type is that it enables the emphasis in teaching to shift away from an over-preoccupation with vocabulary as the vehicle of *topic*; it underlines the text-creating and ideological foundations of lexical choice; it makes vocabulary study more sensitive to a top-down view of language; it assists the job of relating higher order categories in the syllabus (such as text-type) to the micro-syllabus elements of grammar and lexis. In sum, it is one example of the integration of different levels of the syllabus which we shall be arguing strongly for in Chapter 5. If a text-type such as *argumentation*, with its subdivisions embracing patterns such as hypothetical-real can be directly related to clearly defined lexical fields (see for example Jordan 1984), then a major step can be taken in the integration of the diverse levels of the discourse process as represented in the syllabus.

Vocabulary cannot be divorced from questions of mode in a truly language-as-discourse approach. Most language teachers work with a fairly reliable intuitive feel for the 'spokenness' and 'writtenness' of individual words, but the evidence from discourse analysis for the patterning of words across modes is scant and sometimes confusing, as we saw in the review of work done on spoken and written language in Chapter 1. We can, for a moment, remain with the problem-solution pattern and see how the signalling words, as much as any other words in a text, can contribute to our perception of mode. Note in Figures 3.1 and 3.2, which are typical of many advertising texts which mix modes (see section 1.3), how neutral words such as *problem* are accompanied by words strongly associated with the spoken mode of talking about problems and solutions.

One lacuna in the otherwise very interesting work done on vocabulary signals of the problem-solution and hypothetical-real type, and one which it would be of immense value to teachers to have filled, is how the signals occur and are distributed in natural conversational data. Such knowledge would enable the further cross-referencing to mode as well as text-type, which would be another step in the integration of levels which we shall hold to be the core of the discourse-sensitive syllabus. When we turn to real spoken language data, we see further interesting dimensions of vocabulary distribution. Two features are worthy of note: first, the prevalence of a more general and vague lexical selection, and second, the occurrence of fixed expressions, including idioms. Some extracts will illustrate this;

NASTY PEOPLE

We have all had the problem of dealing with nasty people. At the office. In school. And, yes, in our own family. There are people, in our everyday lives, who can leave you feeling small, incompetent or insufficient.

Now, a new guide called 'Nasty People' helps you deal with the wide range of people and situations common to most of us. Such as the nasty boss . . . the nasty husband or wife . . . the typical victim . . . what to do if you think you might be one . . . how to break the cycle of nastiness . . . and much, much more.

In the simplest language 'Nasty People' explains how to spot and conquer nasty behaviour. Once you can do that, the people who enjoyed bugging you will actually lose control. You, not someone else, are in control.

Jay Carter, author of 'Nasty People' is a respected psychological counsellor and teacher. He shows you how to spot and conquer nasty behaviour. Best of all, you'll learn that you don't need to turn into a nasty person to deal with one.

'Nasty People' is for anyone who works with, lives with or knows people who use nasty comments or verbal attacks to make others feel bad. To claim your copy — satisfaction guaranteed or your money back, please complete and return the form below.

Figure 3.1 Source: *Observer* 22 March 1992: 6

How BFP membership can help solve your problems

As a member, you can count on the BFP for expert advice with your problems. Uncertain of what fee to expect for a certain picture? A problem with copyright? Need help with a legal query? The BFP experts are on hand to help and assist you whenever you run into problems with your freelancing.

The Bureau can also assist in recovering unpaid reproduction fees. If you ever experience difficulties in getting payment for a particular picture, we'll gladly take up the cudgels on you behalf. The BFP is well known in the publishing world, and has an excellent track record in recovering unpaid fees for members.

Figure 3.2 Source: *Practical Photography*, April 1992: 103

they are all taken from natural sources where people are discussing problems of various kinds.

(3.13)
A: And at first it's all right because you're slightly bewildered and then it gets really annoying and then you get so that you don't know where you are at all.
B: That's right, you don't.
A: And you say, no good, I can't stand it, yes, we've got to get some order into this place, oh.
B: Yes.
A: The teenagers and young adults are the crunch really.
B: Ah, the the the, that's it.
A: Yes, yes.

(Svartvik and Quirk 1980: 314: 641ff)

(3.14)
A: The trouble is, was, they were a lot of people there who sort of felt a . . . used to assert themselves and then that affected the other people there as well.

(Svartvik and Quirk 1980: 667: 838ff)

(3.15)
A: But I thought, the big worry was, how is he going to respond to people and dogs?
B: Yeah.
C: Yeah.

(Per Olsson's unpublished data, 1992)

Example 3.13 is notable not only for general phrases such as 'at first it's all right' and 'no good', but also for its fixed expressions such as the quite lengthy 'you get so that you don't know where you are at all' and 'the crunch'. Examples 3.14 and 3.15 also contain fixed expressions ('the trouble is', 'the big worry was'), and the fixed, 'fossilized' nature of 'the trouble is' is further confirmed by the speaker adding a 'real' verb for the clause (*was*), something which speakers regularly do in modern spoken English with fixed expressions such as 'the problem is', 'the thing is', and so on (see McConvell 1988). But what does this occurrence of idioms and other fixed expressions tell us? What it might indicate is that the occurrence of such elements is not random, and that they may well correlate with particular discourse functions. It is this we shall now consider.

3.4.2 *The place of idioms in a discourse view of vocabulary*

If we can show some meaningful correlation between idioms and discourse, we may go a long way towards understanding one of the most interesting vocabulary questions for teachers, learners and syllabus designers: why should language 'duplicate' ways of saying things, offering us the literal and idiomatic alternatives that so often seem to coexist? The place of idioms in a syllabus and in the vocabulary learning process is usually dealt with rather unsatisfactorily, in description and in practical materials; idioms become a 'fun' element of the syllabus, but no one is quite sure what they are for, and learners have to be warned that they are dangerous minefields which can explode in their faces if they try to use them. In most cases idioms are considered to be something to tag on to the higher levels of terminal stages of language courses, or are often left to the twilight world of (in publishers' parlance) 'supplementary' materials. Advice to teachers in teacher-training manuals and other literature is often, understandably, vague. Gairns and Redman's (1986) otherwise excellent review of vocabulary teaching concludes that students' enthusiasm for idioms should be channelled into teaching those which are 'useful' and which can be incorporated without seeming unnatural into the learner's productive vocabulary (Gairns and Redman 1986: 36). Since such advice would seem to apply to every kind of lexeme (including single words), and since there would seem to be eqцal justification for consigning less useful idioms and single words to the receptive lexicon, the conclusion would seem somewhat otiose. Gairns and Redman (1986: 36) are right, however, in stressing the generally unhelpful nature of morphological and semantic field approaches to idioms.

It behoves us, therefore, to return to the notion of the relationship between macro-level features and these micro-level items. In the problem-solution conversational extracts, idioms and other fixed expressions seem to play a role in *evaluating* the situation and possible responses to it. Without evaluation, the problem-solution pattern is incomplete, as has been argued by the clause-relational analysts such as Winter (1977 and 1978) and Hoey (1983). Is there indeed consistency (at least to the extent that it can support a pedagogically useful statement) in the view that idioms play a major role in evaluation? Are they more than just alternative, non-literal ways of wording the world? If we look at our textual extracts, there does seem to be some correlation. The BFP membership text (Figure 3.2) contains two notable occurrences of idioms: 'take up the cudgels' and 'track record'. Both items may be labelled here as broad signals of the problem-solution pattern (as opposed to being topic-specific): 'take up the cudgels' is a strongly evaluative synonym of *respond*, and 'track record' of the *evaluation* function itself which lies at the heart of the pattern. Examples such as these do raise descriptive problems concerning the borderline between fully institutionalized idioms and extended metaphors which are perhaps not yet fully fossilized and retain some semantic transparency (on this indeterminate border see Fernando and Flavell 1981: 44–7). But this is hardly at issue here, and recent work on the teaching of metaphor anyway stresses the interpersonal and evaluative functions of metaphors which underline their common ground with more opaque idioms (see especially Low 1988). Not least, the study of metaphor must also address the apparent duplication of meaning in the lexicon and attempt to understand its functioning in exactly the same way as the study of idioms should do.

It is a strong claim for the functioning of idioms and other non-literal lexical devices to suggest that they correlate with elements of textual patterns, but it is not without support in general computational analysis of written texts of a wide variety of types, where the evaluative function of idioms seems paramount (see Moon 1992). Nor is there a lack of evidence from spoken data. One of the very few analysts to attempt to describe idiom use in natural spoken English is Strässler (1982). Strässler departs from the tradition of analysing idioms as a semantic problem and looks at the pragmatics of idioms in real data. He finds that they are relatively infrequent (occurring on average once per 1,150 words), which might already suggest that for the teacher wishing to concentrate on spoken skills, they are less of a 'problem' than they are often thought to be. But when idioms do occur, they occur with a high degree of predictability, not randomly. Idioms, claims Strässler, are much more likely to be used to say something about a third person or about an object rather than about the speaker him/herself or about second-person participants (Strässler 1982: 103). This he puts down to their evaluative functions and the risks to face and interpersonal relations which can arise from the self- or other-abasement idioms often entail (Strässler 1982: 103; 109). To say to someone 'I'm sorry if I've put your nose out of joint' expresses a dominance and confidence on the part of the speaker and a potential abasement of the listener which an alternative non-idiomatic rendition (eg 'I'm sorry if I've caused you difficulties/upset you in some way') seems to neutralize. Strässler's data, therefore, point strongly in the direction we wish to go: the potential for the integration of levels between lexico-grammatical form, communicative function (including interpersonal elements such as politeness and face), mode, text-type and genre. The data we shall present here support some of Strässler's conclusions and take us one step further.

We shall try to illustrate that idioms occur with the interpersonal restrictions suggested by Strässler *and* in a clear relationship with certain discourse-types and genres. As before, and as we shall do so often in this book, we turn to oral narrative as a very clearly defined genre with an identifiable discourse structure, and see there that idioms seem to occur at significant points, not randomly.

Idioms in narrative data often occur in segments where the teller is *evaluating* (in the Labovian sense, as we discussed in section 1.6.5) the events of the narrative. They also occur in *codas* (again in Labov's sense). Here are some examples with idioms in italics:

> (3.16)   [A is telling a story about her very old dog]
> A: He's 16, he's very geriatric.
> B: Yeah, our dog was really ill.
> A: I thought he was going to die actually. It would have been awful,
>   actually, just to see, to see him *peg out* on the kitchen floor [laughs].
> >   (Lucy Cruttenden's unpublished data, 1988)

> (3.17)   [A has just told of a series of calamities that he experienced on a
> recent holiday; first, B comments on the events]
> B: Still, pretty horrendous, though.
> A: Oh, it was very unsettling, . . . still, so many other unsettling factors
>   *I didn't know whether I was on my head or my heels* that day.
> >   (authors' data, 1989)

These two examples show idioms correlating with significant features of the narrative pattern. In example 3.16, 'It would have been awful, actually,' with its conditional tense is a typical *comparator*, where the teller evaluates actual events against a possible world; it is in this 'possible' evaluative segment the idiom occurs, and it is predicated upon a third person (the dog). In example 3.17, the idiom evaluates the whole situation, and acts as a *coda*, summarizing all the events. But here it is *first* person. Personal oral narrative is a particular genre where speakers often tell tales that evaluate and abase *themselves* (for humorous effect, to create social solidarity, to create informality, etc), and so we should not be surprised to find first person idioms here. Additionally, as McCarthy (1991: 139–40) points out, story-telling is frequently a collaborative effort, and listeners can evaluate events too (see also Duranti 1991). Here, we might well find idioms, but they will have to be ones that are careful not to abase the teller, unless the relationship between teller and listener is very relaxed and on equal terms. In our data we find listeners doing this:

> (3.18)   [Same speakers as in example 3.17, later in the discourse. B is
> now reciprocating with a story about her old dog being put down]
> B: . . . she wasn't in any pain and she was as alert as ever, that was the

awful thing, but her body was just *giving out*, her leg, and so my Mum
said, thought, 'Right, next day'.

C: *Don't know where to draw the line*, do you?

(Lucy Cruttenden's unpublished data, 1988)

Speaker B uses *giving out* ('ceasing to function') to evaluate the dog's
situation. Speaker C also uses an idiom to evaluate the events, but
predicates it upon an impersonal *you*, thus minimizing risk to face (it
is worth considering the opposite effect of '*you* don't know where to
draw the line' addressed as a personal pronoun to the teller). The
idiom here partakes of that 'retreat or sheltering behind shared
values' that Moon (1992) observes in idiom usage in her data, and
suggests the importance of observing the *cultural* contexts of idioms.

In these examples we can combine Strässler's (1982) observations
concerning the interpersonal nature of idioms and their non-random
distribution with regard to discourse patterning at the higher level.
This is in striking parallel with our statements about grammar in the
earlier sections of this chapter. It seems that, whatever aspects of
lexico-grammar we choose to look at, we cannot really separate them
from the concerns of creating discourse. Matters traditionally thought
of as the domain of semantics and syntax can be placed squarely at
the heart of discourse analysis. Things that we have traditionally
taught as language teachers in traditional ways (idioms being just one
example, being usually approached from their morphological characteristics or from their nature as semantic anomalies), can be
meaningfully reassessed from a language-as-discourse viewpoint. But
we stress that we do not reject the value of syntactic and
morphological approaches where these might be helpful for learning
purposes (see McCarthy 1990: 7). Nor would we underestimate the
potential for increasing cultural awareness offered by semantic-
universal types of approach (eg Makkai 1978). Finally, one can hardly
argue against the value of examining syntactic commutability as
exemplified in work by Cowie (1981) and Alexander (1978; 1984),
when a language like English contains so many expressions of such
varying degrees of syntactic fixedness (as well as a long scale from
almost complete semantic transparency to complete opacity). However, we wish to argue that the study of idioms will be of *greatest* use
to learners the more we know about their occurrence in discourse.

We shall stay with narrative and with idioms for a moment, but
return to written data further to reinforce our argument. Teachers
often face the task of trying to find appropriate textual sources for
areas of language that they wish to teach. Idioms are particularly
interesting in this respect. A kind of narrative data that seems

frequently to contain idioms is the popular horoscope, and, given what we have said above, this should not now surprise us at all. The horoscope is a narrative of the future (a kind of *irrealis* narrative if we subdivide narratives along conventional lines); it is *your* (the reader's) narrative, told and evaluated by the astrologer-writer. The writer is in a dominant role, and may wish to inform you, admonish you, advise you, but not terrify you or alienate you. Also, the horoscope has to be sufficiently general to seem to apply to any reader with that birth sign and must not be too topic-specific. Some examples of horoscopes follow from popular magazines.

> (3.19) Nice aspects to Saturn on 5 and 10 November suggest you'll *make headway* with work or study . . .
> *(More* magazine, 12 November 1991: 64)

> (3.20) You're usually *free and easy* with your money, but it looks like you're determined to save for something special. . . . People and places you thought too dull to bother with *turn out to be a riot.*
> *(More* magazine, 12 November 1991: 64)

> (3.21) From early November you must find ways of your own to overcome obstacles or realise that they're simply not worth worrying about. *Let off steam* as you need to *wind down.*
> *(More* magazine, 12 November 1991: 64)

> (3.22) An unexpected night out with someone close will *add some colour* to your life this week.
> *(Best* magazine, 14 November 1991)

> (3.23) But don't let others tell you how to spend your cash, especially youngsters who *think you are made of money.*
> *(Best* magazine, 14 November 1991)

> (3.24) Since the current Full Moon occurs in your own birth sign, you may well be of the opinion that it is up to others to *proffer the olive branch.*
> (Patric Walker, *Radio Times*, 24–30 August 1991: 89)

> (3.25) However, much depends on the outcome of a family or domestic wrangle and whether or not others really can be persuaded to *let bygones be bygones.*
> (Patric Walker, *Radio Times*, 24–30 August 1991: 89)

The popular personal horoscope, as a genre, is meant to be an intimate conversation between reader and astrologer. It is hardly remarkable then that the genre seems to have taken to itself a high occurrence of idioms that evaluate the reader's character, the behaviour of others towards the reader, and the situations that readers will supposedly find themselves in. In most popular magazine horoscopes (though in British ones there are noticeably fewer idioms in horoscopes in the 'quality' magazines), idioms occur with a much greater frequency than Strässler's (1982) suggested figure of every 1,150 words for spoken data. In a random 300-word sample from the data quoted above, no fewer than 13 idioms occur. So, not only are popular horoscopes an extraordinarily rich natural source of idioms for the teacher but also they show how vocabulary distribution is crucially dependent on genre and register. The discourse syllabus, where notions such as genre, register and text-type are central organizing principles, can choose its data to highlight certain micro-level features within macro-level frameworks and vice versa. It can thus operate by referring both top-down and bottom-up simul-taneously, avoiding the divorce that often occurs between structure and vocabulary lists on the one hand and prescriptions of text-types on the other. The most useful work in discourse analysis for the teacher is that which achieves this integration of levels.

3.4.3   Idioms and culture

We remain with idioms for our final subsection on vocabulary, for they are a good example of the extent to which vocabulary knowledge can place great demands on the cultural competence of the learner, an issue we shall take further in Chapter 4, and which will be relevant in our discussion in Chapter 5 of the various types of 'competences' posited by linguists which applied linguists try to build into language teaching syllabuses and materials.

Anyone looking at British English data in search of idioms, we have suggested, will find their distribution to be uneven and closely tied to discourse-type. Another thing they may well notice is the frequency with which idioms and other types of fixed expressions are *alluded to* rather than used in full. Many common, everyday texts assume that the receiver will be able to pick up such allusions and perceive the cultural references made by them. These references are not necessarily 'cultural' in the sense of referring to great art and literature, but in the sense that they refer to the everyday culture of the mass media, the deep-rooted common cultural store of allusions, proverbs, sayings, idioms and other fixed linguistic forms and the belief-systems these encode. It is a broad notion of culture that we shall take up again in Chapter 4. Examples of various kinds of oblique cultural references found in advertising texts, book and song titles, headlines and other sources follow, with an explanation of the cultural reference.

(3.26)   Twinkle, twinkle, little tsar.
(Headline to an article about Russia)

Reference: 'Twinkle, twinkle, little star', children's nursery rhyme/song.

(3.27)   Dry skin. Irritation. Razor Burn. No wonder shaving's a pain in the neck.
(Razor advertisement)
Reference: 'a pain in the neck', an idiomatic phrase meaning an annoyance, a problem.

(3.28)   Now is the discount of our winter tents.
(Sign advertising a winter sale of camping equipment in an outdoor leisure shop)
Reference: 'Now is the winter of our discontent/Made glorious summer by this sun of York', Shakespeare, *King Richard III*, Act I, Scene 1.

(3.29)   Despite inflation, the wages of sin remain the same.
(On a chapel noticeboard)
Reference: 'The wages of sin is death', The Bible, *Epistle of Paul to the Romans* vi.23.

(3.30)   Junk and disorderly.
(Sign on bric-a-brac shop)
Reference: 'drunk and disorderly', legal term for an offence.

(3.31)   You've never add it so good.
(Sign advertising an accountancy business)
Reference: 'Most of our people have never had it so good', British Prime Minister Harold Macmillan in a speech, 20 July 1957.
This was generally splashed as '*You've* never . . .'

(3.32)   *Spaniard in the Works*
(Book by John Lennon)
Reference: 'to throw a spanner in the works', an idiomatic phrase meaning to disrupt a process or the progress of something.

From this brief selection we can see oblique references to childhood culture, to religion, to the law, to politics, to great literature and simply to everyday idioms. Any reader failing to pick up these references misses not only the humour but also the sense of cultural solidarity, of belonging to a community with shared linguistic and cultural values that such references engender. An ability to refer across discourse worlds, a kind of *intertextuality* (the text referring outside itself to the world of other texts in the common culture), lies at the bottom of this aspect of lexical competence. For the discourse analyst it suggests a widespread penetration of everyday culture into the way we express ourselves and the ultimate impossibility of a theory of language in use that attempts to separate culture from linguistic expression. It is conceivable that, on the most banal level, culture-free versions of natural languages can be created for survival-level communication or for very restricted registers (for example the role of English as *lingua franca* in international business and academic communication), but languages as they are naturally used by human beings for interpersonal, interactive communication probably cannot exist without reference to common cultural norms and without exploiting the potential for creativity those norms offer. The implications of the kinds of data we have looked at for the language teaching context in relation to wider issues such as the teaching of culture in its various different senses will be taken further in Chapter 4. For the syllabus designer our discussion here opens the whole question of the difficulty of separating different types of competence in the learner, a theme we shall return to in Chapter 5.

In this book we place great emphasis on the importance of literary text as discourse; it is also in literary text that we can find examples of the creative exploitation of idioms and their cultural contexts. One notable source is T. S. Eliot's poem *The Waste Land*, in the second section, entitled 'A Game of Chess'. This section of the poem is basically structured on three linguistic registers, a 'high' register, a 'medium' and a 'low' (see Monroe 1990). The 'high' segment begins with an allusion to Shakespeare's play, *Anthony and Cleopatra*, and continues in a rather formal literary register. The second section is somewhat neutral, while the third section attempts to capture the demotic conversation of a pub at closing-time. There we find idioms playing familiar roles in the discourse, but, additionally, we find in Eliot's text face-threatening use of idioms in an aggressive, argumentative context, in a way which contrasts neatly with Strässler's (1982) more co-operative conversational contexts, where threats to face are normally avoided. No stylistic analysis of the 'A Game of Chess' section of *The Waste Land* is complete without a consideration of the role of idioms in creating not only the demotic cultural context but also the sharp edge of the pub conversation and the swaggering, boastful aggressiveness of the narrative voice at that point in the narrative. Literary text in this case, therefore, provides us both with data that re-create the conversational context and with a particularly interesting use of idioms probably otherwise very difficult to gather as naturally occurring data. Twentieth-century English poetry in particular is rich in the mixing of registers, a reaction by poets against the notion of a fixed, stable, homogeneous poetic diction (see the discussions in Leech 1969; Carter 1987b: ch. 8).

The literary text is not some object dwelling in a separate world from other texts, but can, and should, be held up as a mirror to other texts and to the cultures they spring from and be viewed as language used in special ways creating highly focused contexts. It is the very focused and marked nature of these contexts that make literary texts ideal vehicles for raising language awareness and homing in on particular areas of language use which are present in different forms and less focused contexts in everyday texts. This integration of literary text and other everyday texts is something we shall argue for in depth in Chapter 4, and we shall argue in both directions: that literary text is an important vehicle for raising language awareness and for focusing on language and culture, and that literary texts can best be understood when juxtaposed with non-literary texts (for instance, the use of idioms in literary narrative compared and contrasted with their use in oral narrative).

3.5 Naturalness

Not all of the questions that discourse analysts set out to answer are of immediate relevance to language teachers, but one aspect of ethnomethodology which is of interest is the close observation of natural patterns in everyday linguistic events such as explaining, arguing, telling anecdotes, agreeing and disagreeing, inviting, apologizing, requesting and thanking. Working with real data, ethnomethodologists attempt to describe such events in terms of patterned behaviour within particular cultures, especially aiming at the elusive objectivity which can be achieved only by viewing one's own culture as 'exotic'. The kinds of patterns thus observed are sets of elements in sequence, the presence and ordering of which represent an idealized version of a particular culture's requirements for the realization of an activity such as inviting, apologizing or whatever. As such, they are characterizations of different *genres*, in the sense that we have talked about genres in section 1.6. They are not simply realizations of single speech acts in the rather simplistic way that is sometimes conceived in description and in pedagogy; the whole emphasis is on a sequence and an ordering of acts which together perform an activity recognized by members of the speech community. This level of naturalness is just as important in the syllabus and materials as the natural and idiomatic use of grammar and lexis (see McCarthy 1988b).

Let us begin by taking an everyday example: the asking of favours. As with all the other examples of everyday genres mentioned above, the asking of a favour involves the participants in a high degree of interactivity; one can hardly imagine a culture where the simple transmission of information concerning the need of the favour-seeker would be sufficient to enact the event. Participants are involved in risks of loss of face, of imposition, mis-communication and disharmony, and are thus faced with the need to press into service the interpersonal grammar of the language being used and the politeness strategies considered normal by the culture in which the favour-seeking is performed. Favour-seeking, as with so many other genres of this type, takes on the air of a ritual, with participants following predictable steps. It is the ritualistic or genre-constrained framework which discourse analysts try to describe, and which is the important preliminary for the language teacher in deciding what the most useful and indispensable language is in any given case, as well as holding in reserve other, non-essential language which may surround any event. For the learner, knowing 'how to do' such genres in the target language is an enabling vehicle for personal expression; it is more than just a set of robotic procedures and is, we would argue, part and parcel of the powerful folk-linguistic notion of 'getting a feel' for the foreign language.

Data for everyday linguistic genres such as favour-seeking are not always easy to obtain, since such events often take place in intimate personal settings. But dramatized data such as plays and soap operas, not written with any intention of displaying or teaching language forms, are often an excellent source of data considered by consumers to be 'natural'. Additionally, where data are available in published research, teachers with access to the sources can gain great insight from the observations of others, and can develop their skills of evaluating the naturalness of dramatized extracts by analysing them in relation to what research has established to be the norm. Evaluating 'artificial' language data (here meaning simply as opposed to naturally occurring data) is one of the many practical purposes of analysis that we shall propose in this book at various points (see especially section 5.5), and which we feel should be important features of learning-about-language components of teacher-training programmes.

Our data sample for favour-seeking comes from a very popular Australian television soap opera, *Neighbours*, in which everyday families interact in an everyday fashion, agreeing and disagreeing, explaining, arguing, requesting, narrating and so on. In our sample, Clarrie, an elderly man, has come to ask a favour of Helen, an attractive grandmother living next door, in connection with a party Clarrie has suggested Ryan (his teenage grandson) should throw at their home ('number 30') to help Ryan switch off from too much studying (Clarrie's first problem; the favour is his second 'problem'):

(3.33)
CLARRIE: So I said to him, forget your books for one night, throw a party next weekend.
HELEN: A party at number 30! What will Dorothy say about *that*?

CLARRIE: Well, what she doesn't know won't hurt her. Of course, I'll be keeping my eye on things, and that brings me to my next problem. You see, these young people, they don't want an old codger like me poking my nose in, so I'll make myself scarce, but I still need to be closer to hand, you see. So I was wondering, would it be all right if I came over here on the night? What d'you reckon?
HELEN: Oh, Clarrie, I . . .
CLARRIE: Oh I'd be no bother. It'd mean a heck of a lot to those young kids.
HELEN: All right.
CLARRIE: I knew you'd say yes. You're an angel, Helen.
HELEN: Ha! [laughs]

(Neighbours, BBC1 TV, 29 August 1991)

If we examine this extract in terms of sequences of elements, we can see that Clarrie does not actually spell out his favour until 'Would it be all right if I came over here on the night?'; a lot of preparatory work takes place first, which could be expressed schematically:

SIGNAL OF OPENING   'that brings me to my next problem'
EXPLAIN PROBLEM   (marker) 'You see,'
                       (explanation) 'these young people, . . . to hand'
                       (marker) 'you see.'
ASK FAVOUR   (marker) 'So,'
                       (softener) 'I was wondering,'
                       (request) 'would it be all right if . . . night?'
                       (softener) 'What d'you reckon?'

The ball is then in Helen's court; she has to say yes or no. In fact she hesitates, which occasions further elaboration by Clarrie. We can also schematize this phase.

(RESPONDENT) YES OR NO   (hesitation) 'Oh, Clarrie, I . . .'
MINIMIZATION   'I'd be no bother.'
REINFORCE EXPLANATION   'It'd mean a heck of a lot . . .'
(RESPONDENT) ACCEDE   'All right.'
THANK (WITH BOOST)   'I knew you'd say yes. You're an angel, Helen.'
(RESPONDENT) MINIMIZE   'Ha! [laughs]'

We now have a putative structure for favour-seeking sequences. Not all sequences will be the same, of course, and a proper investigation would need to consider occasions where the favour is acceded to *without* hesitation, those where the favour is small enough to dispense with some aspects of the ritual, and those where the favour is declined. Declining requests of any type threatens face and harmony, and elaborate linguistic means will be utilized by interactants for damage-limitation. What will also vary from context to context is actual realization. For instance, Clarrie's 'which brings me to my next problem' is not the only, nor necessarily the most common, way of signalling that a favour is about to be broached. One can easily imagine alternatives:

'Could you do me a favour?'
'I was going to ask you a small/great favour.'
'I wonder if you could help me out.'

Only close observation of real data will provide us with the best range of realizations for the syllabus or materials that we may be seeking to create.

What Clarrie's behaviour seems to suggest is that, in his culture, favour-seeking (at least for significantly large favours) must be preceded by elaborate precautions against loss of face on both sides. Signals must be sent out. Markers will be used to clarify the situation (Clarrie uses 'you see' twice, and 'so'). The request must be softened, made less direct and imposing (past continuous 'I was wondering'; informal tag 'What d'you reckon?'). The asker must reduce his own self-importance in the matter and exaggerate Helen's. Note how Clarrie uses idioms to do this: 'old codger', 'make myself scarce', 'closer to hand', 'no bother', 'you're an angel'; we have already argued the importance of this aspect of idiom use in section 3.4. Helen, for her part, must minimize her action in acceding; this she does by her laughter and dismissive 'Ha!' (see Pomerantz 1978 on down-scaling compliments). All this is what we have called an interpersonal grammar; it is as much a part of the description of English as a basis for a language-teaching syllabus as the 'ideational' grammar that creates the content of the talk; it accounts for the *interactional* elements, while the ideational grammar realizes the *transactional* elements (see Brown and Yule 1983: 1–4).

All languages will have an interpersonal grammar for the creation of genres. In fact, some of the best observations on favour-seeking data come from Held's (1989) study of politeness in requests and thanking sequences in French and Italian, and her data confirm in several important ways what we have observed from our one-sample analysis. Held observes three main stages in favour-seeking: the *preparatory* phase, the *focal* phase and the *final* phase. The preparatory phase corresponds to our 'signal of opening'. The focal phase is subdivided into elements such as 'ego's [ie asker's] reasons', 'constraints' (eg 'I've tried everywhere but can't get one'), the other's face (eg 'You're the only person I can turn to'), and so on. The final phase often consists of anticipatory thanks, promises and compliments (such as Clarrie's 'I knew you'd say yes. You're an angel'). Held's basic sequence of elements gives us confidence that the *Neighbours* extract is reasonably natural and a good model for favour-seeking. Once we have the general structure (or GSP as it was called in section 1.6) for favour-seeking with varying outcomes, we are in a far better position to design activities, choose materials, encode a syllabus or evaluate data relevant to this activity than we might have been by either just making a list of decontextualized speech-acts or an equally abstracted list of grammatical structures and lexical items.

We have dwelt on favour-seeking because it is an excellent example of a common, everyday genre amenable to description using discourse-analytical methods, and one which is likely to be of practical interest to language teachers. Other daily events that can be described in a similar way include complaint sequences, direction-giving, inviting, problem-sharing, etc. Psathas and Kozloff (1976) show how direction-giving is an ordered sequence of actions in the way we have argued for favour-seeking. Three sequential phases of elements are common: the situation-defining phase (where the receiver of the directions is starting from, how well he/she knows the environment and what means of transport is to be used), the information and instruction phase, where the actual directions are given, and the ending phase, where checks are made and mutual reassurances given (eg 'You can't miss it').

Our data and description in this section raise two potential areas for close monitoring in the language teaching context: first, whether learners' performances in realizing particular day-to-day genres are 'natural' in that they contain the basic elements and anticipated sequences required by the target culture, and second, whether learners can handle the interpersonal grammar of L2 with skill, sensitivity and the right 'feel'. Cross-cultural research, while offering the reassurance that phenomena such as face-preservation and politeness are universal (see Brown and Levinson 1987), also produces on occasion tantalizing evidence of differences between cultures in their normal behaviour within genres. Jaworski (1990), for instance, shows some interesting mismatches between elements and sequencing in informal phatic opening phases of conversational encounters in Polish and in American English. In his data, his American learners of Polish transferred some of their cultural habits to Polish, using more ritualistic linguistic formulae than the native-speakers, and using more of them at the *beginning* of the conversational opening phase. Also, some elements recurring to a significant extent in the Polish speakers' performance were rare or absent in the Americans' performance. On eight occasions, the Polish subjects expressed surprise at meeting their interlocutor; only one American subject did this. Jaworski does suggest that differences of this kind may play a part in cultural stereotyping; it is not certain that minor differences in performance will always cause negative effects or have any implications at all, but they should be aspects of the monitoring process by teachers and learners together, a point we shall take up again in Chapter 5. Nor does it need to be the case that the remedy for such cultural gaps be sought in simply 'cramming' knowledge of the target culture in the way that one might learn about the geography of L2's homeland(s). Brown (1990), for instance, argues that it is better to encourage learners in a set of strategies for constructing the target culture in the same way that we all adopt such strategies to infer features of our own, L1 cultures.

Much of what we have been exemplifying and discussing in this section is often considered under the heading of 'politeness', and languages and cultures are often perceived as more, or less, 'polite'. This leads to the cry sometimes heard by teachers of English from frustrated learners: 'I don't want to be polite like English people; I want to be myself'. Politeness is perhaps an unfortunate choice of label for the phenomena we have looked at and much of the negative reaction to inclusion of these features in language teaching programmes may be due to the connotations of the label. The sequential structure of direction-giving is a practical and sensible procedure to ensure successful communication, rather than a series of 'polite' acts. The elaborate behaviour that accompanies something such as the seeking of significant favours is also concerned with proceeding towards a goal in the smoothest way and with sensitivity to one's interlocutors. We would therefore prefer the label *natural interactiveness* to describe the kind of behaviour which will be found, admittedly with distinct realizations, surrounding the basic functions of informing, asking and directing in all human cultures. On the realizational level, what may be perceived as varying sometimes is the degree of *directness* commonly adopted in different languages. Garcia (1989), for instance, found that Venezuelans simulating apology-sequences were more directly friendly and familiar with the person to whom they were apologizing than American subjects, who were more deferent and self-effacing, and that these differences could cause cross-cultural misunderstandings. Both groups, however, were using interactive strategies.

A further problem in examining learners' performances in L2 is that we may make misjudgements about their L1 culture because of the reduced range of interactive strategies that a learner may have at his/her disposal owing to a lack of grammatical or lexical knowledge. In such situations, the learner may fall back on a rather skeletal 'transactional' mode of behaviour, a point we shall pursue further in section 5.4. There is evidence that learners do this. Trosborg's (1987) study of apology simulations with Danish learners of English found that lower linguistic competence threw learners back on basic apology formulae, as opposed to native-speaker subjects, who were able to realize a range of interactive elements, including 'repair offers' (offering to make amends in some way). Without the appropriate linguistic knowledge, we can hardly expect learners to display the full functional range demanded of naturally interactive sequences.

By studying the natural patterns of everyday situations, we can come to a much better understanding of what each one demands of participants in terms of cultural and linguistic behaviour. With such information, we are better placed to design syllabuses and materials, evaluate existing ones and, perhaps most important of all, to understand the interpersonal and inter-cultural areas of language learning that are most sensitive to subtle differences in the manipulation of interpersonal grammars. The ethnomethodological approach enables us to combine the best features of the old 'situational' approach (describing what typically happens in given settings) with communicative approaches stressing the functions that particular linguistic realizations can perform, and with the genre-based approach that tries to encapsulate the elements and sequences of language-forms and functions that together constitute accepted and recognized activities in particular cultures.

Here we have talked about observing everyday spoken situations, but the same generic sequences involving natural interactive behaviour can be observed in written language. In Chapter 2 we emphasized how the same patterns were found in spoken and written modes, so we should not be surprised to find the same urges to interactiveness in writer–reader reciprocity. For example, research has shown that in spoken English, disagreement sequences tend to take the form of partial agreement preceding the act of disagreement and the inclusion of softeners, as a strategy to preserve the recipient's face (eg Pearson 1986). Mulkay (1985) not only finds similar tendencies for 'agreement prefaces' in written texts, but also finds that disagreements are frequent and forceful. He suggests that forceful disagreement may be easier to carry out in writing than in speech. So, while the same patterned elements and sequences may be expected broadly to be found in speech and writing, there may be differences in distribution and realization that warrant separate attention and which may contribute to the creation of distinctions of mode, as we have used the term in Chapter 1. As we argued there, the dimension of mode can cut across other divisions in the syllabus, and this will probably be true for the everyday situations that we have considered here.

Reader activities

Activity 1

In the light of the section on discourse management (3.1), look at this text and consider the function of the cleft construction at the beginning of the second paragraph. In what way can it be said to function both retrospectively and prospectively, as Johns and Johns (1977) suggest? The text is a review of a film about John Lennon (*Imagine: John Lennon*).

> Those who thought Lucy In The Sky With Diamonds was a way of putting LSD into a song title were wrong. It was, in fact, the title of a drawing by John Lennon's son. Such revelations abound in *Imagine: John Lennon* and are no very good reason for going to see David Wolper and Andrew Solt's officially-sanctioned obituary. It's a bit sparse with the secrets, unlike Goldman's recent book.
>   What the film is, though, is a friendly but not entirely uncritical summation of the life and times of a song-writing superstar who received so much adulation, fame and fortune that he could have been easily forgiven for going completely nuts, not just spasmodically eccentric.
> (Derek Malcolm, *Days in the Life*, *Guardian*, 27 October 1988: 21)

Activity 2

Here are some teaching materials prepared by Tessa Moore, of the Centre for English Language Education at the University of Nottingham. In what way has Moore tried to introduce a discourse-oriented approach? What other types of structures could her exercise-type be adapted to?

continued

Activity 2 *continued*

Relative clauses: focus

The information contained in a relative clause is generally less important than that contained in the main clause. What is important will depend on the context or the main subject the writer is talking about. In the following sentences the same information is presented in different ways. Try to decide which sentence is more appropriate after reading the final statement:

(a) Guy Fawkes, who tried to blow up Parliament, was a Roman Catholic.

(b) Guy Fawkes, who was a Roman Catholic, tried to blow up Parliament.

  The plot failed.

(a) Guy Fawkes, who tried to blow up Parliament, was a Roman Catholic.

(b) Guy Fawkes, who was a Roman Catholic, tried to blow up Parliament.

  He was just one of many who were prepared to die for their faith.

(a) Charles I, who was beheaded, was not prepared to give more power to Parliament.

(b) Charles I, who was not prepared to give more power to his Parliament, was beheaded.

  He was the last English monarch to be put to death by the people.

(a) Diane Abbot, who is a black Labour MP, was elected in 1983.

(b) Diane Abbot, who was elected in 1983, is a black Labour MP.

  She is one of only 43 women sitting in Parliament.

Write a paragraph from the notes below; the information in brackets is less important. Remember to include any articles, prepositions, etc, which may be necessary.

The first bicycle in Scotland

  1839: First Scottish bicycle – designed by Kirkpatrick Macmillan. (He was a blacksmith/He lived near Dumfries)

continued

Activity 2 *continued*

Bicycle – based on a French invention (designed by Baron de Sauerbrun in 1818) (consisted of two wheels connected by a wooden crossbar)
Macmillan's machine – useless on Scotland's hilly roads (propelled by rider's feet)
Developed another model (worked with treadles/avoided contact between feet and ground)
Macmillan – not interested in marketing bicycle. Gavin Dalzell (another Scot) sold invention to Lion Bicycle Company (this company sold it under the name of the 'Dalzell')
(Shelagh Young – History KS 3–4, AT 1, Knowledge & Understanding of History as in Bright Spark, 'The Brainchild of a Devil on Wheels', *Education Guardian*, 14 May 1991: 4)

The next stage in this exercise would be to add linkers/markers and look at reduced relative and appositional clauses.

Activity 3

Here is a selection of short news texts. What, if any, patterns of tense/aspect can be seen in them? Do these patterns correspond to a particular sub-genre of news report? What name or label could be given to such a genre? What particular grammatical contrast(s) would they be a useful resource for in teaching?

1   ELECTRICITY CHIEFS TO AXE 5,000

Five thousand jobs are to be axed by electricity generating firm National Power, it was announced yesterday.

Smaller power stations will close but bosses pledged no compulsory redundancies over the next five years.

National Power, the larger of the two generating businesses due for privatisation in February, also announced a £605 million loss last year.

(*Daily Mirror*, 27 July 1990: 2)

2   JUST THE JOB FOR SHILTS

Peter Shilton is to continue his career with the England football team after all.

The Derby keeper, who announced his international retirement after the World Cup, is to carry on in a new role as goalkeeping coach. New England manager Graham Taylor is anxious to utilise Shilton's enormous experience and expertise by passing it on to the keepers battling it out to take over the number one jersey.

Shilton will replace the existing goalkeeper coach Mike Kelly, but the move has not yet been made official.

(Matt Hughes, *Daily Mirror*, 26 July 1990: 36)

Activity 4

Consider this extract from a piece of writing by a non-native speaker of English. The extract comes from an academic essay on the stylistic analysis of an English novel. The essay writer is commenting on the novelist's use of reported speech-acts, and cites a particular part of the novel, where an old man is doing battle with a big fish at sea. Bearing in mind the discussion of tense and genre in section 3.3, what norms or conventions is the writer breaking by using *past* tense?

> To indicate the old man's ordeal and endurance, the verb *promised* is used in his speech while he was trying very hard to kill it [the big fish]. He was very tired and he tried very hard to kill it therefore he *promised* to do it.

Activity 5

In the light of our previous narrative data, how would you explain the occurrence of the italicized idioms in this piece of natural oral data?

The speaker is a school teacher talking about discipline problems with her class and what advice a friend, Gill, gave her:

> Anyway, last lesson today. I'm lucky. I'm only teaching two. Well, I don't know about sixth form, so I've only got one today. My second years and . . . erm, it's the last lesson on a Friday so, erm, Gill said, you know, 'You'll probably have to *blow your top* the next couple of lessons *just to show them* like'. The lesson before, I was quite firm and they talked a lot and we *got on really well*, but she said otherwise *they might push it a bit*, so I *had a bit of a barny* today and I practised my shouting in the classroom and, er, Liz was . . . she . . . Liz reckons she thought my lesson went really really well.
> (Roza Gimenez's unpublished data, 1991)

Activity 6

Underline all the modal items in this text and consider its usefulness for the classroom in terms of which kinds of modal items it best illustrates and what contrasts in the functions of items it best exemplifies.

continued

Activity 6 continued

The road to a world park

To manage activities in the Antarctic without interfering with its ecological balance is one of the greatest challenges facing humankind.

A World Park Treaty could be created as 'easily' as the minerals treaty – by negotiation. An 'environmental convention' could be agreed as part of the Antarctic Treaty system. If negotiations on an environmental treaty started in 1990, Antarctica could begin the next century as the first World Park.

To safeguard the environment, all human activities would be judged against the 'World Park Criteria' of Wilderness, Peace and Cooperation. Minerals mining, nuclear testing and storage or 'disposal' of toxic or nuclear waste would not be acceptable.

An Antarctic Environmental Protection Commission could ensure uniform implementation and enforcement of rules. Any proposed activity would also have to adhere to the 'precautionary principle' whereby those hoping to conduct the activity must show that it would be environmentally benign.

What is needed now is the political will from governments to embark on such a path. Public opinion in many countries has mandated governments to press for an environmental treaty. They are not alone; last year the UN General Assembly called for Antarctica to be declared a World Park.

Britain is one of the very few countries insisting that a mining ban is not in keeping with national interests. If the UK were to change its position other countries would surely reconsider. The US senate is showing significant signs of opposition to the minerals treaty while the West Germans have put off signing it.

The UK government must give global, environmental interests precedence over narrow, selfish interests in Antarctica.

(*Greenpeace News*, Spring 1990: 8)

Notes on activities

Activity 1

The cleft construction at the beginning of paragraph 2 is 'What the film is, though, is . . .'. Retrospectively, this contrasts with the rather negative statements in the first paragraph, which suggest that the film is hardly worth seeing. The cleft construction stresses that the film has positive qualities, and simultaneously signals prospectively that paragraph 2 will tell us what those positive qualities are. This is a typical example of the influence that a cleft construction can have over a considerable stretch of text on either side of it.

Activity 2

Moore's exercises make the point that the choice of a non-defining relative clause has implications beyond its own sentence. In this respect she is looking at the discourse implications of the construction rather than at its internal structure and position. The non-defining relatives in her examples clearly relegate the information contained in them to the level of comment rather than topic; thus the examples where *topical* information (ie information which will be continued as the main topic of the next sentence) is put into the relative clause sound rather odd (eg option (a) in the first set of choices).

Moore's basic principle is that a construction should be exemplified in light of its effect on surrounding sentences and that the learner's attention should be focused on making a choice that takes the surrounding sentence(s) into account. The principle might therefore also be useful for constructions such as clefts, non-finite subordinate clauses, apposition, and so on. It could also be used directly to apply some of the example sentences in Ehrlich (1990), which looks at choices of pronouns or full noun phrases in the second sentence of sentence-pairs similar to those Moore uses.

Activity 3

The news texts display an interesting regular tense pattern: headline and/or initial sentence(s) with the 'future infinitive' construction ('Electricity chiefs *to axe* 5,000'), followed by futures with *will* ('smaller power stations *will* close').

The infinitive construction is used for the general 'abstract' of the news item, while the *will* constructions seem to correlate with the specific details of the stories. So, just as we had a regular pattern of present perfect plus past simple for 'hot news' stories in the past, we seem to have a regular pattern of tense forms for stories about things that will happen in the future. Texts of this kind are excellent not only for showing the functions of different constructions but also for actually offering them together, in contrast, in non-artificial contexts.

Activity 4

This activity underlines a rather fine point, but one which illustrates the fact that genres have internal conventions of grammatical form. It is usual to refer to details of a narrative one is reviewing or criticizing or summarizing by using present tense, not past. Note how book blurbs, film reviews and programme outlines for television and radio films and plays do this. The literary-critical essay also normally follows the same convention. An interesting difference is revealed if one thinks of the answer to the question 'What is *Crocodile Dundee* about?', which would be answered with a present-tense narrative summary, as compared with 'What happened in *Eastenders* last night?', which would be recounted as a typical narrative, in past tense.

Activity 5

Here we have idioms used in the typical way that oral narrators use them: to stand back from the narrative in some way and to evaluate the events. The evaluation here includes quoting what a third party said about events (two idioms: *blow your top*, *show them*), comparing the actual lesson in the story with an earlier one (*got on well*), using a Labovian *comparator*, talking about what *might* happen (*might push it a bit*), and the narrator evaluating her own actions of that day (*had a bit of a barny*). There does seem to be a direct correlation between narrators' use of idioms and the evaluative function in Labov's (1972) sense, and idioms are not merely non-literal alternatives used randomly.

Activity 6

Modal items

> (1.4) *could*; (1.5) *could*; (1.7) *could*; (1.9) *would*; (1.12) *would*; (1.13) *could*; (1.15) *would*; (1.16) *must*; (1.28) *must*

Of nine tokens, three types (*could*, *would* and *must*) are represented more than once. There is a neat contrast here between *could*, *would* and *must* which can be exploited in the classroom. This would be especially useful with Chinese-speaking learners of English, who often have difficulties with *could* and *would*.

Could correlates with the writer's opinions and proposals; *would* expresses the projected *results* of those proposals. The first *must* (1.16) corresponds to a proposed rule or law, while the second *must* (1.28), is the concluding evaluation by the author and represents a strong imperative.

This text is a good one for classroom use since it contains sufficient examples of *could* and *would* in a natural context to illustrate two important contrasting modal functions.

Further reading

An excellent article which takes a discourse perspective on front-placing and which relates to our discussion on discourse management is Hietaranta (1984). Thompson (1985) looks at the discourse implications of initial versus final purpose clauses in English, while

Virtanen (1992) examines fronted adverbials of time and place. Another paper (data-based) on cleft constructions is Collins (1991); on pseudo-clefts with *all* see Bonelli (1992). Another recent, excellent paper on clefts, offering a classification of types, is Delin (1991). Front-placed *ing*-forms are analysed in a data-based study by Erdman (1981). Front-placing and cleft usage in other languages include Källgren and Prince (1989) (Swedish) and Lambrecht (1988) (French). In the same collection as the Lambrecht paper, Myhill and Hibiya (1988) is an interesting study of discourse and clause-chaining. Hinds (1977) gives further arguments for a link between pronominalization and paragraphing. Of relevance to the staging of information and how certain constructions may be overgeneralized in learners' writing, see Schachter and Rutherford (1983), who look at the use of *there is* among Chinese speakers' essays in English. Watabe, Brown and Ueta (1991) look at the use of passive constructions in written data from Japanese and English learners of ESL and JSL, respectively. Further discussion of topic-organization in paragraphs may be found in Giora (1983b).

Fleischman (1985), as well as being an excellent general work on tense and narrative, is of particular interest to scholars of French, as her data are thirteenth-century Old French narratives. Fleischman (1990) is an important extension of her earlier work and contains useful categorizations of narrative types. The papers in Fleischman and Waugh (1991) are useful for those interested in tense usage in French, Italian and Spanish. French tense and aspect contrasts in discourse are also discussed, alongside Russian and Malay, in Hopper (1979). Hopper's paper is interesting from the point of view of *realization* of interpersonal and textual signals in different languages; Malay, for instance, signals foregrounded elements of narrative by using 'passive' voice and the *lah* particle. Hopper (1982) is along similar lines. Other interesting papers on the present tense used in 'past' contexts are Bellos (1978), Bailey (1985) and Johnstone (1987). The special issue of *Linguistics and Philosophy* (1986) on tense and aspect in discourse is also worth consulting.

The whole issue of foreground versus background events and how these are marked by tense and aspect (among other features) is taken up by Couper-Kuhlen (1989), who challenges some basic assumptions, especially that which holds that simple aspect in English signals foregrounding while continuous signals background. Another paper on aspect and foregrounding is Ehrlich (1987). Polanyi (1981) also looks at foregrounding and backgrounding and relates these to evaluation in narrative. Paprotté (1988) examines the use of perfective and imperfective aspect for foregrounding and back-grounding in Greek oral narratives and compares this with English. Those interested in tense and aspect in Spanish oral narratives should consult Silva-Corvalán (1983). Silva-Corvalán's paper is of interest not only to Hispanists, for she takes to task the view expressed in Wolfson (1978; 1979) that the historical present serves to separate events in a narrative rather than to dramatize particular events. Silva-Corvalán inclines to the latter view (as does Schiffrin, 1981) and sees historical present as an internal evaluation device. The use of historical present tense and past tense for marked and unmarked features in narrative has recently been re-examined by Fludernik (1991). The historical present in colloquial Japanese narratives is considered by Soga (1983: 46–8), who concludes that its function is similar to historical present in English, but that shifts between tenses seem to be freer and less bound by tense sequencing rules.

In the LSP field, the general concerns of genre and ESP texts are explored in the collection of papers in Dudley-Evans (1987), which are strongly influenced by Swales's work. LSP teachers will also find interesting material in Riddle (1986), who considers the discourse function of the past tense in English and who takes a brief look at the problem of tense choice in learned citations (eg when does one say 'Chomsky (1957) claims/claimed/has claimed'?). Malcolm (1987) is an important paper on tense usage in scientific articles, and more recently, Salager-Meyer (1992) combines an anlysis of verb tense and modality in medical English texts.

Papers on vocabulary at the discourse level include McCarthy (1988a; 1992b) and Carter and McCarthy (1988a). Hoey's recent work is significant in the study of lexical patterning, in general (1991a) and in legal texts in particular (1988).

Among the many good recent papers and books on modality are Coates (1983; 1990), Holmes (1983; 1988), Ghadessy (1984), Westney (1986) and the papers in the special issue on modality of *Folia Linguistica* (1987). Powell (1992) strongly supports the evaluative nature of idiom usage. More on idioms in the works of Eliot and the American poet John Ashbery may be found in Monroe (1990). The kind of word-play we have looked at in oblique references to idioms and cultural entities is investigated from a phonological point of view by Zwicky and Zwicky (1986). Moeran (1984) is good on hidden cultural allusions in advertising texts.

On ethnomethodological approaches to everyday situations, Gar-finkel (1967) is a good introduction. The standard work on politeness as a universal is Brown and Levinson (1987); Lakoff (1973) is also a good, basic source. Brown and Levinson have recently been criticized for lacking generalizability by Matsumoto (1988). The *Journal of Pragmatics* (1990) has devoted a special issue to the study of politeness. Butler (1988) is a good study of politeness in modalized directives. A contrastive approach to politeness formulae may be found in Davies (1987). Myers (1989) is a good example of the application of Brown and Levinson's work in the written context. Cherry (1988) also deals with the written context.

Studies of the particular activities of apologizing and requesting can be found in Blum-Kulka (1989a) and in the papers in Blum-Kulka, House and Kasper (1989). Blum-Kulka's own paper (1989b) in that collection has examples of realizations of requests, which include favour-seeking, in Australian English, Canadian French, Hebrew and Argentine Spanish. Openings, requesting and complimenting in German and English and Polish and English are studied in Edmondson et al (1984) and Olesky (1989). Other contrastive studies of politeness across and between particular languages include El Sayed (1990) (English and Arabic), Walters (1979) (English and Spanish), Watts (1989b) (Swiss German and English) and Khanittanan (1988) (Thai).

On the phatic phase of conversational openings, see Laver (1975). The basic framework for studying agreement–disagreement sequences is found in Pomerantz (1984).

Comparisons of native speaker and non-native speaker performances in realizing activities such as inviting and thanking can be found in Scarcella and Brunak (1981) and Eisenstein and Bodman (1986), respectively.

Psathas (1986) continues his earlier work on direction-giving (Psathas and Kozloff 1976) and also gives very precise examples of grammatical and lexical realizations which are useful for language teachers. Myers Scotton and Bernsten (1988) look at the implications of direction-giving data for the evaluation of textbook dialogues.

4 Literature, culture and language as discourse

4.0 Introduction

In a paper on the learning of languages, Michael Halliday (1987) suggests a three-part division of emphasis:

1 learning language
2 learning through language
3 learning about language.

Learning a language involves an acquisition of the appropriate rules and conventions for using that language. Learning through language involves using language as a means of learning something else, for example, learning how language construes our experience or learning a curriculum subject such as physics or history. Learning about language involves learning something about the nature of language as a system, about how it works and about the kinds of functions it fulfils. Learning about language involves conscious reflection and understanding as opposed to an active linguistic engagement and interaction with the world. The three-part division is in one sense artificial since language learning is a process in which the three dimensions are integrated and an emphasis on any one dimension necessarily requires attention to the other two. However, learning *about* language is more obviously a process of analysis, of explicit attention to language, of conscious reflection on the forms and functions of language and on the means by which meanings are made by language.

In this chapter we devote attention to learning *about* language. We focus in particular on learning about language as text and discourse; our overall argument is that not only teachers but also learners can benefit from becoming discourse analysts. We hope to establish that processes of reflection on language and the development of more explicit knowledge about language can generate skills and competences which can feed into the process of learning to use language more proficiently. In Chapter 5 we look at how such language awareness at the discourse level can be incorporated into the syllabus. We present these arguments, however, in the knowledge that much contemporary language teaching theory emphasizes unreflective exposure to rich language environments and the creation of opportunities for using the language as fluently and as un-self-consciously as possible.

The central strand in our discussion is that the introduction of more literary texts into the language classroom can foster both processes of reflection and skills of analysis. The chapter is thus not directly concerned with the teaching of literature *per se* – a curriculum area in its own right (see further reading section) – but with literary texts as components of the language curriculum. Such a position does not so much diminish as enhance the role of literature in the curriculum. In spite of much debate since the early 1980s, this is a position which literature teachers do not always readily understand or accept.

The approaches that we consider in this chapter are all united by a common concern with the analysis of naturally occurring connected language. Literary texts are examples of language in use. They are instances of real communication in real social contexts. Consequently, discourse analysis can reveal meanings and patterns in literary text that are not normally revealed by the more traditional commentaries based on grammatical, lexical and phonological analysis. Increasingly, literary texts are becoming a subject for discourse analysis; indeed, the term *discourse stylistics* now refers to the practice of using discourse analysis in the study of literary texts (see Carter and Simpson 1989: 11). Through a contextually oriented approach of this kind much can be revealed: for example, the relationships between characters in novels and plays; the nature of the spoken voice in both prose and poetry; patterns in narrative organization; the differences and similarities between literary and non-literary texts as social discourse in contexts of use. This approach also means that questions concerning the relationship between language and culture cannot be ignored. Such questions naturally lead us to consider the relationship between language, text and ideology. In turn, discourse analysis cannot really avoid the question: what *is* literature? Such questions also have important implications for the use of literature in the classroom, especially in the context of language teaching. Answers to these questions affect the criteria for the division of the world of discourse which was the subject of Chapter 1, the subsequent selection of texts for the syllabus, the sequence in which they are studied, teaching methodology and the nature of the literature curriculum.

4.1   Conversational analysis: pragmatics and style

Two good starting-points for the analysis of literary discourse are fictional and drama dialogue since the functions of such stretches of language normally require explanation by reference to language organization beyond the sentence or the single conversational turn. Quite often, this will involve 'making sense' of language which on the surface appears to make no sense at all. Modern dramatists, in particular, draw extensively on such patterns of discourse. For example, the famous ending of *Waiting for Godot* by Samuel Beckett (1956):

VLADIMIR: Well. Shall we go?
ESTRAGON: Yes. Let's go.
   They do not move.
          (Beckett 1956 *Waiting for Godot*, London: Faber & Faber, p. 94)

can be shown to be ill-formed because the dialogue does not result in the expected action of leaving. A principle of adjacency seems to be deliberately violated. The dramatist relies on the absurdity inherent in the dialogue to point up a 'theme' of absurdity which is one of Beckett's main preoccupations in the play. Indeed, such dialogue is characteristic of a whole school of drama, called, not unexpectedly, 'the Theatre of the Absurd'. The management of the interactive dimension of speech is important, for it is from such interactions that we understand characters' behaviour and the situations that they are in. Central to this interaction management is the notion of turn-taking.

As we have seen in Chapter 2, systems of turn-taking have been extensively investigated within domains of study termed eth-nomethodology and conversation analysis (CA). Among the aspects of turn-taking studied are transitions from one turn to another; turn rights, including the current speaker's right to self-select for the next turn or allocate the turn to another speaker; the functions of extended turns; interruptions; speakers overlapping with one another, and so on. Dramatic criticism has tended to concentrate on the verbal *content* of character speech but a little thought will reveal how significant such aspects of turn-taking can also be for the interpretation by an audience of a speech situation (see Herman 1991). Dramatic dialogue is, on one level, tidied up talk; otherwise, an audience would not be able to follow the movement of a play. But it is also clear that dramatists will employ all the resources available to them for the practice of their art. In particular, they may 'overload' their discourse, so that the basic information content of a dialogue is supplemented by a wealth of other rhetorical and dramatic devices in order to provide as dense and rich a set of possibilities for interpretation as is commensurate with the dramatist's intention. In this connection, we can learn a lot about the management of 'ordinary' conversation by studying the way in which the rules and conventions of such discourse are creatively exploited by the great dramatist. This is also one of the main reasons why drama texts can be used to considerable effect in contexts of language teaching, especially the teaching of a second or foreign language.

Here is an example of a dramatist exploiting some conventions of turn-taking. The extract comes from Alan Ayckbourn's *Woman In Mind* (1986). Susan, the main character, suffers an accident which leaves her in a disturbed mental state. She 'imagines' a parallel family to her real family. Her real husband is Gerald; the other characters are fantasy characters. Note how it is the turn-taking that suggests the irreality of the characters. Real people in normal conversations do not simply echo each other's turns, people who are not addressed or are not participants in the conversation do not take turns, and utterances are not chopped up between speakers in the peculiar way that the last few turns are:

(4.1)   Alan Ayckbourn: *Woman In Mind*

GERALD: Why didn't he tell us?

SUSAN: I should have thought that was fairly obvious.

GERALD: Yes. I suppose so. All the same, I don't think it's fair to lay all the blame at your door . . .

TONY: What?

LUCY: What?

SUSAN: What?

GERALD: There are probably two sides.

LUCY: Mother, don't stand for this . . .

SUSAN: My door? Did I hear you correctly?

LUCY: Her door?

SUSAN: My door?

TONY: Want me to shoot him?

SUSAN: No.

GERALD: No, I'm saying, there are usually two sides –

SUSAN: How dare you?

LUCY: How dare he?

TONY: Perfectly easy to shoot him . . .

SUSAN: (*To* TONY) No. (*To* GERALD) How dare you stand there and –

GERALD: Now, Susan, I'm not going to start on this. We have argued our lives away over that boy and we're not going to do it any more. I refuse to become involved –

SUSAN: You smug –

LUCY: Self-satisfied –
SUSAN: Self-satisfied –
TONY: Conceited –
SUSAN: Conceited . . . bastard!
(LUCY *and* TONY *cheer and applaud this last effort of* SUSAN*'s*)
(Ayckbourn 1986 *Woman In Mind*. London: Faber & Faber, p. 58)

It is not so much *what* is said, which is only occasionally bizarre
(Tony's 'Want me to shoot him?'), as *how* the turns are constructed.
In relation to Sacks et al's (1974) principles for co-operative turn-
taking, this is a strange conversation indeed, which takes place as
much in Susan's *mind* (hence the punning title of the play) as in the
'real' world.

Another related example occurs in Harold Pinter's play *The
Caretaker* (1960). The dramatist exploits aspects of interaction
between the characters of Davies and Mick to underline a sense of
menace and psychological tension which is thematically significant.

(4.2)   Harold Pinter: *The Caretaker*
DAVIES: You been playing me about, you know. I don't know why.
           I never done you no harm.
MICK: No, you know what it was? We just got off on the wrong foot.
           That's all it was.
DAVIES: Ay, we did.
(*Davies joins Mick in junk*)
MICK: Like a sandwich.
DAVIES: What?
MICK (*taking a sandwich from his pocket*):   Have one of these.
DAVIES: Don't you pull anything.
MICK: No, you're still not understanding me. I can't help being
           interested in a friend of my brother's. I mean, you're my
           brother's friend, aren't you?
DAVIES: Well, I . . . I wouldn't put it as far as that.
MICK: Don't you find him friendly, then?
DAVIES: Well, I wouldn't say we was all that friends. I mean, he done me
           no harm, but I wouldn't say he was any particular friend of
           mine. What's in that sandwich then?
MICK: Cheese.
DAVIES: That'll do me.
MICK: Take one.
DAVIES: Thank you, mister.
MICK: I'm sorry to hear my brother's not very friendly.
DAVIES: He's friendly, he's friendly, I didn't say he wasn't.

While most normal conversations are co-operative events between
equals, the encounter here is subtly unequal and asymmetrical. As
the dialogue progresses, Mick emerges as the dominant partner.
There are several strategies by which he assumes power over Davies.

First, Mick controls the process of questioning, thus determining the direction in which the topic moves and the ground on which they talk. Davies is not allowed any such opportunity and is permanently cast into the role of respondent. Second, Mick refuses to allow Davies to shift the topic of conversation. Davies is not prevented from taking his turn but he is subjected and controlled by Mick's questioning. Third, Mick reformulates Davies's replies, thus allowing his interpretation to prevail. The submissiveness of Davies is also illustrated by his greater politeness, and by his compliance with Mick's instructions. For example:

MICK: Take one.
DAVIES: Thank you, mister.

The dialogue concerning the sandwich is merely a cover for the exercise of dominance.

At other points in this play silence is employed as a deliberate strategy in the exercise of continuing power when Mick refuses to answer Davies's questions. Deliberate suspension of a turn can be profoundly unsettling and can be as effective in the assertion of dominance as the refusal to allow a turn to someone else. Remaining silent can be construed as impolite, non-committal or threatening depending on our interpretation of that silence in the context of the particular sequence of dramatic exchanges.

Pauses, too, can produce similar effects. In the opening sequences of Samuel Beckett's play, *Happy Days* (1961), the only two characters, Winnie and Willie, are on stage against a backcloth of an unbroken plain and covered to their waists in a mound of earth. This visually disturbing scene is reinforced by a 'dialogue' in which the characters, as it were, talk past each other. Willie is reading a paper; Winnie is reviewing long past experiences. Her memories and his reading out of a newspaper do not appear to meet dialogically. There are many pauses.

(4.3)   Samuel Beckett: *Happy Days*
WILLIE *turns page.* WINNIE *rummages in bag, brings out small ornate brimless hat with crumpled feather, turns back to front, straightens hat, smooths feather, raises it towards head, arrests gesture as* WILLIE *reads.*

WILLIE: His Grace and Most Reverend Father in God Dr Carolus
          Hunter dead in tub.
     Pause.
WINNIE [*gazing front, hat in hand, tone of fervent reminiscence*]:   Charlie
          Hunter! [*Pause.*] I close my eyes – [*she takes off spectacles and does
          so, hat in one hand, spectacles in other,* WILLIE *turns page*] – and am

sitting on his knees again, in the back garden at Borough
Green, under the horse-beech. [*Pause. She opens eyes, puts on
spectacles, fiddles with hat.*] Oh the happy memories!

Pause. She raises hat towards head, arrests gesture as WILLIE *reads.*

WILLIE: Opening for smart youth.

*Pause. She raises hat towards head, arrests gesture, takes off spectacles, gazes
front, hat in one hand, spectacles in other.*

WINNIE: My first ball! [*Long pause.*] My second ball! [*Long pause. Closes
eyes.*] My first kiss! [*Pause.* WILLIE *turns page.* WINNIE *opens eyes.*]
A Mr Johnson, or Johnston, or perhaps I should say John*stone*.
Very bushy moustache, very tawny. [*Reverently.*] Almost ginger!
[*Pause.*] Within a toolshed, though whose I cannot conceive. We
had no toolshed and he most certainly had no toolshed. [*Closes
eyes.*] I see the piles of pots. [*Pause.*] The tangles of bast. [*Pause.*]
The shadows deepening among the rafters.

*Pause. She opens eyes, puts on spectacles, raises hat towards head, arrests
gesture as* WILLIE *reads.*

WILLIE: Wanted bright boy.

The Norton Anthology of English Literature Vol. 2 5th Ed p. 2272

The pauses are indeterminate and the audience must actively fill
them out with significance. Beckett manipulates pauses here so that
certain unspoken thoughts and feelings exist as subtexts.

Comparing stretches of dialogue and conversational exchanges
can be valuable to language learners. For the more advanced student
it can provide a basis for the stylistic analysis and interpretation of
drama texts. For less advanced learners it can stimulate reflection on
the nature of conversation. The conversations in language course-
books are inevitably neat and tidy events, symmetrical, polite and
geared towards a co-operative exchange of ideas and information.
Dramatic texts challenge assumptions and the language embedded
within those assumptions and can, by breaking or extending them,
serve to enhance learners' awareness of the rules and conventions of
conversational behaviour. The process may even stimulate awareness
of the differences between conversations in dramatic texts, conversations in language course-books and real conversations in naturally
occurring contexts. Later in this chapter we argue that such
conscious awareness is not only valuable in itself but can also
empower the learner to use the language with greater confidence.

4.2   Analysing narratives

In section 1.6.5 above an explicit framework for the analysis of
narratives was introduced. In this section we look at how such
analysis might reveal differences in structure and organization

between narratives and at how and why language learners might be made more aware of such differences.

Two narratives are compared: one narrative, 'The Auto-pilot', is taken from a widely used EFL/ESL textbook (Figure 4.1); the other is a naturally occurring narrative recorded at a dinner party (without the teller of the tale being aware that she was being recorded though permission to use the material was subsequently given: example 4.4). There are general similarities in the content of both narratives which allows a clearer focus on structure and organization.

The unit of the course-book contains valuable and imaginative activities designed to prompt learners into recounting, in narrative form, experiences which they have themselves undergone. Section (b) presents a narrative entitled 'The Auto-pilot', which is designed as a possible model on which learners would base their own narratives of a 'frightening flight' (Section (c): see Figure 4.1).

In this connection it is worth analysing the narrative in terms of Labov's (1972) narrative model (see section 1.6.5). It will help us to assess the extent to which it conforms to norms of narrative organization, particularly given its exemplary status in this part of the course book.

First, there is only minimal 'orientation' in this narrative. The flight is particularized only in so far as 'this particular flight' is made to serve as an exception to the general rules governing 'the flight'. We know the flight runs several times a week and we know the habits of the captain who would (habitually) come to meet passengers while leaving the plane on auto-pilot. Such information contributes to orientation – indeed, iterative verbs are, according to Labov, different from main narrative action verbs in that they supply orientating background to habitual events. But we are not given any more detailed orientation in this narrative. There is little to inform us of 'who, when and where'.

Second, the 'complicating action' or the main burden of narrative action, which is introduced by the adverb 'unfortunately' and which signals the problem around which most narratives revolve, does not really issue in any 'resolution'. In this respect the narrative appears somewhat truncated, with the reader or listener left asking 'what finally happened?' Similarly, there is no attempt made by the narrator of this story to reflect on the action. Although inferences can be reasonably drawn, there is no discernible 'evaluation'; there is certainly no 'coda' which might offer a moral, based on these events, on the part of either the captain or the narrator. In other words, and at least according to a Labovian account, the text is incomplete as a

A frightening flight

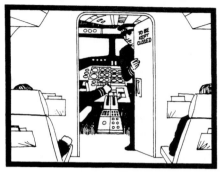

a   Which of the following can you find in the picture? the pilot/captain, the crew, the controls, the cabin, the cockpit/flight deck, the passengers, the security door, the aisle.

b   Have you ever heard a story like this before?

THE AUTO-PILOT
The flight ran several times a week taking holiday makers to various resorts in the Mediterranean. On each flight, to reassure the passengers all was well, the captain would put the jet on to auto-pilot and he and all the crew would come aft into the cabin to greet the passengers.
Unfortunately, on this particular flight the security door between the cabin and the flight deck jammed and left the captain and crew stuck in the cabin. From that moment, in spite of the efforts to open the door, the fate of the passengers and crew was sealed.

Here is another story on the same subject. Can you think of words that would fill the gaps?

JUMBO JET PILOT
A show-off Jumbo Jet ——— put the controls on ——— in mid-flight and took his entire ——— for a stroll back down the aisle to meet the ———. He then discovered the cockpit door had ——— itself and he had ——— the key.

☐   Listen to the two stories and see if you chose the same words for the second one.

Do you think these stories are true?

Word study

Match the words or phrases on the left with the words/phrases with similar meaning on the right.

their fate was sealed	lost
mislaid the Keys	jammed shut
then *discovered*	whole
locked itself	nothing could be done
his *entire* crew	attempts, trying
his *efforts* to open	found

---

c   Discuss in groups any frightening flight you have had or have heard about or seen on TV. Choose one story to tell the class.

Figure 4.1   A frightening flight. Source: Collins COBUILD English Course, Student's Book 2: 52

narrative. This is strange since in a teaching unit ostensibly concerned with the development of skills of narration, the example offered is not obviously one which might assist learners in the full development of those skills. Comparison with the naturally elicited example 4.4 underlines such structural and organizational incompleteness:

(4.4)
Well, I'll always remember that time we were struck by lightning coming back from Hong Kong, well landing in Bahrain actually, do you remember? I suppose we were about 50 miles out and like dropping all the time. It was pitch black outside, they'd dimmed the lights for landing and you could see flashes of lightning right across the sky . . . it looked like we were flying right into it. It was really frightening; it made you seem you weren't going to make it. Suddenly there was a loud bang and the whole aircraft shook; a few people started screaming; what was really unnerving was that the crew were nowhere to be seen. Anyway, the plane kept descending; the whole plane was, you know, really quiet . . . it was quite eerie . . . then the pilot came through to say we were about to land. Then guess what happened . . . he didn't tell us the plane would start shuddering; and next thing we knew, all the overhead lockers started rattling. In the end we landed safely with a real thump. Then the crew, stewardesses and things, suddenly appeared all smiling and we filed out all looking a bit pale. When we looked at the tail of the plane there was a gaping hole on the sort of fin bit. It made me realize how lucky we were. I'm not sure I'd fly with that airline again ever. Ever since, I've never felt all that happy while a plane's landed.

(authors' data, 1991)

This text is a more complete and rounded narrative. There is fuller and more detailed orientation (eg 'coming back from Hong Kong'; 'landing in Bahrain'; '50 miles out'); a resolution is signalled in a single sentence ('In the end we landed safely with a real thump'); and a coda, involving some reflection on the experience, is offered ('Ever since, I've never felt all that happy while a plane's landed').

If this naturally occurring narrative is a more prototypical narrative, then it will probably also be noted how much more it is a prototypical *spoken* narrative than 'The Auto-pilot'. For example, this narrative demonstrates a richer range of realizations or markers of the key elements in narrative structure. For example, 'I'll always remember' indicates the onset of the abstract to the narrative; 'then guess what happened' marks the transition to a problem which in turn introduces a sequence of complicating action. 'Ever since' and 'It made me realize' signal coda and evaluation respectively. There are, of course, many other features of spoken discourse which the narrative illustrates but the point to underline here is the extent to which this narrative is closer to the norms of narrative shaping identified in his research by Labov (1972).

This comparison raises many questions for language teaching pedagogy which cannot be dealt with here. Some are, however, covered in other parts of this book. For example, differences between spoken and written discourse and associated questions for the teaching of discourse are explored in sections 1.1 to 1.2; questions of 'naturalness' in the use of examples in language course books are very complex and are in part investigated in section 3.5; issues in the teaching of narrative using narrative models are discussed in section 1.6.5; also McCarthy (1991:141) discusses the interactive and collaborative nature of story-telling and the implications of this for activity design in language teaching materials.

Our intention is not to criticize a single section of one unit of a complete course-book, which is itself part of a carefully graded sequence of such books. It is instead to raise questions to which easy answers are not possible but which the analysis of language as discourse forces upon us. Among the main questions are: the extent to which real data should be mined for examples of narrative discourse markers which can then be taught directly to learners; the extent to which completely formed narratives should be used in connection with activities which require story-telling skills; the extent to which, at different levels appropriate to different learners, different narrative types and styles can be explicitly analysed and discussed as a way of increasing learners' conscious understanding of a central and ubiquitous language – making resource in what is probably the most core of all genres of language use.

4.3   Repetition and rhetoric

Repetition is a resource by which conversationalists together create a discourse, a relationship, and a world. It is the central linguistic meaning-making strategy, a limitless resource for individual creativity and interpersonal involvement.

(Tannen 1989: ch. 3)

All conversations contain repetition. Indeed, repetition occurs in all kinds of discourses. We often repeat the words of others; we notice repetitions in everything from political speeches to TV and radio news broadcasts: we accept repetitions as basic components of songs and poetry. Yet repetition can be regarded negatively and to be told 'you're repeating yourself' is normally heard only as a criticism. In this section, following, in particular, leads given in the work of Deborah Tannen, we explore the nature of repetition in texts, literary and non-literary. If repetition is a central resource in language use then it should be given full attention in language learning and development and in the selection of texts made to support such development.

In her book *Talking Voices* (Tannen 1989) Deborah Tannen devotes a chapter to repetition in conversation. She cites the following piece of talk (example 4.5) as evidence of the density of repetition which can be found in everyday instances of naturally occurring language.

(4.5)

CHAD:	I go out a lot
DEBORAH:	I go out and eat
PETER:	You go out. The trouble with ME is if I don't prepare and eat well, I eat a LOT. . . . Because it's not satisfying. And so if I'm just eating like cheese and crackers, I'll stuff myself on cheese and crackers. But if I fix myself something nice, I don't have to eat that much.
DEBORAH:	Oh yeah?
PETER:	I've noticed that, yeah.
DEBORAH:	Hmmm . . . Well then it works, then it's a good idea.
PETER:	It's a good idea in terms of eating it's not a good idea in terms of time.

(Tannen 1989: 76)

Repetition here involves self-repetitions and repetition of the words and phrases of others; it involves degrees of verbatim repetition and paraphrase; it involves paraphrasing the words of others with varying degrees of delicacy. McCarthy (1988a) found in his data that the interplay between exact repetition and reiteration by other means such as using synonyms occurred regularly within speakers' own turns, across their turns and between different speakers (see also Norrick 1987). It can be seen in Tannen's data that repetition also embraces syntactic structures:

I go out a lot
I go out and eat
You go out?

. . . if I don't prepare and eat
. . . if I'm just eating
. . . if I fix myself something

as well as fixed phrases:

it's a good idea
it's a good idea
it's not a good idea

and lexis (verbatim repetition of words and reiteration with a synonym, *stuff*):

eat / eat / stuff

and discourse markers:

Oh *yeah?*
I've noticed that, *yeah*

In short, repetition within a turn and across turn boundaries can involve phonemes, intonational and rhythmic patterns, words, idioms, phrases, sentences or discourse structures.

Tannen establishes repetition as a key aspect of discourse but goes on to argue that conventional views of repetition as somehow inefficient or ill-formed are inappropriate. Tannen argues that repetitions, of the kind witnessed in her data above, are not a negative feature, are not a waste of breath and are not merely a mark of having nothing to say. Repetition is not a signal of non-creative automaticity. Instead, repetition contributes to the mutual intelligibility of conversation. It signals rapport between speakers who use repetition actively to create interpersonal involvement. McCarthy (1988a) comes to precisely the same conclusion. Tannen puts it as follows:

> Analysis of repetition thus sheds light on our conception of language production. . . . In short, it suggests that language is less freely generated, more prepatterned, than most current linguistic theory acknowledges. This is not, however, to say that speakers are automatons, cranking our language by rote. Rather, prepatterning . . . is a resource for creativity. It is the play between fixity and novelty that makes possible the creation of meaning.
>
> (Tannen 1989: 37)

The subtitle to Tannen's third chapter of *Talking Voices* is 'Towards a poetics of talk'. One of Tannen's related arguments is to show similarities between patterns of repetition in naturally occurring talk and many standard literary devices. She points out how repetition is, for example, the most marked feature of poetry. Repeated patterns of sound, syntax and meaning either across poetic lines, refrains or whole stanzas are essential prosodic devices serving to create the active participation and involvement of the listener or reader.

Repetition is endemic to poetry in all its many forms from a formal ode to a popular limerick. Rhythmic and phonological repetition can embrace patterns of language at all levels, as we can see from the following poem by the late-nineteenth-century British poet Gerard Manley Hopkins:

(4.6)   Heaven-Haven
  I have desired to go
    Where springs not fail,
To fields where flies no sharp and sided hail
  And a few lilies blow

  And I have asked to be
    Where no storms come,
Where the green swell is in the havens dumb,
  And out of the swing of the sea.
            (G.M. Hopkins *Poems and Prose*. Penguin Classics, 1985, p. 5)

Repetitions here are phonological (eg end rhymes such as fail/hail and alliterative patterns such as 'To *f*ields where *f*lies no sharp and *s*ided hail'); they are syntactic (eg 'I have desired to go'/'I have desired to be') with the variation of the structure emphasizing the significance of the newly introduced verb 'to be'; and they are cohesive with the conjunction *and* foregrounded by its line-initial position.

The following passage from D.H. Lawrence's novel *Lady Chatterley's Lover*, which describes the mining village of Tevershall and which allows an unambiguous attitudinal marking on the part of the author, contains numerous different kinds of repetition: lexical; phonological; syntactic and discoursal.

(4.7)   D.H. Lawrence: *Lady Chatterley's Lover*
The car ploughed uphill through the long squalid straggle of Tevershall, the blackened brick dwellings, the black slate roofs glistening their sharp edges, the mud black with coal dust, the pavements wet and black. It was as if dismalness had soaked through and through everything. The utter negation of natural beauty, the utter negation of the gladness of life, the utter absence of the instinct for shapely beauty which every bird and beast has, the utter death of the human intuitive faculty was appalling. The stacks of soap in the grocer's shops, the rhubarb and lemons in the greengrocers! the awful hats in the milliners! all went by ugly, ugly, ugly, followed by the plaster-and-gilt horror of the cinema with its wet picture announcements, 'A Woman's Love!', and the new big Primitive chapel, primitive enough in its stark brick and big panes of greenish and raspberry glass in the windows. The Wesleyan chapel, higher up, was of blackened brick and stood behind iron railings and blackened shrubs. The Congregational chapel, which thought itself superior, was built of rusticated sandstone and had a steeple, but not a very high one. Just beyond were the new school buildings, expensive pink brick, and gravelled

playground inside iron railings, all very imposing, and mixing the suggestion of a chapel and a prison. Standard Five girls were having a singing lesson, just finishing the la-me-doh-la- exercises and beginning a 'sweet children's song'. Anything more unlike a song, spontaneous song, would be impossible to imagine: a strange bawling yell that followed the outlines of a tune. It was not unlike savages: savages have subtle rhythms . . . it was not like animals: animals *mean* something when they yell. It was like nothing on earth and it was called singing.
    (D.H. Lawrence: *Lady Chatterley's Lover*. Penguin 1928/1961, p. 158)

In the opening sentence the word *black* is repeated four times, in each case in a different grammatical category:

blackened brick – modifier (past participle)
black, slate roofs – modifier (adjective)
black with coal dust – post-modifier
the pavements wet and *black* – complement

The word *black* occupies every available grammatical position. It pervades possible grammatical structures in the same way as it pervades every interstice of the town of Tevershall. The repetition is motivated not simply to create a pattern of sound to involve the reader or to persuade the reader to adopt a similarly negative view of the village; the repetition is also motivated to reinforce particular meanings. It is this density of effects which characterizes specifically literary as opposed to non-literary functions of repetition. Repetition is commonly found in many kinds of texts but in the more literary texts the effects are the result of an iconic relationship between form and meaning. The repetitions create deeper levels of meaning which also reinforce the overall semantic design of the text.

Repetition is also a regularly recurring rhetorical strategy, an essential component in the art of persuasion. Rhetorical strategies are found in a wide range of public discourses from editorials to political speeches (see the data in Grady and Potter 1985), and different forms of argumentation. In all cases, repetition of key structures serves to reinforce a particular point of view in a way which involves the reader or listener in as direct and co-creative a role as possible. One of the best known examples is Abraham Lincoln's Gettysburg address on 19 November 1863:

(4.8) . . . It is for us, the living, rather to be dedicated here to the unfinished work they have thus far nobly advanced. It is rather for us to be here dedicated to the great task remaining before us, that from these honoured dead we take increased devotion to that cause for which they here gave the last full measure of devotion: that we here highly resolve that the dead shall not have died in vain, that this nation, under God, shall have a new birth of freedom; and that government of the people, by the people, and for the people shall not perish from the earth.

One reason for repetition is that it is an artful aid to the memorability of key ideas. It is one of the reasons why the final clause and its associated phrases have passed so distinctively into the everyday lexicon of English.

As an aid to memorability, advertisers regularly exploit repeated linguistic structures. Examples of such patterns of repetition in the language of advertising are legion and some have entered the lexicon of fixed phrases now established as part of the common currency of Modern English. Recently, however, this practice has been extended to include *once-removed* allusion to these established phrases. A recent advertisement for a Rover executive car contained the headline

You can be sure it's Schnell

which repeats by allusion a phrase associated with British advertisements for Shell petrol: 'You can be sure it's Shell'. The use of a German word *schnell* (*fast*) also creates a link with fast German cars using that association to promote a parallel image for the British Rover 820i.

One of the main implications for language teaching of work in the analysis of repetition in naturally occurring texts is that appreciation of literary functions of language may not, paradoxically, always be best stimulated by an exclusive focus on literary texts. First, it is important to recognize that 'literary' uses of language routinely occur in all kinds of texts. For teachers interested in helping to develop students' sensitivity to such uses of language, a bank of texts is available in familiar everyday contexts which can be exploited in the classroom. Furthermore, students need not feel intimidated by the mystique which can sometimes surround canonical literary texts. Literature can thus be demystified. Considerable degrees of confidence can be derived from pedagogic strategies which engage students in reading and appreciating a variety of texts each of which displays varying degrees of literariness. Second, there are real benefits in showing that all language, including the language produced by students themselves in everyday conversations, involves *patterns*, that these patterns are creative of meaning and that these patterns serve to generate emotional and psychological responses on the part of the writer/reader or the speaker/hearer. *All language users are creative users of the language.* Pedagogies for the teaching of language and literature are likely to be all the richer for recognizing this.

4.4   Situations across cultures

The examples we have given so far are taken not only from the English language but also exclusively from the English used in a narrow range of contexts. These contexts are further associated mainly with native speakers and are confined to British and North American cultures. If we extend our view beyond these data, different values are seen to attach to it. For example, our analysis of pauses in example 4.3 assumed specific cultural norms on the part of the playwright. We observed that pauses serve to underline uncertain relationships between participants and to create an atmosphere of tension and apprehension. However, silence is a cultural variable. In some cultures, for example the culture of Lapps and Finns, it is quite normal for conversational participants to remain silent for long periods across conversational turns. Silence has also been studied for its cultural significance in Japanese (see Lebra 1987). In Burundi in Central Africa clear divisions of caste and of seniority affect who speaks to whom first and who should remain silent. For the most senior member of a group to remain silent can signify strong disapproval of the other members of the group. In a related way, repetition (see example 4.7) is a cultural variable. In the data we have cited, repetition takes different forms and can in its many forms signal rapport between speakers. However, Becker (1984: 109) quotes examples of 'savouring repetition' in East Java where an audience at a lecture will, for example, repeat phrases to their neighbours (both *verbatim* and while the lecturer is *still* speaking) as a mark of their appreciation of the lecture. It is a culturally different function of repetition which in many Western cultures would be interpreted as rudeness or at best lack of attention.

To adopt a cultural view of language is to explore the ways in which forms of language, from individual words to complete discourse structures, encode something of the beliefs and values held by the language user. It is entirely in keeping with a discourse-based view of language. Our aim in this section is to discuss the relationship between culture and context and to evaluate the relevance of such understandings for language teaching and for the nature of the learning of a second or foreign language. In particular, we examine the significance of greater *awareness* on the part of learners of both language and of culture.

Culture can be generally defined as the set of values and beliefs which are prevalent within a given society or section of a society. In the practice of language teaching, however, more specific definitions can be discerned. At least three main meanings of culture obtain.

First, *culture with a capital C*   This refers to the most prestigious artistic achievements of a society: its art, music, theatre and, especially, its literature. Indeed, some approaches to language teaching have a main goal of learning the language in order that learners may read canonical literary texts as well as develop skills in translating literary passages. For example, grammar-translation methods of language teaching, which are prevalent in many parts of the world, particularly in universities, are valued for the intellectual disciplines such contact with literary texts is believed to promote.

Second, *culture with a small c*   This refers to the habits, customs, social behaviour and assumptions about the world of a group of people. Although this is a vast area, some textbooks attempt to provide some coverage either integrated into the main course material or as a supplement. Such coverage can range from family eating habits to the institutions of the society, eg Church, police, education. Literary texts (culture with a capital C) can often be exploited as a source of information about such domains. Other relevant 'cultural' forms within this definition include: advertisements, magazine stories, popular TV series, jokes, newspaper articles and feature stories.

Third, *culture as social discourse*   This refers to the social knowledge and interactive skills which are required in addition to knowledge of the language system. There may be marked differences here with a learner's own cultural norms. For example, part of a learner's communicative competence involves a familiarity with generic and rhetorical conventions in writing as well as with conventions of politeness, uses of silence, repetition and appropriate discourse markers. We mentioned silence in Japanese above; back-channel behaviour also seems to be a significant cultural feature of Japanese, to the extent that American interlocutors have been observed to *accommodate* towards Japanese levels of back-channel when interacting with Japanese partners (White 1989; see also Maynard 1990). Language users, therefore, can be sensitive to cultural divides and may try to bridge them when feasible. Communicative competence (see section 5.1) of this kind may also include sensitivity to paralinguistic codes such as use of eye-contact, intonation, gesture and interpersonal 'distance'.

The extent of the texts and discourses which are embraced by culture in its three main definitions make the selection of representative examples a difficult task. However, in keeping with the main orientation of this chapter towards written texts and the kind of awareness required for reading and interpreting them, two brief examples are given here. Example 4.9 illustrates the difficulties that face readers when a topic and related choices of language are deeply embedded within a set of culture-specific practices and when knowledge of the *denotative* meaning of words has to be supplemented by an awareness of precise cultural-*connotative* associations. The article raises difficulties which occur as a result of metaphoric analogies. The analogies presume of readers the ability to draw on particular background knowledge into which are encoded culturally specific social and ideological values. An example is the first sentence of the text.

> (4.9)　**Hunters under fire from two fronts**
> Huntin' shootin' types are under fire from both hunt saboteurs and the European Parliament. As the saboteurs announced that they would have more groups than ever out on Boxing Day, the British Field Sports Society warned its members about draconian measures planned by the parliament to restrict their fun.
>
> The Hunt Saboteurs Association, which will have 120 local groups out on Boxing Day, is concerned at the mounting violence of attacks on saboteurs by hunt supporters.
>
> Saboteurs say that they have been beaten up with pick-axe handles and fence posts, run over by a tractor, and had a minibus overturned.
>
> The Field Sports Society said: 'Sadly many Euro-MPs show a deep lack of understanding of the role well-organised field sports can play in the successful conservation of wildlife.'
>
> A strengthening of wildlife laws, with an extensive shooting ban and catch limits for anglers, has been proposed.
>
> (*The Guardian*, 15 December 1988)

Not one of three major EFL dictionaries (COBUILD, OALD and LDOCE) explain the metaphoric compound *hunt saboteurs* although all three provide entries for each separate word. Included in the various meanings of the noun 'hunt' is the British English sense of chasing wild animals, usually foxes, to catch and kill them using a pack of dogs and on horseback. To identify this meaning as the one appropriate to this article a reader needs to be able to recognize its particular cultural context. Additionally, the fixed phrase *huntin' shootin'* (with its fixed spelling pattern) refers to the activities of a specific social group (usually aristocratic or upper class).

Similarly, the term 'sabotage' is defined in the three EFL dictionaries. The emphasis in the definitions is on the sense of deliberate damage to property, its secret nature and its purpose of hindering the activities of one's opponents. Examples given of contexts of use refer to war or to industrial or political disputes. However, these meanings are not entirely relevant to the compound *hunt saboteurs*. The saboteurs here are using sabotage as a mark of protest (rather than of war or of political dispute); nor are these saboteurs operating in secret. On the contrary, they are eager to publicize their activities.

It might also be expected that the activities of these saboteurs, engaged as they are in intentional damage to property, would be described in negative terms. However, considerable space is given to an airing of their grievances in relation to the violence they suffer in pursuit of their protest. In order to make sense of this apparent contradiction, the reader must have sufficient background information on a range of cultural practices such as British attitudes to wildlife conservation; the operation of pressure groups within society; the ideological stance of a liberal, left-wing newspaper such as *The Guardian*.

The second set of texts is drawn from *jokes* in English. It is often argued that jokes do not translate and the ability to comprehend a range of different kinds of jokes in any language, especially in a foreign language, marks an ability to fuse linguistic and cultural understanding. Jokes in any language range from straightforward punning such as the following:

(4.10)
'Mummy, Mummy, I don't like Daddy!'
'Then leave him on the side of your plate and eat your vegetables.'

which, Hockett (1977) argues, can be translated and seen as a joke by all who share similar eating habits. Categories go on to include jokes which are less translatable because the puns depend on homophones:

(4.11)
Is the tomb of Karl Marx just another Communist plot?

A further category are those jokes which for their understanding require background knowledge (in fact, the preceding joke demands encyclopedic knowledge of Karl Marx) and an explicit knowledge of the two languages across which they work. For example:

(4.12)
Q. What do Frenchmen eat for breakfast?
A. Huit-heures-bix
(*Weetabix* is a popular British breakfast cereal)

(4.13)
Sum ergo cogito
Is that putting Des-cartes before de-horse?

In fact, Chiaro (1992) identifies a marked poetic competence in the ability to construct and appropriately process the latter joke:

in this case the reader has to a) know the quotation b) see what has been inverted c) know that Descartes was the author of the quotations and that he was French d) recognise the idiom as the punch-line e) link the marked form of 'the' /də/ as indicative of a French accent . . . in order to perceive the allusive and creative homophony involved: what we have defined as a poetic competence.

(Chiaro 1992: 13)

We can also see culture operating as a substratum of text in language teaching materials, and we do not even have to look at different languages to perceive how cultural assumptions within texts are not necessarily shared by all members of one linguistic community. Our examples come from British and American English. Algeo (1989) has pointed out the difference between the more obvious *lexical* differences in British and American English (eg *lift* vs *elevator*, *rubbish* vs *garbage*), the lexical *gaps* that can often exist (eg British *fortnight* has no 'lexicalized' equivalent in American English), and genuine *cultural* gaps (eg the domestic British *airing cupboard* may be a puzzling concept for most Americans). But cultural references may be even more subtle and apparently innocent assumptions may be challenged when 'translation' of British language teaching materials takes place for the American market, and vice versa. The extremely popular *English Grammar in Use* (Murphy 1985), in its British version, contains the following sentences:

(4.14)
'Did they change trains?' 'No, it was a through train so they didn't have to change trains.' (p. 65)
'Chuck came to Britain from the US nearly three months ago.' (p. 21)

The American version (Murphy 1989), clearly reflecting different cultural assumptions, translates these as:

(4.15)
'Did they change planes?' 'No, it was a direct flight so they didn't have to change planes.' (p. 63)
'Sue went to Canada from the U.S. almost three years ago.' (p. 21)

In example 4.14 the British version assumes a society where people largely travel between national destinations by train; in example 4.15 the American version translates this to one where such travel is mostly done by air. The second sentence, in the British version, puts the reader-learner in Britain as the 'deictic centre' of the text by the use of *came*. The American version neutralizes this with *went*, which does not necessarily have any direct implications for where the reader is when actually using the book. These are small changes, but not insignificant in terms of our arguments concerning language and culture.

The examples of the cultural contexts of texts help us to pose the following main questions for language teaching.

1 What kinds of cultural knowledge are required by a language learner? How is this best provided in the context of a language course?
2 Is there such a thing as a cultural syllabus?
3 What are the implications of the above questions for the selection of texts and associated text-based teaching strategies which are developed?
4 What cultural assumptions are contained in sentences and/or texts used in language teaching?

We explore these questions in the following sections, and in particular in section 4.7.

4.5   Text and ideology

In section 4.4 we discussed the ways in which cultural practices can be embedded within language use in texts. We also argued that understanding a text can depend not simply on knowledge of word or sentence meaning but also, crucially, on cultural frames of reference and meanings. Implicit in our analysis was a view that language is not unproblematically transparent and neutral; language is a site in which beliefs, values and points of view are produced, encoded and contested.

Culture itself cannot be neutral. The existence of English as a world language and the provenance of certain cultural products which this entails is not unconnected with economic, military and political power at a particular point in history (see Bailey 1992; Phillipson 1992). Similarly, when textbook authors and publishers select particular cultural situations, in which language use is illustrated – for example, a white middle-class family in a London suburb – then this conveys a view of British society and of standard southern British English which is not unconnected with the power of those values in 'naturalizing' a view of culture. Even course-books which offer a 'neutral' mix of cosmopolitan contexts such as international airports and hotels, express inter-country trains and uniformly similar beach resorts which in turn serve as background to reading texts and dialogues centring on international leisure pursuits (pop music, discos, keep-fit, photography) cannot be culture- or value-free. Such course-books only sidestep the problems of the frames of cultural reference needed for effective use of a language. At the same time, they insert a set of materialistic values and an ideology of hedonism to which it is tacitly presumed that learners will be able to and will want to aspire. In this section we examine more closely the relationship between specific linguistic choices and some ways in which cultural values and ideologies are conveyed. Newspaper headlines are frequently cited as key texts in this connection. The forms of language which have received most attention in the course of such analyses are confined to a restricted set: mainly transitivity relations, distinctions between the active and the passive voice and the functions of tense (eg Montgomery 1986). As an example we present three headlines taken from (1) the *Guardian*, (2) the *Daily Express* and (3) the *Morning Star*:

1   NCB chief fit after incident at pit
2   Coal supremo felled in pit fury
3   MacGregor scraps pit visit in face of angry demo.

The Guardian is a liberal independent newspaper, the *Daily Telegraph* is a right-wing newspaper, the *Morning Star* is a communist newspaper.

There are several features of language which merit comment here. These include the characteristic conventions of newspaper headlines, such as omission of articles; the deletion of a main finite verb; abbreviations (*demo*) and alliterative patterning (*pit/fit*; *felled/fury*); the formality differences marked by lexical choices eg *incident/demo* and by naming devices: *Coal supremo*; *MacGregor*; *NCB chief*, and so on. Also relevant here would be features not immediately recognized when the headlines are laid out as above, such as typography, or the placement of the main caption in relation to pictures as well as to other headlines. Of some significance in this connection, for example, are the styles of sub-headlines which in some newspaper designs support the main caption.

But analysis of language in and for itself does little to reveal the contrasts between these headlines in terms of ideology. The relationship in this case between language and ideology is not a transparent one; it is signalled with some subtlety and works to subject the reader to a particular interpretation of events. In the case of headline (3), for example, MacGregor is placed in the role of main actor in the clause and is made responsible (*scraps visit*) himself for the act of cancellation (*scraps* is a transitive verb). There is no reference to his physical position or disposition. By contrast headline

(2) represents MacGregor *acted upon* (*coal supremo felled*) and underlines the lack of agency by use of a passive verb with no agent specified (*felled by whom?*), and marked emotive lexis (*felled/fury*). Headline (1) seeks to be altogether more neutral by use of the word *incident* and the use of a complement structure (*NCB chief (is) fit*) avoids a passive/active distinction with its necessary assignment of agency. In other words, each headline inserts a different view of events. In (3) there is no suggestion that those taking part in the demonstration are directly responsible for action by MacGregor whereas in (2) MacGregor is the object of an action which we assume is initiated by the fury of the miners at the pit. In the opposition between *coal supremo* and *miners* the headline subjects the reader to a position which is limited by a preordained interpretation of events. In (1) there is no overt taking of sides, although in the case of such struggles neutrality usually signals greater allegiance to those political forces which seek to maintain a status quo. In all three headlines there is a relationship between stylistic choice, text structure and the ideological construction of a particular reading position. In each case different grammatical and other choices encode markedly different ideologies.

Recent work using Hallidayan grammar (Halliday 1985) also highlights the significance of *grammatical metaphor* in encoding ideologies. For example, the following two headlines, taken from provincial newspapers but which also report events at the time of the miners' strike in Britain in 1984, offer interesting points for further analysis:

1 Coal Board closes 30 pits. Miners protest
2 Pit closure sees violent scenes.

The word *closure* is a grammatical metaphor. Nominalization has turned the verb *close* into the noun *closure*. What was a *process* when expressed as a verb has become more like a *participant* in the clause when expressed as a noun. The grammatical metaphor here is significant since it allows reference to the action of closure to occur without any assignment of agency. The nominalized *closure* deletes any reference to those responsible for closing the pits. Its effect is not dissimilar to the use of the passive voice.

Also significant in the second headline is another transitive verb *sees*. The subject of the verb *sees* is normally an animate, human agent; here it is an abstract noun (*closure*). The effect is again to appear to attribute agency but without naming who the agents are. Responsibility for the closure is assigned elsewhere and the violence is accordingly inscribed as somehow motiveless and undirected. The newspaper which carries headline (2) above purveys an ideology which aligns it more directly with the Coal Board than with the miners. In neither case are the linguistic choices simply for purposes of a neutral or factual report of events.

Example 4.16 is from a magazine which is specifically targeted at women readers. It is revealing to compare here the ways in which patterns of transitivity are associated with the two main characters.

(4.16)   It had been so different three years ago, the night she'd met Stefan de Vaux. There'd been a party. Bella always threw a party when she sold a picture because poverty, she'd explained, was a great inspiration. She'd been wearing a brilliant blue caftan, her fair hair twisted on the top of her head, the severity of it accenting her high cheekbones, the little jade Buddha gleaming in its silver chain round her neck.

Claire, pale from England and the illness that had allowed her to come to Tangier to recuperate, had passed from guest to guest – 'Ah, you're Bella's cousin' – like a plate of canapés, she thought ruefully, attractive but unexciting. Until Stefan de Vaux had taken her out onto the balcony and kissed her.

'Well?' he'd said softly, in his lightly accented voice, letting her go at last, and she had just stood there, staring at him, at his lean, outrageously handsome face, his laughing mouth, amber brown eyes. 'Angry? Pleased? Shocked?' And she'd blushed furiously, feeling all three.

(*My Weekly*, 1 March 1987)

The transitive verbs are associated with male actions (*[he] kissed her*; *[he] had taken her out onto the balcony*; *[he let] her go*); the intransitive verbs are associated with female actions. Stefan de Vaux takes actions and takes initiatives; Claire just *stood* there and *blushed*. (In such fiction sentences such as 'she kissed him' are almost impossible to find.) She has things done to her and is cast in a passive and helpless role ('had been passed from guest to guest'). The syntactic choices here encode a conventional gender positioning of men and women, one frequently patterned in romances and stories in similar genres. It is often in such sources as popular fiction that critical discourse analysis, which aims to see through language to underlying ideologies, can help us to begin critically to interpret such texts.

The above examples explore, in particular, a relationship between language and the exercise of power on the part of an 'author' in establishing a point of view or a particular interpretation of events. The grammar involved is in one sense a sentence-level grammar. On another level, that of genre, grammar plays a large role in creating the headline as a text-type in itself and in creating or reproducing a specific discourse world.

4.6   Teaching literature with a small l

One of the implications of previous sections of this chapter is that the term *literature* is not defined in any exclusive sense. Instead, we adopt an inclusive view of the texts which might constitute the 'literature' component in a language curriculum. Indeed, the texts examined so far have included a poem by Gerard Manley Hopkins and an extract from a novel by D.H. Lawrence, an advertisement, newspaper headlines, jokes, a political speech and a piece of popular fiction from a women's magazine. Some of these texts might be termed *canonical* (Hopkins and D.H. Lawrence, for example); in other words texts by such authors are likely to be defined as literary by the literary academy for purposes of school and university study of literature. Others may not be so defined but contain features of language which are to varying degrees literary in purpose and function. Our position here is close to that established by Carter and Nash (1990) and developed more fully in pedagogy by McRae (1991). It is that of recognizing the existence of literature with a capital L and of literature with a small l (the latter is the title of McRae's book). It parallels the distinction we made in section 4.4, between culture in both its upper and lower case meanings.

Such a position may be felt by some, especially teachers of literature, to demean the texts valued by a cultural community to be of canonical status; our argument is that, far from demeaning 'literary' texts, it reveals and endorses the creativity inherent in much ordinary language use. Recognizing the 'literariness' of a wide range of texts, asserting the value of literature with a small 'l' and developing sensitivity to language in a range of cultural contexts is central to learning about language and the development of a reflective language learner.

4.7   Discourse and cultural awareness: implications for the language learner

Since the late 1960s, language has begun to be viewed increasingly in social, pragmatic, and semantic terms. Sociolinguistics as a discipline has established itself. Discourse analysis has related language to interpersonal realities. In other words, a whole area which in the past had been one of the main justifications for a cultural emphasis is now part of the treatment of language itself.

(Stern 1992: 211)

What are the theoretical implications of this kind of analysis? What is its relevance to language teaching? We begin with the first question.

In other words, what does learning about language in relation to language teaching look like? What can we learn from it? How does it relate to existing theories of language teaching?

The first observation is that native speakers of a language and advanced learners of a second or foreign language react to language mainly unconsciously and unreflectingly. In normal circumstances of communication – where there is successful uptake – most language users do not analyse language in this way. There is no need to. It can be argued that, for example, analysing jokes can destroy their effectiveness. By analogy, therefore, many language teachers would argue that we should not encourage our learners to analyse the target language. It is often said that too much self-consciousness can restrict opportunities for language acquisition and can inhibit the learner. They point to the prevalence of communicative language teaching practices which are designed not to help learners to analyse the language but to experience it *in use*. Communicative methods do not actively encourage reflectiveness on language.

Opponents of language awareness also argue that in order to analyse language a considerable range of metalanguage is needed – that is, you need language to talk about language. (Notice in this connection the terms that we have employed in section 4.6 such as *active, passive, theme, transitivity*.) It is said very forcefully that language learners have a long journey to take: we should not make it more difficult for them by giving them extra luggage to carry. If language awareness is extra luggage, then learning a metalanguage is definitely excess baggage.

The rejection of analysis by communicative language teaching theorists is part of a reaction against traditional structural methods in language teaching. For example, grammar-translation methods involve a lot of conscious metalingual naming of grammatical parts. There is no corresponding attention to helping learners use the language fluently in authentic contexts. Audio-lingual methods do not draw attention to language structure as explicitly as grammar translation methods. But audio-lingual methods are based on an isolation of language structure – a declarative knowledge which teachers seek to convert into procedural knowledge (see Chapter 5) by pattern practice and the use of drills.

Conscious language learning has traditionally been largely a form-focused activity, focusing on the structures of the language in an explicit way and emphasizing accuracy. Language is taught as if it were a product, a static, machine-like entity. Such learning results in learners knowing *that* rather than knowing *how* – knowing that, for example, certain rules obtain in particular uses of language. Knowing *that* is conscious knowledge. It is language awareness. Such knowledge may act as a monitor or editor of language in use but it is not and cannot be equivalent to language use.

We can observe some familiar contrasts and dualisms creeping into our discourse:

explicit learning about language	v.	implicit learning about language
form-focused	v.	meaning-focused
declarative	v.	procedural
conscious	v.	unconscious
knowing that	v.	knowing how
product	v.	process
language as static	v.	language as dynamic
accuracy	v.	fluency

Our view of such familiar dualisms in discussions of language is that they lead to what has been termed the pendulum theory of language teaching. Once a pendulum has swung one way, then it should swing at least as far the other way. In this respect communicative methodology is at one swing of the pendulum; structural analysis, grammar-translation and audiolingual methods are at another swing of the pendulum. During the 1970s and 1980s the pendulum swung firmly away from language awareness and learning about language.

Instead of adopting a dualist perspective, we wish to explore the possibilities of integration of these seemingly opposed theories of language learning. We believe that the development of a particular form of language awareness can serve such integration. Such integration can bring together conscious and unconscious approaches to language development. In this argument we are supported by Widdowson (1990):

> it seems on the face of it to be likely that with some learners a conscious awareness of how language works and the subjection of their experience to analysis would suit their cognitive style, increase motivation by giving added point to their activities, and so enhance learning. It would enable them to make comparisons between the language they are learning and their own language, and engage in the kind of rational enquiry which is encouraged in other subjects on the curriculum.
>
> (Widdowson 1990: 97)

And by Bialystok (1982):

> In unanalysed representations of language, only the meanings are coded; in analysed representations, both the meaning and the relationships between the forms and those meanings are coded. Such analysed

representations permit the learner to manipulate those for-meaning relationships to create particular structured uses of language. While conversations may proceed perfectly well from unanalysed representations . . . other uses of a language involved in reading, writing, lecturing, explaining depend on greater analysis in linguistic structure.

(Bialystok 1982: 97)

Like Widdowson and Bialystok, we argue that explicit and implicit knowledge need not be in opposition and that under certain conditions explicit knowledge can facilitate acquisition. An important contributor to this debate is Rutherford (1987), who makes a key point:

whatever it is that is raised to consciousness is not to be looked upon as an artifact or object of study to be committed to memory by the learner . . . what is raised to consciousness is not the grammatical product but aspects of the grammatical process . . . C-R (consciousness raising) activity must strive for consistency with this principle.

(Rutherford 1987: 104)

If we accept that consciousness-raising or language awareness can and should be more extensively introduced into the language classroom, then how is this best achieved? If we accept that it is likely to be more successful if it is not seen as a separate classroom activity but rather integrated into the ongoing process of language learning, then how is this best achieved? If we accept that learning about language can inform not only language learning but also learning in the broadest sense of the word, then how is *this* best achieved? This brings us to our second main question. What is the *relevance* of greater language awareness to language teaching and what does this mean in the context of the language classroom? We would argue that there are three broad parameters of language awareness:

1 a parameter of *form*
2 a parameter of *function*
3 a parameter of *socio-cultural meaning*.

4.7.1 A parameter of form

Activities within the form parameter involve a focus on formalistic aspects of language. They involve looking at language as a *system*. Examples might include strategies which draw attention to the *-ed* ending in 70 per cent of English past tense verbs; the frequency of plural in *s*; the phenomenon of *th* ($/\theta/$, $/ð/$) in English phonology;

the contrast between count and non-count nouns in English. Control of such forms is important for accurate use of the language. Such aspects of form can be usefully foregrounded by comparisons between the target language and the learner's language and/or interlanguage. Numerous activities exist or could be developed which might foster enhanced awareness of these formal properties of language.

There is always a certain arbitrariness both to forms of language and in the relations between form and meaning. Lexical collocations are a good example of this. Thus, in English you can have *a strong argument/a powerful argument* and *a powerful car* but not **a strong car.* You can have *dry ground/wet ground* and *dry bread or toast* but the opposite is not **wet bread or toast.*

These kinds of lexical gaps can be best exploited within activities which highlight the contrasts and gaps internal to the target language and which bring into conscious awareness related or contrasting patterns within the learner's language. An important component of the contrastive principle is the need to draw attention both to what *is* there and what is *not* there in and across languages.

4.7.2   A parameter of function

Activities within the parameter of function are designed to raise awareness of what language *does*, particularly in communicative contexts. They involve looking at the relationship between language and contexts of use. There are several classroom possibilities here:

1   comparisons between spoken and written texts (especially spoken and written versions of the same content or theme)
2   comparisons between different international Englishes
3   comparisons between different *translations* of the same stretch of language (cf Duff 1990)
4   comparisons between contrasting styles – designed for different purposes or functions (eg real language versus textbook language; scripted versus unscripted talk; real and made-up examples in dictionaries).

More specifically, it can be productive to generate awareness of the functions of words and phrases in texts, especially conversations. Studying the ways that words are used to close down conversations can set up perceptions of how words can have different meanings and functions in different contexts (often, once again, underlining in the process an arbitrariness in the form/meaning relationship). It can also be an enjoyable and revealing task to work out how words like *right, okay, well, good* or phrases like *I'll let you be going then* or *this call must be costing you a lot of money* can be used to signal a desire to finish a telephone call. Activities of this kind illustrate the importance of understanding how closely language function and situation are intertwined (see Bardovi-Harlig et al 1991; Holborrow 1991).

4.7.3   A parameter of socio-cultural meaning

Awareness within the parameter of socio-cultural meaning is also best achieved by invoking the contrastive principle. Examples here might include activities which generate awareness of language cross-culturally. As we have seen, differences in newspaper headlines are an obvious starting-point but within different newspapers and magazines the language of horoscopes, agony aunt letters or 'wanted' columns involve different cultural and social assumptions. Indeed the *absence* of such items within a particular English language newspaper in different parts of the world or within the newspapers of the learners' cultures can raise numerous points for contrastive cultural and ideological analysis.

The existence of three parameters should imply neither that they are exclusive nor that they are wholly separate or discrete (see section 5.6 for arguments towards their integration in the syllabus). The Gulf War of 1991 has, for example, made us more aware of the finite nature of oil resources. Yet *oil* is a non-count noun (like *water, air, petrol*). The form contains an implicit perception that such a resource is limitless and unbounded. The twenty-first century may determine a change in the grammar. We may have to talk of units of *oil* or *petrol*, an *oil* or a *petrol*, or *oils* and *petrols*. Cross-linguistic examples of this kind also exist which may suggest subtly different cultural perceptions: *nuclear waste* in English is uncountable; the near equivalents in Spanish – *desechos radiactivos* and *residuos radiactivos* – are both countable and plural. The examples illustrate the interconnection between formal, functional and socio-cultural parameters with grammar and ideology closely embedded within each other. Thus, teaching about the system of count/uncount nouns as forms can also be an opportunity to integrate cultural and language awareness. All the three parameters provide rich opportunities for cross-lingual comparisons. Such opportunities should, it must be said, arise within the context of meaningful classroom activity; otherwise language awareness can appear to both teacher and pupil as something a little too mechanistic and contrived.

4.7.4 The reflective language learner

One final related argument is the argument for greater learner autonomy which goes with increased language awareness. Consciousness-raising in the area of language form and structure is closely connected with the movement in recent years to give to learners greater control over their own learning. One particular domain here is learner training, the notion of 'learning to learn', as promoted in the work of Ellis and Sinclair (1989). The aim of the materials developed by Ellis and Sinclair is to encourage greater awareness on the part of learners of the learning strategies which they use. Such greater consciousness will, it is argued, help make learners more reflective, flexible and adaptable. A more reflective language learner is a more effective language learner.

So far we have argued in this section for the following main points:

First, learning a language also involves *understanding* something of that language. In both mother-tongue and second/foreign language situations it is unlikely that such understanding can be wholly developed by naturalistic exposure. It also has to be explicitly taught.

Second, learning about a language also involves understanding something of the culture within which the language is embedded. This involves aesthetic understanding, appreciating the creative play and invention of language use. Knowing a language involves appreciating how and why its rules can be broken or creatively manipulated. It involves appreciating jokes and ironies, responding to puns, seeing through language to the points of view and ideologies which language can reveal and conceal.

Third, such language awareness assists in the development of interpretative and inferential skills. It is impossible to teach in detail about the literature, the culture or ideologies of the societies which use the target language. There is neither time nor curricular space to allow this. What can be taught is the procedural ability, the ability to learn how to learn such things, the capacity for interpretation and inference in and through language.

Fourth, in this way, we would assert, language learning and teaching become indistinguishable from language *education* in the broadest sense of the word. Learners are better learners if they are able to analyse what they are doing and *why* they are doing it. Language teaching has for too long been seen as training in the instrumental functions and purposes of the language; and for too long there has been a strong anti-intellectualism associated with communicative language teaching. A learner, educated in the use of language, is aware of the language as a cultural artefact, and is a student/analyst of the language as well as a user. Such awareness can be stimulated at all stages in the language development process and courses should make greater provision for developing such awareness – from the earliest stages to the most advanced levels.

4.8   Teaching texts: curricular principles

In this section we offer five main principles which we believe should be central to text-based language teaching. The principles are derived from the preceding discussion in this chapter and are formulated in order to prompt further discussion and argument concerning curriculum design for language teaching in which texts are central. They are by no means the final word, but they do serve to summarize and encapsulate a position.

4.8.1   The contrastive principle

This principle has been illustrated throughout the book. It states that awareness of the operation of language in all texts is usually best stimulated when texts are compared and contrasted. The contrasts can take innumerable forms: contrasts in genre or text-type, register, narrative structure, point of view, grammatical and lexical choices or phonological patterning can reveal different meanings, especially if the content or subject matter of the contrasted texts can be kept constant. Contrasting treatments of the same or related content enable a focus on language difference and can do much to promote language awareness. Pedagogies which invite students to rewrite a text from one style or mode to another or to construct a text with contrasting stylistic choices reinforce the same principle, turning perception into productivity through the process of writing and on the basis of the process encouraging reflection on language.

4.8.2   The continuum principle

This principle is related to the contrastive principle and is particularly germane to the teaching of literary texts. It states that students' language development is best supported when students are exposed to both literary and non-literary texts but that these terms are not exclusive. A continuum of texts including all kinds of examples of creative and purposeful play with the resources of language needs to be presented, preferably with the texts organized around related themes. Such texts will include work by canonical writers, bilingual writers choosing English as a creative medium and writers whose creative uses of language are explored for a range of purposes from persuasion to simple pleasure.

4.8.3   The inferencing principle

This principle states that it is preferable to teach strategies for cultural and literary understanding. It accepts that almost everything in a language course is capable of carrying a cultural load of some sort and that most texts require a combination of linguistic and cultural knowledge for their reading. It accepts that it is impossible to teach all the cultural facts necessary for interpreting discourse in a second or foreign language and extremely difficult to grade cultural content in such a way as to differentiate significant from less significant knowledge. It accepts the difficulties of teaching courses in literature which adequately represent the literatures of a culture without resorting to factual surveys and chronological overviews.

The principle emphasizes the need to design language courses in which some curricular time and space is devoted to teaching actual procedures for making sense of texts. The focus on interpretative procedures and on learning how to *inference* should result from some overt and explicit reflection on processes of textual understanding. To this end, discourse stylistic analysis can be a significant support. The pedagogic goal of this principle is to develop greater autonomy in learners, to generate a confidence to deal with new texts and contexts, and to give all learners a capacity to work out cultural and literary meanings for themselves.

4.8.4   Familiar to unfamiliar principle

This principle is well established in theories of learning. In terms of language learning it states that learners are more likely to be motivated to learn a second or foreign language if the texts and contexts designed into a course are culturally familiar. The principle can be manifested in many ways. For example, instead of the more usual native speaker to native speaker discourse, course-book 'situations' for language use in certain countries might include interactions between non-native speakers, or between non-native and native speakers (interactions with which learners can more readily identify). A course in literary studies might begin with texts drawn from local literatures in English which deal with familiar contexts. Students might be encouraged to examine dialogues in which they themselves had been involved. The patterns created across turns, the rhetorical skills deployed, the sense of involvement generated could be a prelude to learning how similar patterns are deployed in canonical literary texts.

4.8.5   The critical principle

This principle has underlain much of this chapter. Language awareness can be generated according to the above and other related curricular principles. However, learners are likely to gain more interest and to be more empowered as educated citizens if they also develop a critical capacity to see through language to the ideologies and values which particular stylistic choices encode. The critical principle provides a basis for language learning to become language education.

4.9   Learning about language: some questions for discourse analysis

Teaching and research in the area of learning about language have been so far relatively limited and, in consequence, it could be said that this whole domain of language development raises at least as many questions as it answers. We list here a number of these questions. They serve as a conclusion to the chapter by suggesting some areas for further investigation by teachers and applied linguists. The areas suggested may be of particular relevance to the analysis of texts and discourses.

First, is the development of learning about language justifiable mainly in its own right and as a means to the development of inferential and interpretative skills? What evidence can be gathered of explicit knowledge about language feeding in to greater competence in using language? What particular teaching methods are more likely to enhance this relationship? Is the relationship between learning about language and language use stronger in the area of reading, or writing or speaking and listening? At what linguistic levels is the relationship most successful: at the level of phonology, of lexicogrammar, of text and discourse? How relevant to this process is the Australian work on the teaching of genres of writing (see section 1.6)?

Second, what does progression in learning about language look like? Is a student's awareness of language best activated at the level of words and sounds moving up to larger structures and patterns (bottom-up awareness)? Or is it best activated at the discourse level moving down to the lower levels of clause and word (top-down awareness)? Or is it preferable to see the development of learning about language in terms of a dynamic interaction between such levels: a combination of top-down and bottom-up awareness, a simultaneous shuttling back and forth between different kinds of language patterns? How necessary is increased metalanguage to progression and development in language awareness?

Third, should learning *about* language be assessed? Can it be effectively measured? If so, how is this best done? What are the advantages and disadvantages?

Fourth, given that teaching language awareness is seen as a necessary component in language teaching practices, what further *descriptions* of language are going to be most useful to teachers, and why?

Fifth, to what extent can literary texts best foster learning about language and what particular *kinds* of reflection on language are promoted by literary texts in the language classroom? Can language awareness be more effectively stimulated if language use in a wide *range* of texts and cultural practices is investigated by students?

Finally, is there any place in the language classroom for aspects of culture such as ways of life, social organization, historical facts which are 'beyond language'? Are there points at which a 'cultural syllabus' has to be introduced separately from a discourse-oriented language syllabus?

Given the open-ended and research-based nature of these questions, specific activities and commentaries are not supplied for this chapter.

Further reading

On drama dialogue, Burton (1980) is a classic text in the tradition of Birmingham University approaches to discourse analysis. The following collections of papers contain numerous studies of dialogue and interactiveness in relation to a range of dramatic, fictional and media texts: Carter and Simpson (1989); Hickey (1988); Van Peer (1988). A wide range of approaches across the domains of conversational analysis, pragmatics and discourse analysis are illustrated in these volumes. An interesting paper on repetition is Ishikawa (1991).

The most useful account of narrative from a linguistic point of view is Toolan (1988). Toolan's study covers narrative as a socially situated discourse in a range of texts from canonical literary narratives, to narratives written by primary school children, to narrative formations in newspaper reports and courtrooms. Farrell (1985) is another paper which looks at narrative in conversation. Livingstone (1990) is an interesting article on the interpretation of television narratives.

For studies of rhetoric as the art of persuasion, see Leith and Myerson (1989); Carter and Nash (1990); Nash (1989). The classic work on contrastive rhetorics and on discourse across cultures is Kaplan (1966); more recent studies are Smith (1987) and, with particular reference to language teaching contexts, Valdes (1986). Contrastive-rhetoric works which suggest particular differences between languages (eg on Arabic–English differences: Akram 1989; Hatim 1991) are balanced by Taylor and Chen (1991) who warn against over-generalizations concerning cross-cultural differences in discourse. An ideological study of the growth of English in the world is Phillipson (1992).

Illustrations of the notion of literariness and of literariness in relation to the teaching of literature in EFL are extensive in Carter 1987a; Carter and Nash (1990) and Carter and Long (1991). Arguments for the place of literature in language teaching and for the role of language analysis and study in the teaching of literature have been numerous throughout the 1980s. More theoretical accounts include Brumfit and Carter (1986) and Short (1988); much practical exemplification is to be found in Collie and Slater (1987). Relevant textbooks include Durant and Fabb (1990) at an advanced level and, at a more intermediate level, McRae and Pantaleoni (1990). For arguments, parallel to those in this chapter, on the importance of the development of inferential and interpretative skills on the part of language learners see Widdowson (1983); Brown (1990). Widdowson (1990) contains extensive discussion, in the context of language teaching, of the need to recognize the place of 'Schemata', cultural and otherwise, in the processing and production of language.

In the area of 'intercultural' studies Loveday (1982), Thomas (1983) and Kasper (1984) all explore instances of communication difficulties which result from misunderstanding and misinterpreting pragmatic or discoursal dimensions of language use. Thomas's study is a particularly revealing examination of cross-cultural pragmatic 'failure', distinguishing failure which can be overcome by explicit teaching of appropriate linguistic formulae and 'codes' and failure which results from misalignment with the belief systems and practices of the target language culture. A relevant summary is Strevens (1987); Robinson (1985) contains many empirical investigations.

For general discussion of the roles of language awareness or knowledge/learning about language in relation to language teaching see Donmall (1985); Carter (1990b); James and Garrett (1992). Carter (1990b) covers work in this area in relation to English in the National Curriculum in England and Wales. For a book containing over thirty classroom-based case studies of pupils' learning about language, see Bain, Fitzgerald and Taylor (1992).

Important studies on culture and language teaching and on the teaching of culture in and through foreign languages have been undertaken by Byram. (Byram 1989 and Buttjes and Byram 1990) Valdes (1986) offers a good balance of general and more specialised papers on culture and language teaching; Harrison (1990) is another collection of papers on this topic. Adaskou et al (1990) is a detailed exploration of cultural context design in relation to English language textbooks in Morocco. Riley (1987; 1992) advances valuable arguments concerning the plane of cultural knowledge in relation to language teaching and learning. On newspaper headlines as a text-type, see Iarovici and Amel (1989). For further discussion of the cultural significance of silence in Japanese, see Loveday (1982).

There is a tradition of work on language and ideology in the 1980s influenced by the work of Fowler et al (1979) and Kress and Hodge (1981). Valuable studies include Fairclough (1989 and 1992); Kress (1989); Fowler (1991) and Knowles and Malmkjaer (1989). In a series of papers Candlin (1987; 1989; 1990) argues for the importance of critical language awareness in relation to curriculum organization and planning (see also Fairclough 1992).

5 Designing the discourse syllabus

5.0 Introduction

During the course of this book we have constantly stressed the importance of adequate description as the precursor of language teaching syllabuses. At the macro- and micro-level, from issues of genre down to individual grammatical and lexical choices, we have suggested that our findings have implications for how we look at the syllabus and, consequently, its content and the kinds of activities that it generates in the class. It is now appropriate, in the closing chapter of our book, to concentrate our efforts on taking those implications further. This we shall do, not only in the case of general syllabus proposals, but also by looking in detail at learner data and materials and evaluating them in the light of all that has gone before.

5.1 The notion of 'discourse competence'

Ever since Chomsky (1965) made the distinction between **competence** and **performance**, that is what a person knows about his or her language as opposed to what can be observed from manifestations of actual use, linguists have debated just what 'competence' might mean. Chomsky was concerned with the fact that native-speakers have an underlying knowledge of what constitutes a well-formed sentence in their own language, and he set about trying to account for such knowledge. But it was not long before the notion of competence was expanded to embrace what a speaker needs to know about how a language is *used in particular situations* for effective and appropriate communication, in other words **communicative competence** (see Hymes 1971).

The notion of communicative competence has had a very powerful influence on language teaching, both in terms of methodology and the goals set by syllabus planners which learners are supposed to achieve. Thus the term **communicative syllabus** is a familiar one to most language teachers. Typically, a communicative syllabus will set out a variety of communicative abilities that the learner should be able to demonstrate at the end of a prescribed course or period of learning. One such English Language syllabus, a pioneer in its day, recommended that learners should be able to (among other things) make and receive telephone calls, handle friendly and social correspondence, make short notes to record salient information, ask questions and make comments for gleaning further information, and so on. This was the Malaysian (1976) Communicational Syllabus for Forms 4 and 5 of secondary school (see British Council 1983; 1986). The syllabus was a classic communicative one, with no real emphasis on correctness in grammar and vocabulary, and every emphasis on the ability to communicate and achieve goals, a balance of priorities for which it came into much criticism in its own country (see Mohideen 1991). It was criticism of this swing of the pendulum away from linguistic (ie grammatical and lexical) competence to a preoccupation with communicative competence alone, not just in Malaysia, which led applied linguists to question whether competence could ever be seen as a monolithic concept. Might it make more sense to think of the learner developing a **set of competences**, each one essential to using language effectively, but each one separable in terms of what could be described and prescribed for the syllabus and learning programme? Thus grammatical and lexical knowledge as one of the several competences came to the fore again as an issue in language teaching. Applied linguists argued that communicative ability was a hollow notion without knowledge of the grammatical system that enabled actual realizations of communicative acts (but also vice versa; see Canale and Swain 1980). Equally, there was a return of interest in the problem of vocabulary-building, without which little real communication was possible (McCarthy 1984; see also Carter and McCarthy 1988: ch. 3 for a survey of these arguments). Linguistic competence, it was argued, was a necessary, though not sufficient, condition for communicative ability. From such pressures has come what most would agree is a healthier balance between the development of competence in the language system and competence in its use, as exemplified in so-called **eclectic** syllabuses (the Swan and Walter 1984 *Cambridge English Course* is a good example), and in what Yalden (1983) calls the **proportional** syllabus, where the proportions of system-oriented knowledge and com-munication-oriented skills are increasingly altered in favour of the latter as the learner progresses from beginner level. The lexical syllabus (Sinclair and Renouf 1988; Willis 1990), based on a faithful description of how words are used, represents another move in the direction of integrating knowledge of the system and knowledge of use.

But other questions remain for the language teacher. If the

description of language is incomplete without a description of the level of discourse, and if discourse-level constraints operate simultaneously with lexico-grammatical ones, as we have attempted to demonstrate throughout this book, then is there something akin to a **discourse competence** that can be described and articulated as a set of goals for the syllabus to aspire to? Recent debates in syllabus design have tended to assume that there is. Those linguists and applied linguists who have moved away from the idea of competence as a monolithic concept have already added to the basic notion of communicative competence subdivisions such as socio-linguistic competence and strategic competence. As Canale (1983) uses these terms, they may be briefly glossed as follows:

> *Socio-linguistic competence*   an entity consisting of two sub-components: socio-cultural rules of use and rules of discourse. Socio-cultural rules are concerned with appropriacy of use with regard to such features as topic, roles, attitude and register. Rules of discourse are concerned with features of cohesion and coherence.

> *Strategic competence*   verbal and non-verbal communication strategies for solving problems in communication, whether lexico-grammatical problems or problems associated with sociolinguistic appropriateness.

Among the problems facing the language teacher who tries to interpret these notional divisions and subdivisions are not least that of whether 'socio-cultural' concerns can be separated from 'discourse' and whether such notions can ever be viewed as items or entities 'to be taught', if we are faithful to the view that a syllabus is indeed a list of things to be taught and goals to be achieved. The first problem, the separation of socio-cultural features from discourse ones is especially problematic given that, in this book, we have argued that such things as register and mode are integral to the creation of discourse, not in some way 'parallel' or complementary to it. We have also sought to demonstrate that isolated lists of speech acts are insufficient to describe what speakers/writers do and how they manage interaction over extended language events (see especially Chapter 2 and section 3.5). In other words, we see the chaining together of functions or speech acts as inseparable from the creating of larger patterns and genres in discourse (Chapters 1 and 2). By the same token, we see the realization of registers, attitudinal features and topics as inseparable from coherence and its manifestations in surface cohesion. Even more to the point, we have argued in Chapter 3 that grammar and vocabulary knowledge should involve how these aspects of linguistic *form* create discourse; in other words, linguistic competence cannot be separated from discourse competence.

These views have a direct bearing on the second concern, whether things can be itemized for teaching and given socio-cultural, strategic or discourse labels and thereby allotted their rightful place in the syllabus inventory or check-list. How we analyse and classify language for our syllabus necessarily affects our methodology and what we do in the classroom.

5.2   Analysis and classification

Some notable writers on syllabus design follow the view that the analysis of language into its various levels and the classification of features within those levels is a feasible basis for syllabus specifications. Yalden's (1983) description of syllabus components seems implicitly to accept this with a section entitled 'A further component: discourse structure' (1983: 78), and her syllabus check-list (1983: 169–72) includes the following discourse components:

A.   Cohesion and reference (based largely on Halliday and Hasan 1976)

B.   Operations on text (for example extracting salient information, expanding a text)

C.   Rhetorical organization (textual functions such as generalisation, classification, etc)

D.   Overt transactional skills in spoken discourse (for example initiating, introducing topics, closing, turn-taking).

These categories certainly represent innovative elements in syllabus specifications and are faithful to what discourse analysts have described as above-sentence features. We should note, though, that categories A and C seem to be language features, while B and D would seem to fit better under the heading of skills or strategies. This is no mere hair-splitting, and is at the heart of the process of analysis and classification that precedes specification and itemization. For instance, it could be argued that a feature such as lexical cohesion is an aspect of the language system and can thus be taught as language knowledge, just like teaching the grammatical facts about tenses or determiners. This would mean not only telling learners what the synonyms and hyponyms of a particular word or set of words are, but also demonstrating that synonymy and hyponymy *in use* are often involved in the creation of well-formed text and interactive speech (see McCarthy 1984; 1988a). However, another view might be that lexical cohesion is a language universal; as such, it becomes more a matter of skill-training, practice and training in an intuitive skill in order to improve one's proficiency in its use, without any need to 'present it' as knowledge or fact. This is a crucial decision in the categorizing of syllabus components: Yalden (1983), for example, has clearly flagged features such as turn-taking and closing as 'skills', suggesting a different emphasis from that attached to cohesion and reference, while 'operations on a text' are unambiguously things we 'do' with language, rather than features which 'exist' in the language system. But separating the 'what' of the language system from the 'how' of language skills and strategic use can also be misleading: there is every reason to suppose that knowing 'what' can inform and support knowing 'how', an argument we have propounded in Chapter 4, in our discussion of language awareness.

Munby (1978) has a similar, though much more detailed, specification of discourse *features* (cohesion, initiating, developing the discourse, etc) mixed in with textual operations ('reading between the lines', extracting salient points, skimming and scanning the text, etc), which, among many other things, form a continuum from basic phonemic and graphemic discrimination through to macro-planning, all under the heading of 'language *skills*'. 'Discourse level units' (Munby 1978: 27) are still seen, though, as separate from language micro-functions and grammatical/lexical realizations, and discourse is a level or layer of language rather than integral to its entire operation.

Although, as we shall see, ways of implementing the notion of a discourse element in the syllabus vary considerably, there does seem to be widespread agreement that the idea of discourse cannot be ignored; syllabus templates and check-lists as offered by applied linguists such as Munby (1978) and Yalden (1983) have a discourse element built in. But we must now consider how more integrative views of discourse influence the nature of the syllabus and the teaching that evolves from it.

One problem with the views of communicative competence as implied by the syllabus specifications that we have looked at so far is that they have assumed that language use can be analysed and described as a set of components of various kinds. This assumption often creates difficulties in that the separation of components can produce a false picture of their role in creating the overall message. A good example of this is the sort of list often found in syllabus specifications of speech acts or functions, such as *promising, directing, enquiring, apologizing*, etc. As Candlin (1976) points out, an inventory of speech-acts of this kind 'cannot serve any more than sentences as the direct endpoint of a communicative syllabus'. Any syllabus consisting solely of such a list would fail in two directions simultaneously: it would fail to provide the learner with a clear view of the interrelated and structured nature of elements of the language *system* such as modality and mood, and it would fail to show how apologies, enquiries, promises, and so on are actually realized in interaction and as part of a *sequence* of utterances and how such realizations depended on higher-order constraints of genre. In other words, we would be guilty of dealing with (some of) 'the *components* of discourse, not with discourse itself' (Widdowson 1979: 248). Widdowson and Candlin both come at the problem from the other direction: communicative competence is not a list of learnt items, but a set of strategies or procedures 'for realizing the value of linguistic elements in contexts of use' (Widdowson 1979: 248), and, just as learners may be expected to perceive grammatical regularities in sentences, so they should be given the opportunity to interpret pragmatic clues for the attachment of value to utterances in discourse, and become themselves analysts of discourse (Candlin 1976).

One approach to incorporating discourse into the syllabus but without separating it so much as a 'layer' or component of the syllabus, is that developed by the International Certificate Conference (ICC 1986) for its European adult language-learning syllabus at higher level ('stage 3'). The key to understanding the place of discourse in this syllabus lies in the notion of **discourse strategies**, which are defined as being concerned with 'how we make use of linguistic and other kinds of competence in order to achieve our communicative aims, and at the same time present a picture of ourselves' (ICC 1986: 47). Discourse strategies are employed in the *process* of writing and speaking (ICC 1986: 47). They are choices made by the speaker/writer at all stages of production which pay regard to how the receiver will experience the message, what speech-acts are necessary and desirable, which patterns of interaction are appropriate, and so on. This approach seems to come nearer to Widdowson's view of the importance of 'dealing with the discourse itself' (1979: 248; see also Widdowson 1983: 34).

In this sense, discourse strategies subsume lexico-grammatical choices and socio-cultural constraints and become the dominating feature in linguistic choice. Their specification in the syllabus therefore looks rather different from the more product-oriented components such as lexical cohesion or 'operations on a text'. They include not only the overt management of features such as topic and turn-taking, which the syllabus specifies under the general heading of *coherence-related strategies*, but also *self-help strategies* (part of what was referred to earlier as 'strategic competence'), *anticipatory strategies* (anticipating and dealing proleptically with aspects of the interaction, not just in retrospect), and *politeness strategies* (which are not only concerned with 'being polite', but also include choices for being impolite, reciprocating strategies and expanding the discourse for various functional ends, eg persuasion).

One crucial point must be made about the ICC syllabus specifications, however: because discourse strategies are seen as *process* choices, they cannot be taught or presented prescriptively or proscriptively, even though they may be listed and itemized in the syllabus. Not least of the factors one has to bear in mind in evaluating this particular syllabus is that the whole syllabus and its accompanying methodology are conceived as task-based. We shall return to the relationship between language-as-discourse and task-based approaches to learning in section 5.3.

Another highly innovative approach to incorporating an integrative view of discourse into the syllabus is provided by Aston (1988b). One of Aston's concerns is to redress the imbalance towards transactional language common in much language teaching (which we comment on in section 5.3) and to get to grips with the problem of creating the contexts for interactive discourse in the classroom. Aston too moves away from simply adding discourse as an extra component in the syllabus and effectively builds his syllabus around central and fundamental features of interactive discourse. For Aston (as we have argued) interactive discourse is concerned not only with illocutionary uptake (the realization of speech acts), nor just with 'cognitive convergence' (achieving shared knowledge and perlocutionary effect), but also with affective convergence (an essentially humanistic notion), with the processes of creating such convergences and with the global and local strategies negotiated in individual contexts for achieving them.

Aston recognizes the problems created by analysis and classification as the precursor of syllabus specifications: any analysis claiming to describe competence and to itemize it for a syllabus will fail to capture the fact that discourse is realized by the creative exploitation of the resources that constitute competence (Aston 1988b: 163–4). In this sense, the learner can engage properly with discourse only by *doing* it. This would seem to be a strong argument in favour of the task-based approach as expounded by Prabhu (1987). In the task-based classroom, language is *used* in the process of solving preordained tasks, with the purpose of promoting and enhancing uptake and learning, rather than presented and learnt in order to be used later in exercises or outside in the real world.

Aston, however, sees many problems arising from more extreme views of the task-based approach (the extremest form of which would be the completely negotiable syllabus, with nothing preordained and everything open to negotiation among learners and teachers, which Clarke (1991) claims would be unworkable anyway). Aston seeks to build a syllabus wherein the learning process is not just left to get on with itself in unpredictable ways, but in which teaching can operate as a guidance. To this end, it is not sufficient just to specify a set of tasks for learners to undertake. For one thing, many of the task-types advocated by task-based syllabus designers fall into the same trap as the information-gap activities of communicative approaches, in that they encourage a transactional view of language at the expense of the interactional. Furthermore, simply specifying tasks ignores the fact that learners can be guided in the *procedural* knowledge (the 'how things are done' in particular speech communities) as well as the *declarative* knowledge of 'what is done', both of which are essential to the creation of coherent discourse. Aston, therefore, favours a task-based approach that does not shy away from specifying the discourse strategies that the learner will need; these will be specified in a **strategic pre-syllabus**, which he sees as a 'content-based' one (Aston 1988b: 188). But even with this pre-syllabus, tasks involving the learner in creating discourse as the main syllabus are not enough. For Aston, the main syllabus is two-stranded, and the second strand involves the learner in becoming a discourse-analyst, or indeed a sort of anthropologist (1988b: 184), *observing* and *deconstructing* how discourse is created.

Aston's final model therefore, looks like this:

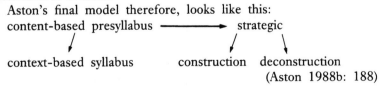

(Aston 1988b: 188)

Aston's view of the syllabus seems to recognize that discourse is a process rather than a product (which tends to be the view of those who see 'discourse-as-a-layer' in language use), but, sensibly, he sees the value both of an analysis and classification of discourse strategies as a precursor to selecting tasks for the classroom (rather as the ICC syllabus did), and of making the learner stand back a little from language and become an observer of it, though as a discourse-analyst rather than as the sentence-parser and rule-discoverer of some approaches to traditional grammar-based syllabuses. We support this view in Chapters 3 and 4.

Ours is also an integrative view, wherein the over-arching perspective of language-as-discourse will affect *every* part of the syllabus, including any conventional 'system' (lexico-grammatical) components and functional/speech-act components, however they are treated, whether as a series of layers of language, or as realizations within general specifications of discourse strategies.

5.3   Analysis as the precursor of tasks

Aston's programme favoured a 'pre-syllabus' oriented towards strategic issues in discourse. Specifying strategies is something that can be done in different ways and at different levels. We have seen how the ICC syllabus specified a general set of strategies, but it is also possible to conceive of a highly detailed set which translate some of the more traditionally conceived 'features' of language use into the strategic domain, and this is what we would like briefly to consider in this section. The overall set of discourse strategies that we feel are of maximum usefulness and generalizability in the pre-syllabus (which in our case will be understood as the criteria for a very wide range of task and activity-types that fall under Aston's construction and deconstruction syllabuses) arise out of our entire analytical and observational preamble of Chapters 1–3. We offer them as programmatic; we cannot claim to have put them into practice in any actual syllabus. What we propose here are a set of strategy-headings that can act as a sort of filter between the learning group and its needs and the specification of tasks. Each heading is followed by example questions that are raised by each one and the sort of practical issues that are likely to be encountered in the detailed specification of discourse *features* that might be encountered in the subsequent tasks. We say 'likely' because we cannot always guarantee what the outcome of a task will be. It will be noted that the global set of strategy headings can subsume what has previously been seen as a separate discourse 'layer' by some syllabus designers. The most general headings are as follows.

1   **Genre-related strategies**
     What are the media and modes that the learners will encounter?
     What genres are likely to be most useful?
     What patterns of interaction are most useful (eg narrative, problem-solution)?

2   **Coherence-related strategies**
What aspects of topic management, turn-taking, etc, will be involved?
What types of cohesion (eg stronger emphasis on across-turn lexical cohesion for interactionally oriented tasks; different types of ellipsis in different media)?

3   **Politeness strategies**
What aspects of face will need to be addressed?
What forms of address will be involved (eg pronoun systems, mood systems)?
How important will reciprocity be (eg very important in interactional tasks)?

4   **Planning strategies**
What sorts of anticipatory strategies will be useful (eg enumerative labelling, cataphoric uses of articles)?
Will special conditions for reference apply (eg anaphora across paragraph boundaries in written medium)?
What sequences of tense, aspect and voice are likely to be involved (eg conventions related to genre)?
What degree of *creativity* and risk-taking with language is feasible and appropriate?

5   **Convergence strategies**
Informational or cognitive convergence: what aspects of categories such as theme, mood and modality will be involved?
Affective convergence: what adjacency-pair types are likely (eg solidary routines, problem-sharing, agreement-disagreement)?
What transaction-boundary features are likely (pitch-sequencing, markers)? What role will repetition play in creating convergence in different modes and genres? What degree of cultural convergence will be required? How will 'knowing about' language and culture assist in solving convergence problems?

6   **Repair strategies**
What are the risks of communicational problems or cultural misunderstandings?
Is repair likely to be largely self-repair, or more global, negotiable repairs?

Strategies invariably overlap. For example, repair strategies may involve politeness, which in itself involves cultural awareness and the problem of convergence, and so on. But given the practical exigencies of dividing the discourse process, we would argue that the strategic list represents a manageable and reasonably faithful framework for syllabus and task design. What one does with a list of strategies for a particular learner group depends on one's philosophy concerning methodology. The discourse-based approach (ie where we *start* with discourse as the overall driving force of our syllabus) lends itself best, we have implied, to a task-based methodology, in that, in this way, language is not atomized and treated as product, thus destroying the basic notion of discourse as engaging with language as *process* and meaning as negotiated and contextual. However, in the real world, teachers often have to work within clear and restrictive constraints where they are expected to work to explicitly stated classroom input and to achieve explicitly measurable output, in other words, syllabuses that say *what* is to be learnt and in what order.

We see no contradiction between our proposed list of discourse strategies and the subsequent specification of the syllabus in terms of a set of specific performance goals, only that we start from a different premise: that all such goals can, and should be, expressed as discourse goals rather than as lexico-grammatical or notional-functional ones. For example, we might envisage a 'learners should be able to . . .' feature including something like the following (with reference to section 3.5).

Ask significant favours of others in appropriate sequences involving
1   signals of opening
2   explaining the problem
3   asking
4   minimizing
5   reinforcing
6   acceding
7   thanking.

The asking of a favour is thus conceived of as a *genre* rather than as a function or speech-act, and involves not only speech-act realizations at the micro-level, but also a strategic level involving politeness strategies (face), planning (opening), convergence (reinforcing), and so on. At the lexico-grammatical interface, one could specify modality and (depending on level) use of idioms. The point is that the conventional syllabus-as-inventory view can still be meaningfully adapted to a language-as-discourse approach without just adding discourse as a layer upon the other layers. Equally, such an inventory, in our opinion, does not necessarily preclude additional use of well-chosen tasks in class that can subscribe to Aston's (1988b) conditions of construction and deconstruction, nor does it necessarily preclude some sort of proportional syllabus approach such as Yalden (1983) advocates. For us, it is the analysis of language needs through a discourse perspective which is most important as a precursor to tasks and activities, whether such tasks are additional to a more conventional communicatively oriented syllabus or whether the analysis is merely a pre-syllabus for the selection of open-ended tasks that will form a whole task-based syllabus in themselves.

If analysis from a discourse point of view is to the pre-syllabus for a task-based one, then we would strongly support Aston (1988b) in his view that an analysis based on *interactional* language is just as important as one based on transactional uses of language. Real data show that the two types of language use rarely occur discretely (see section 3.5; see also Belton 1988; McCarthy 1991: 136–7). For an interactional view of language to have an input into task design, the understanding of how natural conversation works, how speakers/writers orient towards reciprocity and convergence, how they do so using systematic resources such as lexical cohesion and how features such as topic management are realized are all central. It is here, we feel, that syllabus designers have most to learn from what discourse analysts can offer. It is why we have spent so much time in this book exploring their findings.

Designing tasks is no easy matter, and much useful literature exists which treats with more rigour than space allows us here the factors which can make or break tasks (see especially Nunan 1989). It does seem worth underlining here, however, that tasks which promote only or mainly transactional uses of language (eg information-gap tasks) are unlikely to engage learners in a full range of discourse strategies. Discourse strategies, we have argued, are concerned with human beings presenting a picture of themselves, not just conveying information to one another. Chapter 3 was essentially concerned with those humanistic and creative aspects of discourse as manifested in literature. Therefore, if 'gaps' or 'problems' are the core features of tasks which motivate their completion, then we need to build in much more than just information or 'opinion' gaps (see Aston 1988b: 192–9 for a critique of information- and opinion-gap approaches). Gaps in rapport, problems of sensitivity, convergence towards acquaintance or friendship, gaps in self-image, problems of face, all of these will assume as much importance as gaps in places on a map, or gaps in agreeing on where to spend a Saturday night, the stock-in-trade of many present classroom tasks. Tasks *can* fulfil some of these interactional criteria by deliberately 'designing in' unpredictable reactions, 'difficult' participants, goals where conversational well-being is more important than informational transaction, and so on.

An example of an attempt at building into a task interactional constraints demanding politeness and convergence strategies, taken from the International Certificate Conference's teacher-training programme for teachers intending to use the discourse-strategy and task-based syllabus mentioned in section 5.2 (ICC 1986), involves participants in a consensus activity to agree on the arrangement of furniture for a school open-day. Much of the task is transactionally oriented, culminating in leaving instructions for the school caretaker to execute the furniture plan. However, the person who role-plays the caretaker is required to take offence at the tone of the instructions and the task therefore cannot be completed until oil has been poured on troubled waters and 'affective' convergence has been achieved, even though cognitive convergence is already present in the written instructions for the furniture plan. This is only one small example, but it shows how task design can attempt to replicate a wider range of discourse conditions, and how the 'pre-syllabus' might feed into the constructional syllabus in a more controlled way, if the desire is to follow a task-based approach. The most important thing is to be aware of the factors that can constrain or free the uses of language we would like our learners to engage in. Raymond Brown (1991) demonstrates quite clearly how differences in the degree of *procedural* work (decisions about how to do the task) and *interpretative* work (having to interpret or evaluate data) that a task specifies for participants can produce quite different outputs. For example, interpreting a poem pushed the learners involved into making hypotheses, a feature entirely absent from the more procedural tasks that Brown set his learners.

We can, it is apparent, extract from what discourse analysts have demonstrated about language use, features that can be enumerated and strategies that can be listed. But it is also crucially important to be able to evaluate our syllabus and its implementation in terms of learners and the discourses we engage them with. In other words, what are the *outcomes* of tasks in terms of real learner data, and how can we measure these from a discourse point of view. Section 5.4 takes some real examples of learners engaging in discourse and examines some of the questions raised in evaluating learner output using the tools of discourse analysis.

5.4   Putting analysis into the learner context

In the previous sections of this chapter we have considered the problem of building discourse into the syllabus. But what of the *output* of learning programmes, and how does the learner's *performance* relate to our desire to engage with the discourse process? Can we use discourse analysis not only to form the basis of the syllabus but also to evaluate its products and to assist learners to evaluate themselves? Analyses of natural data using the kinds of models we have outlined in previous chapters, once completed, may look appealing on the page but may leave the teacher-analyst feeling 'what next?' The most important question for many teachers is: how do I make data analysis relevant to the teaching context? In this section, we shall look at how analysis can be made relevant to the context of the learner. To do this, we shall first take data involving native speakers and non-native speakers of English doing similar tasks, analyse both sets of data and see if the differences at the discourse level offer any pointers towards alternatives or improvements in approaches to the syllabus and to methodology.

For our analysis, we use a modified version of the exchange-structure model proposed by Sinclair and Coulthard (1975). The model works with the basic unit of *exchange*, which consists of an *initiating move* (from whoever speaks first), a *responding move* (from whoever responds in some way, either by word or action) and, in many cases, a *follow-up* move (in which the initiator commments on the response in some way). A simple example would be:

(initiating move)	A:	Where did you go for your holidays?
(responding move)	B:	Oh, we went to Norway.
(follow-up move)	A:	Mm, that sounds nice.

Further details of exchange-types can be found in Sinclair and Coulthard (1975) and in McCarthy (1991: 12–22). For our analysis here, we have extended the follow-up move to take in a checking type of follow-up very common in ordinary talk. These we label Follow-up 1 and 2 (F1 and F2):

I(nitiation)	A:	Where did you go for your holidays?
R(esponse):	B:	Oh, we went to Norway.
F1	A:	Norway?
F2	B:	Yes, Norway

In the Sinclair–Coulthard model, the moves themselves can be subdivided into *acts*. These are the discrete communicative functions performed by individual parts of the move, such that the following move may be said to consist of four acts:

A:	Hey, Mary, you know that bottle-opener, what did you do with it?	
	Hey:	summons
	Mary:	nomination
	You know that bottle-opener:	starter
	What did you do with it?:	elicitation

Sinclair and Coulthard (1975) list over twenty acts commonly found in classroom discourse, and others have extended their list (eg Burton 1980; Francis and Hunston 1992). This is not surprising, since an enormous number of potential communicative functions can be imagined for everyday talk, and a good deal of subjectivity is often involved in labelling this level of the discourse structure. What matters when examining data and comparing transcripts is consistency of labelling; it matters less what differences there might be in the various approaches advocated by linguists. The names of the acts we have labelled here are, we hope, self-explanatory.

Our initial data consist of example 5.1, an adult native speaker interviewing another adult native speaker in English on the subject of 'holidays', and example 5.2, a Spanish, adult non-native speaker of English interviewing a native speaker on the same subject. Both interviewers were following the same brief, and for the purposes of comparability, twenty turns of speech are analysed in each case. Our purposes in doing the analysis will be to address the following questions:

1   What quantitative differences are there between the two data sets?
2   What differences are there in *exchange* structure?
3   What specific differences are there in the structure of *moves*?
4   How is the *topic* structure developed?
5   How do 1–3 relate to the non-native speaker's own perceptions of her performance?
6   What areas of discourse competence need to be concentrated upon to bridge the gap between desired and actual performance?
7   To what extent does this (primarily) transactionally oriented task enable learners to talk interactively and to 'present a picture' of themselves?

5.4.1   Transcript data and analyses

(5.1)   Transcript A: native–native (N–N)
Maureen (M) and Jason (J)

1	M:	Hello, what's your name, please?
2	J:	My name is Jason Lucas.
3	M:	Hello, Jason. I want to ask you a few questions and I'd like you just to tell me how you feel. Can you tell me where you went on holiday last year?
4	J:	I went to Wales last year for a week.
5	M:	To Wales?
6	J:	Yes.
7	M:	Which part of Wales did you go?

8   J: North Wales. Bala.
9   M: Ah yes, and was that an organized holiday through a tourist company or was it with family or friends or . . .?
10 J: That was just by myself visiting a member of the family.
11 M: Oh, that was nice, and what member of the family was it?
12 J: That was my aunt, auntie Serrina.
13 M: [laughs] Auntie Serrina. Where does she live?
14 J: She lives in Bala.
15 M: In a house or cottage?
16 J: Oh yes, in a house, yes.
17 M: And what did you do when you were there? Did you look round the area or . . .
18 J: I just went walking and lazed about, basically.
19 M: Very nice. And where else did you go? Did you go somewhere special every year or to the same place?
20 J: Nowhere special particularly, usually Wales or perhaps Cumbria.

(ICC data, 1991)

(5.2)   Transcript B: non-native–native (NN–N)
Maria (M) and Sarah (S)
1   M: Good afternoon.
2   S: Good afternoon.
3   M: What's your name?
4   S: Sarah.
5   M: Okay, Sarah, I'd like to know where did you spend your holidays last year?
6   S: Last year I went to Tenerife.
7   M: Oh, really?
8   S: Yes, and my grandfather lives in Tenerife, so I went to see him for two weeks.
9   M: Oh, I see. Do you usually go there?
10 S: More often than not, yes.
11 M: Mm, mm. What do you think about the people?
12 S: Well, they're lovely people, really friendly and helpful and . . .
13 M: And about the food?
14 S: Very good, very good.
15 M: Yes, you liked it?
16 S: Yes, lovely.
17 M: Nice. So, what about this year?
18 S: This year no plans as yet, hopefully I might go away for Christmas to see my granddad again.
19 M: I see. Do you sometimes spend holiday in Britain as well?
20 S: Not very often, no. There's not the weather for it. I prefer to go away and get some sun.

(ICC data, 1991)

The number of words in transcript A is 186 and in transcript B is 144. Transcript A contains 11 per cent more words than B. The average number of words per turn in A is 9.3 and in B is 7.2. Looking solely at the interviewers themselves, the gross number of words for Maureen is 125 (67 per cent of total words); for Maria it is 63 (43.7 per cent of total). The gross number of words tells us that Maureen 'does more talking' than Maria, but it does not tell us exactly how. What we must look at is how the words are distributed in the discourse structure.

Transcript A has nine exchanges; transcript B also has nine exchanges. Transcript A has twenty-five moves and B has twenty-six moves; the distribution of move-types is as follows.

Move-types	A	B
Initiations	9	9
Responses	9	9
Follow-ups F1	6	7
Follow-ups F2	1	1

There are no significant differences here either; both transcripts seem about equal in exchange-structural terms. What differences remain to account for the disparity in output between Maureen and Maria? Let us examine the internal structure of the moves used by the two interviewers.

Counting the number of discrete acts, Maureen used twenty-one, while Maria used nineteen. We can analyse the various act-types in the following way.

Act-types	Maureen	Maria
Greetings	2	1
Elicitations	9	8
Starters	1	1
Expanders	3	—
Nominations	1	1
Acknowledgements	1	5
Checks	1	1
Comments	3	1
Markers	—	1

It now becomes clear that what differences there are here are in the 'fine tuning' with regard to acts, what we might expect at the advanced level. Maureen's questioning is more complex: she begins the interviewing procedure with a starter (turn 3: 'I want to ask you a few questions . . . etc') and uses expanders (turns 9, 17 and 19) to ask for specific information. Maria uses a simpler starter (turn 5: 'I'd like to know'), and no expanders, but she does use a marker (turn 5: *okay*).

Maureen's follow-up moves include comments on the inter-viewee's responses (turns 11 and 19: 'Oh, that was nice'; 'Very nice' and the laughter and repetition of the aunt's name in turn 13). Maria's follow-ups include one comment (turn 17: 'Nice'), but are otherwise minimal vocal acknowledgements ('Mm') or non-commenting minimal verbal acknowledgements (turn 15: 'Yes'; turns 9 and 19: 'I see').

It is interesting to note that Maureen's slightly more complex behaviour in her elicitations and follow-ups are all concerned with *interactional* aspects of the discourse, in that they are not essential to the bare informational or *transactional* structure of the encounter. Her expanders encourage the interviewee himself to be more expansive in his reply, opening up possible areas that he might wish to talk about, while her comments involve her more in the evaluative process that is ever-present in interaction. Maria's elicitations and follow-ups do the basic job and do it efficiently, but, seemingly, without as much involvement.

The analysis underlines nicely Maria's own feelings about her performance as interviewer. When we interviewed her after the task, she said that she had wished she could have said more, and wanted especially to follow up on Sarah's replies, but had lacked the ability or confidence to do so. Maria is a quite advanced speaker of English (indeed, she teaches the subject), but even here we have a small but not insignificant gap in discourse competence which may well have come from an exposure to an impoverished range of discourse roles and functions at earlier stages of her learning.

Maureen's performance is not only relevant as data to contrast with the non-native speaker. In the mother-tongue teaching context, a discourse analysis of the kind we have done could be just as relevant for the measurement of the speaker's interviewing skills in any situation where such training is important, and 'contrastive' data in this case might be recordings of speakers commonly accepted as being highly skilled at interviewing, such as good broadcasters. The use of such skilled performances in the L1 or L2 context either for awareness-raising or as models is something we shall return to below.

Maria is a case of an advanced learner interacting with a native speaker. If we look at interview data between learners themselves and at a considerably lower level, we find even more marked contrasts with the discourse structure of our N–N data. Example 5.3 is a transcript of two lower-intermediate learners, Chortip (Thai) and Zenab (Libyan), again doing an interview about holidays. We could not transcribe twenty turns here since the participants managed only thirteen turns between them. We follow it with the same kind of analysis already used.

(5.3)   Transcript C: non-native–non-native (NN–NN) (whole interview)
Chortip (C) = Thai
Zenab   (Z) = Libyan
1   C: Er, what do you do when you have a holiday?
2   Z: When I have a holiday I like going to visit my friends in another
         countries. I went to Egypt er because I have friends in Egypt.
         Also I going to . . . I like shopping. Sometimes er . . . er I like to
         er stay in my house for er I like house er working, I work in my
         house I like cooking (C: Mm) I make cooking and er . . . er . . .
3   C: Erm . . . what er do you enjoy travelling . . . travel to . . . in
         Egypt?
4   Z: Yes, I am enjoying because I visit many place in Egypt and er it's
         very nice country, I think so, er and because it's near to my
         country, easy go and come (C: Mm) no problem.
5   C: What are you interested in Egypt?
6   Z: I interest to old building.
7   C: Building?
8   Z: Yeah (C: Mm) and er . . .
9   C: Pyramid?
10 Z: Pyramid, yeah . . . er . . .
11 C: And how about the weather ⌈ in Egypt?
12 Z: ⌊ Oh, in Egypt, weather is er very
         nice in the spring, but in summer is very hot (C: Mm) er if
         anybody go to Egypt must go in spring, not in summer, also it's
         nice in winter.
13 C: Thank you.

                                                  (authors' data 1991)

The total number of words is 168.
Total interviewer: 35 (20%)
Total interviewee: 133 (80%)

                                                  (authors' data 1991)

Moves (interviewer/interviewee) Total		13
Initiations		5
Responses		4
Follow-ups F1		2
Follow-ups F2		2
Acts (interviewer) Total	11	
Elicit	4	
Check	2	
Thank	1	
Back-channel	4	

We see that a very impoverished range of discourse functions is
realized in comparison with transcripts A and B, especially on the
part of the interviewer, who makes no acknowledgement or
comments on the interviewee's utterances, nor does she use any
starting or expanding acts. However, she does use a checking follow-
up and a help, and thanks her interviewee at the end, which shows an

interactive engagement with the discourse. She also makes four *back-channel* sounds ('Mm') during Zenab's answers. We might well conclude that, with minimal resources, Chortip has made a reasonable job of producing an interview with at least some interactive elements, even though the interview is very 'transactional', compared to transcripts A and B.

However, we must be careful not to read too much into data: our last interview may have been influenced by the very different cultural background of the participants. Moreover, never forgetting our arguments in Chapter 1, that speakers orient themselves towards *genres*, until we know what Chortip and Zenab saw as the exact nature of the activity, using these data to judge their discourse competence might be considered a little previous. The interview genre is sufficiently broad to take in a variety of sub-types from minimally interactional, maximally transactional events (eg formal political interviews) to maximally interactional personal encounters (eg chat-shows, therapeutic interviews, getting-to-know-you routines with strangers, etc). Sometimes, the data will give us evidence of how the participants see things. Note Maureen's 'market researcher-cum-psychiatrist' style:

M: Hello, Jason. I want to ask you a few questions and I'd like you just to tell me how you feel. Can you tell me where you went on holiday last year?

Other data in our collection of interview activities are also revealing of how participants might be viewing things, as with this Turkish learner (Hulya), interviewing a native speaker:

(5.4)
HULYA: Hello, Sue, I'd like to have an interview about you. What sort of holidays do you like?

(authors' data, 1992)

In addition to the clues in the data, the best way to find out how participants view the activity is to ask them directly. What matters is that we should not judge unfairly a piece of learner discourse which might not be exactly what we (the activity promoter) think it is. Nor should we expect too much interactional content from interviews of the kind generated here.

The interview activity has no interactional features built in other than stressing to the participants that they were not role-playing journalistic interviewing. The non-intimate interview as a *genre*, though, is certainly not well attuned to interactional features: reciprocity and affective convergence are not at all among its goals, and topic control is usually in the hands of the interviewer. Our data are presented rather as an example of how analysis can be applied and how it can raise important questions for teachers and learners and how it can suggest directions of investigation for the solving of real problems perceived by them. Maria would have *liked* to be more 'human', more interactive, but we may have restricted her by setting her a primarily transactional task.

Limited analysis of data should naturally be backed up by more extensive analysis or reaffirmation in the work of other researchers. In the case of the present data, for instance, our analysis is supported in the work of Aston (1988a; 1988b) and Belton (1988), who both conclude that over-emphasis on the transactional aspects of communication in language teaching at the expense of the interactional may be detrimental. But at the same time, contrastive data between different languages sometimes reveal that *cultural* differences may lie behind differences in realizations in discourse. For example, Edmondson et al (1984) found that, in making requests and complaints, German speakers seem to be more direct than English speakers, and concluded that German, in this particular discourse domain, seems to be more content-oriented, while English is more interpersonally oriented. This may be read as close to our distinction between the transactional and the interactional. And the distinction may go beyond requesting and complaining, to embrace an activity such as interviewing. It could therefore be that the English-speaking analyst may be expecting too much in the way of interactional behaviour on the part of German-speakers in an interview situation. British and American English certainly seem to demand fairly elaborate configurations of speech acts for actions such as requesting (see Gibbs and Mueller 1988), and it may be that personal interviewing is also marked by more elaboration at the interactional level than in other cultures. The point here is that the teacher-analyst not only should rely on the surface evidence of the text or transcript, but also should seek explanations for quantified phenomena in the work of others and, above all, should explore the cultural context of the learner. Interviewing learners and recording their own perceptions of their performance and exploring their possible cultural motivations is just as important as analysing the product of their performance of a specified task. We should remember, too, that we have argued strongly for *not* separating cultural competence from the discourse process.

The value of the quantitative analysis is really no more than its ability to pinpoint differences in discourse structure and to make explicit what may be felt only intuitively. It does not provide any explanations or solutions. What happens after analysis of this kind is a matter of practical decision-making between teachers and students. One possibility for follow-up is the kind of monitoring of group- and pair-work advocated by Kehe and Kehe (1989), where the teacher uses a check-list of discourse features (eg how many follow-up moves, or 'listener responses' as Kehe and Kehe call them, that the learner uses), which are reported back to the learner at a later point. Another possible next step in the investigation of particular areas of discourse competence in the learning context, we suggested earlier, was to look at how members of the target speech community considered to be skilled in those areas perform similar activities to those often demanded of learners. The example we shall examine was worked out in the context of a teacher-training course, where the participants set themselves the task of finding out what discourse strategies accomplished interviewers in English used. The task was done as a follow-up to a viewing of the video of transcript C (example 5.3) and was intended as something which could be replicated directly, with learners, in a task-based class. The participants chose a British television chat-show (*Wogan*), in which the chairman, Irishman Terry Wogan, interviewed media celebrities in a fairly relaxed and informal way. In terms of popularity, Wogan was one of the most successful TV chat-show interviewers of his time. Video recordings were made of several interviews and analysed especially with regard to the structure of exchanges and the internal structure of moves. Resulting from the analysis, a list of strategies was drawn up, which Wogan had used, along with simple examples of how these might be realized in interviews (based on Wogan's questions but not necessarily using his words).

5.4.2   Discourse strategies of the skilled interviewer

1   Use a lead-in to the question ('*You've made three films now*; what's your next one going to be?')
2   Expand after the main question ('So, why do you work so hard? *Is it for the money, or for enjoyment?*')
3   Reinforce your question to get more from the other person (A: Why don't you come back to Britain? B: Well, I love New York A: *But you love Britain, too, surely?*)
4   Use a conventional expression to take the other person back to an earlier question to get more from them ('*Going back to* your family, how important are they to you in your work?')

5   Link your next question to the last answer ('I see, live theatre,
    well, speaking of live theatre, when are you going to come back to
    the stage?')

(ICC teacher-training seminar, 1988)

The list should not be looked upon as a set of behaviour to be aped
in a robot-like fashion. It is rather a resource bank of examples and
actual language which teachers and learners can use for their own
perceived needs, either as a pre-syllabus (see section 5.3) or simply
regard as an awareness-raising phase, a stage in a task-based class
which might involve interviewing at some later point, in other words,
as a deconstruction activity in Aston's (1988b) terms. Its value in the
particular context in which it was produced is that it provided
examples of the very things that were lacking in the data being
evaluated: the elaboration of moves and the creation of fluid
exchange structures with a high level of interactional content. The
teacher-training group that produced the list saw it as a next practical
step in translating analysis into the learner context and as a very
valuable exercise for themselves. However, many teaching situations
will not have the opportunity to obtain rich natural data of this sort to
promote discourse awareness, and many teachers will have to rely on
available materials. What role, then, can analysis play in the
evaluation of materials? It is to this that we turn next.

5.5   Analysis and materials evaluation

The question we address here is: to what extent can a discourse
analysis of available materials help in bringing the discourse process
to the fore or at least providing more discourse-oriented materials for
the classroom? We have stressed that, although we see task-based
approaches as lending themselves best to engagement with the
discourse process (albeit simulated), we recognize that many teachers
(probably the majority) work within constrained syllabuses and with
pre-selected material. It is therefore important that teachers and
learners become critically aware of what the materials are offering
them, and that they should perceive opportunities to adapt them
where they are felt to be lacking in the features of natural discourse.
We are talking principally of textbook dialogues and ready-made
speaking and writing activities. We are not suggesting that every
example sentence or gap-filling exercise be condemned and
defenestrated; where lexico-grammatical rules and meanings are in
need of demonstration and exemplification, sentences and drills are

often the clearest and most economical media for doing this. But in places where the material does claim (or at least implies) that discourse is being presented, we should be able to evaluate its status in relation to what we know from discourse analysis. We shall use as our examples some dialogues from textbooks currently in use in some secondary schools in Japan. They are intentionally simple in lexico-grammatical terms but are constructed as simulated talk. Example 5.5 is a simple interview-session between a native speaker of English (Miss Fields) and various pupils in a Japanese classroom.

(5.5)   Lesson 1 Let's talk in English (review)
1   AHIKO: Is this your first visit to Japan?
2   MISS FIELDS: Yes, it is.
3   HIDEO: Do you like Japan?
4   MISS FIELDS: Yes, I do. Japan is really clean and safe.
5   TAKESHI: Where do you live in Canada?
6   MISS FIELDS: I live in Toronto.
7   JUNKO: Are you staying with Mr. Mori's family now?
8   MISS FIELDS: Yes, I am. They are very kind to me.

(Sato 1989: 2)

It is very easy to find all sorts of features here that would be odd in a *conversation* in the real world. There seems to be no proper opening, there are no follow-up moves, the repetition of *Japan* (rather than *it*) in turn 3 may be a bit odd, and because of the lack of follow-ups, the questioners sound rather impersonal and the subtopics jump around somewhat. But this is not a conversation; it is something akin to an interview, and, once again, there is no reason for the interviewer(s) to do more than fire questions at Miss Fields. Also, this is a classroom; in classrooms, children normally follow rigid discourse norms, among which is that they do not usually produce follow-ups to responding moves; following up in the classroom is traditionally done only by teachers (Sinclair and Coulthard 1975). Within its limits, then, and as a model for the 'foreign visitor to the classroom questioned by the pupils' genre, it is probably quite a faithful and natural dialogue. It is neither our desire nor our place to judge whether this is a good dialogue for its target group or for particular teaching situations; we simply wish to demonstrate how a discourse analysis of the text can illuminate its qualities and enable the users of the textbook to evaluate the dialogue more rigorously. The teacher who is looking for a model of natural conversation may conclude that this is not one; the teacher looking for a model of how pupils might deal with a foreign visitor to the classroom might be quite happy with it; any teacher simply wishing to use the text as a vehicle for lexico-grammatical rule-demonstration would not even need to consider it from a discourse point of view.

Example 5.6, from the same book, seems to portray a conversation rather than an interview.

(5.6)   Lesson 2: Nancy visits London
It is a fine spring morning. Tom is running along the river with his dog.
He sees Nancy there.

1	TOM:	Hi, Nancy. You were absent from our club yesterday.
2	NANCY:	I was in London.
3	TOM:	In London?
4	NANCY:	Yes. I was there for a week.
5	TOM:	Were you with your father?
6	NANCY:	No, I wasn't. I was with my mother.
7	TOM:	Was London interesting?
8	NANCY:	Yes, it was. There were many famous places, such as the Tower of London, Big Ben and the British Museum.
9	TOM:	What was interesting in the museum?
10	NANCY:	The Rosetta stone.

(Sako 1989: 6–7)

As a model of conversation, there are problems here. Nancy does not reciprocate the greeting, Tom does not use any commenting follow-up moves to his questions (though he does use one of the checking type in turn 3) and his questions are purely transactional in nature. Nancy does not reciprocate with any questions to Tom, and so the whole dialogue has, once again, the characteristics of an interview rather than a conversation. As before, it is for the individual user to evaluate the usefulness of this dialogue; the discourse analysis simply positions it within a spoken genre. However, with only small adaptations (and we have used this as an activity on teacher development courses), for example by adding follow-ups and a reciprocal section for Nancy to ask things of Tom, the dialogue can be made more discoursally natural without increasing the lexico-grammatical load. Adaptation of materials is often the only realistic option for teachers working within the rigid constraints of school-syllabuses, and we would argue that skill in discourse analysis is a very useful prerequisite to this kind of adaptation.

Finally, example 5.7 shows how even lower level dialogues, if carefully composed, can have a reasonably natural discourse structure. It is also a currently used Japanese one.

(5.7)   Lesson 2 On the road

| 1 | JACK: | Are we on the right road? |
| 2 | JILL: | I think so. |

3	JACK:	You think so. Aren't you sure?
4	JILL:	No, I'm not sure. I've only been along this road once before.
5	JACK:	Then we'd better ask someone, hadn't we?
6	JILL:	Yes, that's the right thing to do. We don't want to lose our way. Look, there's a mailman. He'll know.
7	JACK:	Does this road go to Henfield?
8	MAILMAN:	Yes, this is the Henfield Road.
9	JACK:	Is it very far?
10	MAILMAN:	No, not very far. About an hour's walk.

Ueyama and Tamaki 1988: 7–8)

Here we have follow-up moves from Jack (turn 3) and from Jill (turn 6), with a comment in turn 6 from Jill. Jack uses a connector (*then*) and a checking tag (turn 5), giving the sequence a natural set of features. The questions to the mailman then become, quite appropriately, more interview-like, without the follow-ups and other interactional features. As an example of two kinds of talk, this dialogue, although simple, seems to capture natural speech with a certain degree of success. It shows that even lexico-grammatically simple dialogues can yet be relatively faithful to natural patterns of interaction.

The question of materials evaluation obviously goes far beyond simply evaluating dialogues, but, for many teachers throughout the world, concocted dialogues are the only models available for L2 speech, and it is for this reason that we have concentrated on them. The same criteria for evaluation clearly apply to written texts, in terms of how faithfully they reflect common patterns, how they express mode, what patterns of cohesion are visible, and so on. Example 5.8 is a text written to illustrate the uses of present simple tense forms, for false beginners' level, from a current EFL textbook:

(5.8)   Read and answer the questions
Vidal Sassoon is a famous British hairdresser. He is in his fifties and lives in Bel Air in California with his third wife.
He wakes up at six and swims for about half an hour each morning, almost a mile. If he doesn't swim he exercises, using a machine to develop his muscles. For breakfast he has a bowl of fruit salad with orange juice or herbal tea. He never drinks coffee or eats sugar.

(Lonergan and Gordon 1986: 36)

In evaluating this text, we might consider whether the patterns of syntactic repetition are natural for this sort of 'personal profile' genre. Also, there is the problem of reiterated theme (*he*) which dominates the text; is this normal or not for personal profiles? Reiterated theme is certainly found in some types of advertising text (see McCarthy

1991: 56), but do naturally occurring personal profile texts typically use it? Furthermore, the text (at least as much as we have here) does not contain any sentence connectors. Is this desirable? The text is intended to illustrate present simple tense forms, but are these necessarily the way habituality is expressed in such a context? Evidence from the Birmingham University Collection of English Text suggests that (at least in first-person spoken accounts of daily routines) speakers mark habituality not only on the verb but also with *adverbs* such as *usually* and *generally* and the lexical verb *tend* (see Belton 1988 for a discussion and transcripts). Only by closely scrutinizing how personal profile texts are normally realized as a genre can we appropriately judge the concocted one. Following our evaluation, we may simply decide that the text is adequate for its purposes as an illustration of grammatical regularity, or we may decide to adapt it discoursally, while still retaining the essential grammatical features. In the proportional syllabus, it may well be sufficient at this lower level simply to see the text as part of the system-knowledge component.

The same textbook later gives an example text to illustrate simple past tense forms, this time in the form of a letter from an 8-year old to his grandmother, recounting a day at the zoo.

(5.9)   We saw all sorts of animals – penguins, monkeys, polar bears, lions, sealions. My favourite animal was the giant panda. Mum bought us all an ice-cream. After the zoo she took us to McDonalds. I ate a hamburger, a bag of French fries and a chocolate milk shake.
                                    (Lonergan and Gordon 1986: 65)

We may well feel that the textbook writers have been very skilful here in utilizing a genre (a child's personal narrative) that *naturally* has a very simple discourse structure, with simple sentences and few distractions from the verb-forms that are to be focused upon. The job of illustrating grammar is efficiently done, yet within a fairly natural discourse context.

Here we have offered just some examples of how a discourse approach might influence our evaluation of textbook materials. We now turn to the more general problem of implementing and evaluating the syllabus as a whole.

5.6   Refining and realizing the syllabus

Most teachers will find themselves most frequently in a position where they have a certain amount of scope for refining and adapting materials, for example the rewriting of dialogues, the editing of texts, designing activities where learners themselves can make dialogues more natural, adding on exercises to bring out features of interaction not present in the available material, and so on. More rarely, teachers will have the opportunity to provide some input into or to adapt a syllabus, and here many practical decisions may have to be made if the desire is to incorporate a discourse-dimension of the kind this book has been advocating. Some questions that will undoubtedly have to be addressed include the following.

First, will *discourse* be a separate section or layer of the syllabus, grafted on to existing ones? All our arguments so far have suggested that such a choice gives a false picture of the integrated nature of language: grammar is not something separate from discourse, nor is vocabulary, nor are the language 'skills' and 'strategies', nor is cultural competence.

Second, is the idea of *syllabus* separable from *methodology*? In other words, even if a syllabus tends to break language up into elements or layers, does this necessarily exclude the possibility of an integrated approach to *implementation* of the syllabus through methodology? Our view on this is that, in many situations around the world, it is the syllabus that dominates, setting the agenda for much of what happens in the classroom, and that methodology, however innovative, struggles to serve the needs of the goals enshrined in the syllabus and tested in examinations that attempt to measure the outcome of learning in terms of the syllabus. Therefore, the more the syllabus itself can reflect the integrated nature of the discourse process, the more likely it is that classroom practices and assessment will follow along. Refining the methodology without refining the syllabus is likely to create tensions difficult to resolve for the teaching-learning community.

Third, a syllabus has to be divided somehow, so what are the divisions that best reflect the notion of language-as-discourse? Certain broad top-down divisions, we hope, will have emerged in the course of this book:

1 divisions of mode and genre
2 the notion of discourse strategies
3 the cultural continuum.

If we take these as broad divisions, then practical outcomes can be foreseen: mode and genre involve specific identifications of grammatical and lexical elements, as well as discourse elements such as markers, choice of macro-patterns and institutional constraints of genre. Discourse strategies not only involve the traditional areas of 'communicative functions', but also include key lexico-grammatical features that can be listed and focused upon, such as choices of ellipsis, thematization, strategic use of idioms, etc. The cultural continuum suggests a better integration of literature into the syllabus; so often, at the present, literature is viewed as an optional element, or the icing on the cake, or even as an irrelevance to purely 'communicative' needs.

The value of such an approach to the syllabus is that it never fails to recognize the centrality of grammar and lexis, but suggests a reorganization of the purposes for learning structures and vocabulary items. The syllabus may still contain lists of structures and lexemes, but they will be cross-referred to their functions in the larger headings that attempt to capture the discourse process more faithfully. An example of a syllabus that retains the lexical inventory but which presents it in the service of a strategically oriented programme is the ICC *Higher Certificate* lexical inventory (ICC 1986), where primary importance is given to a 'systematic' inventory (ie one based on interactive functions), but where a more conventional, alphabetical inventory is also included. The systematic inventory includes headings such *intensifiers, downtoners, focusers* (eg *as for, come to think of it, what I'm getting at is* . . .), *no-equivalents* (eg *forget it, by no means*), *directives, summatives*, and so on. The labels all reflect the aim of the inventories: to flesh out the discourse-strategy headings which provide the overall structure of the syllabus. The alphabetical inventory places no less emphasis on strategic function, including many words and phrases and word-formation devices for the creation of interaction. For instance, under 'M' we find:

merely: I was merely asking.
mind: I've forgotten it. Well, never *mind*. I don't think we'll need it.
Mind you don't break it.
Mind you, she must be over eighty now, I suppose.
Most people think it's a question of morals, but to my *mind* it's a question of power.
Mini-: minicab, miniguide, miniskirt, etc.

Pragmatic and interpersonal functions are foregrounded rather than the traditional denotative semantic functions associated with lexical lists.

Getting from general principles to refinements and realizations is never an easy task, but a language-as-discourse approach offers exciting possibilities for reworking the material we already have as teachers, our stock of grammar and lexis, and our syllabus frameworks that already exist. No possibility, from minor adaptations to fundamental realignment of the syllabus, should be dismissed without careful thought and experimentation. Syllabuses tend to reflect our view of language at any point in history; the language-as-discourse view has yet to make itself fully felt, but description now offers us the opportunity to take a closer look at how we organize language for teaching purposes.

We have already, in earlier sections of this chapter, looked at the evaluation of syllabuses and tasks, and all our efforts, we hope, point to the same conclusions: that awareness of discourse and a willingness to take on board what a language-as-discourse view implies can only make us better and more efficient syllabus designers, task designers, dialogue-writers, materials adaptors and evaluators of everything we do and handle in the classroom. Above all, the approach we have advocated enables us to be more faithful to what language *is* and what people use it for. The moment one starts to think of language as discourse, the entire landscape changes, usually, for ever.

Reader activities

Activity 1

Here is a transcript of two lower-intermediate German-speaking learners who were asked to interview each other to get to know each other and find out what each was doing before they came to their present language course. Do a rough analysis of it as was carried out on transcripts A–C (examples 5.1 to 5.3) in section 5.4. How does this performance compare with the others? What can we learn about the range of discourse functions realized here? What pitfalls might there be in comparing this transcript with the others?

1   A: What did you do before?
2   B: Before what?
3   A: Before this course of course.
4   B: Oh . . . erm . . . you see, I . . . erm . . . just came back from living in Rome. I have been in Rome for three months and I went to school to learn how to speak Italian. It's almost like English courses at IKAB.

continued

Activity 1 *continued*

5	A:	And before this Italian?
6	B:	Oh, before that I had a job as a social worker.
7	A:	A social worker. It didn't suit to you?
8	B:	It suited me but I had a . . . this was, oh . . . I don't know the word . . . there was a lady going on holiday and I replaced her.
9	A:	And so you, you're . . .
10	B:	So it was a limited job.
11	A:	You have been dismissed, or . . .
12	B:	That was before [laughs].
13	A:	After your licence had . . . they putted you off, off the door?
14	B:	I lost my job.
15	A:	You lost the job, yes, I mean you lost the job.
16	B:	I lost my job, the job before the other one, I lost . . .
17	A:	They took another?
18	B:	I was a social worker, and I, we had big fights together, and we couldn't find . . . erm . . . well, we ended up that they, they told me to leave, to go. So I had to go.
19	A:	How many years did you work?
20	B:	There?
21	A:	At the social branch.
22	B:	Oh, erm, thirteen years, . . .

(ICC data, 1987)

Activity 2

Evaluate this textbook conversation in terms of the presence or absence of natural discourse features. How appropriate is it as a model for the kind of conversational context it is set in?

Angie is talking to Carl, a neighbour [they are both young people]

1	ANGIE:	Hi, Carl! What are you doing here? Aren't you supposed to be at school?
2	CARL:	No, we've got the afternoon off. I wanted to go swimming at the sports centre but the pool's closed all this week.
3	ANGIE:	Isn't there a pool in Lansbury Park?
4	CARL:	Yes, but it's no good. It's too shallow and anyway all the kids go there.
5	ANGIE:	What about the Oasis at Mile End? The 49 bus goes there, doesn't it?
6	CARL:	Yes, but it takes so long.
7	ANGIE:	Come on, lazy bones! I'll take you on the bike. Grab this helmet and jump on!

(Abbs and Freebairn 1989: 44)

Activity 3

Here is a dialogue typical of the kind often found in English language teaching materials. It does not contain follow-up moves on Jane's part (she does not comment on what Rob says, she simply goes on to her next question).

1 What do you think natural follow-up moves might be for Jane?
2 How could you adapt the dialogue for use in class, either rewritten by you, or worked into some sort of exercise or activity which would bring out natural features not originally included?

JANE: Hi, Rob, did you have a nice holiday?
ROB: Yeah, we went to England.
JANE: How long were you there?
ROB: Six weeks.
JANE: Isn't that rather a long holiday?
ROB: Well, it was a sort of language course too.
JANE: Were you working hard all the time?
ROB: Just in the mornings, not all day.
JANE: Did you learn a lot?
ROB: Yeah, a fair bit.

Activity 4

Here is an extract from an outline of communication objectives as offered by Canale (1983). Given the discussion in this chapter, what view of the place of *discourse* in the syllabus objectives does it imply? What areas of overlap are there between 'socio-linguistic competence' as described here and a language-as-discourse (integrative) approach?

2 SOCIOLINGUISTIC COMPETENCE
2.1 Expression and understanding of appropriate social meanings (that is, communicative functions, attitudes and topics) in different sociolinguistic contexts
2.2 Expression and understanding of appropriate grammatical forms for different communicative functions in different sociolinguistic contexts (where functions and contexts are

continued

Activity 4 *continued*

selected according to analysis of learners' communicative needs and interests)

3 DISCOURSE COMPETENCE

3.1   Common oral and written genres selected according to analysis of learners' communication needs and interests:

3.1.1 *Cohesion in different genres*:

3.1.1.1 Lexical cohesion devices in context (e.g. repetition of lexical items, use of synonyms)

3.1.1.2 Grammatical cohesion devices in context (e.g. co-reference of nouns with pronouns, ellipsis, logical connectors, parallel structures)

3.1.2 *Coherence in different genres*:

3.1.2.1 Oral discourse patterns, e.g. the normal progression of meanings (particularly literal meanings and communicative functions) in a casual conversation

3.1.2.2 Written discourse patterns, e.g. the normal progression of meanings in a business letter

(Canale 1983: 23–4)

Activity 5

Study a copy of the syllabus that you work to or any other language-learning syllabus and consider it from the point of view of the following questions.

1 Is there a discourse level or element(s) included in the syllabus? Which elements are considered to be discourse ones (eg cohesion, discourse markers)?

2 Is discourse considered a separate 'layer' of language or is there any attempt to integrate it?

3 If there is a list of grammatical structures and a lexical list, are these related in any way to discourse functions?

4 Is there any attempt to build in genre and/or text-typologies?

5 Does literature feature at all? If so, what is its status relative to other kinds of text?

6 Could the syllabus be adapted to have a language-as-discourse orientation? For example, is it possible to make the grammar and lexical inventories more discourse-sensitive? If there is a list of 'functions', are these just isolated speech

continued

> **Activity 5** *continued*
>
> acts? Could they be combined to form generic patterns (as we did in Chapter 1 with favour-seeking), and could they be reorganized under 'strategy' headings (see section 4.2)?

Notes on activities

Activity 1

Here is our analysis:

Total words: 215   A: 66 (30.7%)   B: 149 (69.3%)
Exchanges: 8   Moves: 23
Move-types:
Initiations   8
Response-initiations   2
Re-initiations   2
Responses   8
A Follow-ups   2
B Follow-ups   1
Number of discrete acts used by A: 13
Act-types
Elicitations   8
Re-elicitations
   (following a prompt from B)   2
Acknowledgements   2
Comments   1

This is a different picture from our data sets for transcripts A and B, and also from transcript C. We must bear in mind that the subject-matter is not the same; however, in some ways it may seem even more inclined to favour a good mixture of interactional (getting to know each other) and transactional talk. The data show that the interviewer expends fewer words than the interviewee, and the range of discourse functions realized is restricted. Of eight exchanges, only two have follow-up moves (turns 7 and 15), and the exchange structure is complicated by the need for re-initiations caused by communication problems. The only F1 – F2 follow-up sequence (turns 15 and 16) also seems to be concerned with a communication problem (the interviewee losing her job). The range of acts is also meagre, with elicitations dominating, and only one comment (turn 15: 'I mean you lost the job'), again concerned with communication problems. This means that the interactional content of the interviewer's talk is low. The interviewee does better: she uses interactive markers ('you see'; 'well') and signals her problem directly on one occasion ('I don't know the word'), as well as being more expansive in her answers, evaluating her information (turn 4: 'It's almost like English courses at IKAB').

The two sets of data at the lower level do raise the question of possible stages in the development of discourse competence. At lower levels of general linguistic competence, the exchange structure may be problematic, and a narrow range of acts may be realized, with speakers concentrating their efforts on producing the transactional discourse. At the higher level, the exchange structure seems sound, but development of follow-up strategies and command of the full range of acts may still be incomplete.

Activity 2

On the face of it, there do seem to be a number of natural discourse features here. Both Angie and Carl expand on their core utterances (Angie in her opening question, Carl in his first two answers). But Angie does not follow up on Carl's replies; she simply goes straight on to the next question, which we might consider a bit unnatural. It certainly has the effect of unbalancing the conversation a little, making it more like an interview than a reciprocal encounter. This is further underlined by the fact that Angie asks all the questions and Carl simply answers. No discourse markers occur, which is not normal in naturally occurring talk.

If you feel the lack of follow-up moves *is* unnatural, then the dialogue could be edited slightly for class use, or could be the basis of a language-awareness activity in which students discuss places where natural features such as follow-up moves and discourse markers could be added, and what types would be most suitable.

Activity 3

Possible follow-up moves for Jane include the following in bold type.

JANE:	Hi, Rob, did you have a nice holiday?
ROB:	Yeah, we went to England.
JANE:	**Really? / Oh, right.** How long were you there?
ROB:	Six weeks.
JANE:	**Six weeks! / Really?** Isn't that rather a long holiday?
ROB:	Well, it was a sort of language course too.
JANE:	**Oh, I see / Oh, right.** Were you working hard all the time?
ROB:	Just in the mornings, not all day.
JANE:	**Yeah.** Did you learn a lot?
ROB:	Yeah, a fair bit.

Which markers one actually chooses depends on a number of factors, not least that a younger person is more likely to say *right* (as an alternative to *yes*) than an older person. Also, repetition of the same discourse marker in every case would be rather unnatural.

Using the dialogue in class can range from simple gap-filling/ multiple choice exercises concentrating on the follow-up slot to acting out the dialogue from memory using follow-ups provided by the student or by the group. The student playing Rob could also be encouraged to reciprocate Jane's enquiries in some way. Another possibility is to have a fast, fluent recording of the dialogue *with* follow-ups and have students spot the differences between the spoken and written versions.

Activity 4

The notion of discourse competence here suggests that *genre* is central as a selection criterion for the discourse element of the syllabus, as we have argued throughout this book. There is a clear separation of cohesion and coherence, though, which might threaten to lose some of the genre-creating functions of cohesion which we argued for in Chapter 3. However, the cohesion section does stress that cohesive devices will be taken *in context*, which may offer the bridge between devices, texts and genres. 'Socio-linguistic competence' (see section 5.1) includes some things that we would class under discourse, such as variation in topic and attitudes. Equally, we would consider the relationship between grammatical form and communicative function to be central to a discourse view of language. Canale's (1983) headings are deliberately fairly general; one would want to know, for instance, what the 'normal progression of meanings in a business letter' is, and it is here that detailed analysis of data is necessary, or recourse to available studies. Having said this, Canale's outline is a significant contribution towards bringing discourse-level preoccupations into the syllabus.

Activity 5

This activity depends on the individual syllabus being studied.

Further reading

Almost any of Widdowson's and Candlin's writings on aspects of discourse, syllabuses and methodology are thought-provoking and relevant here; see Widdowson (1984; 1987), and Candlin (1984;

1987) in addition to their works already cited. For excellent arguments on task-based syllabus design see Nunan (1988) and Long and Crookes (1992). Breen's work in the area of task-based syllabuses is also essential reading (especially 1984; 1987). Melrose (1991) takes a meaning-negotiation approach to the syllabus, including examples of a 'topical-interactional syllabus' and Chapter 9 has a useful evaluation of discourse and the syllabus. An interesting paper on the lexical syllabus and issues of discourse is Tripp (1990). Willis (1990) is also important for the study of the lexical syllabus. Canale (1983) should be read to follow on from Canale and Swain (1980). For more on issues of competence, see Le Page (1975). Bachman (1991) considers the components of competence from the point of view of language testing. Shaw (1992) stresses the variability and tension between universality and culture-specificity of the elements that go to make up communicative competence. Ranney (1992) also opposes the single-speech-act view criticized in this chapter and emphasizes whole speech events in the study of socio-linguistic competence. The papers in Section 1 of Harley et al (eds) (1990) are all relevant to the general notion of communicative competence, especially Schachter's. Paulston (1992) also deals with the notion of communicative competence in language teaching in general.

Not much is available from a discourse analysis point of view on the informal, personal interview situation. However, Tolson (1991) is a very useful analysis of chat-show interviews and Greatbatch (1988) also includes a short section on chat-show interviews as contrastive data to his main purpose: the analysis of news interviews. News interviews are also the subject of Jucker (1986), but the genre model for the structure of news interviews found therein may be adaptable to the analysis of non-news interviews. Blum-Kulka (1983) also deals with political interviews, while Harris (1991) looks specifically at the question of evasiveness in political interviews. Corner (1991) has some fascinating historical television interview data. Yule (1990) contains some relevant remarks to situations where learners of unequal proficiency in L2 (as in transcript C, example 5.3) are engaged in interaction and suggests that success in negotiation of the interaction may depend on which partner takes which role. On the importance of looking at learner data as input to curriculum design, see Nunan (1990). Our analysis in section 5.4 used an exchange-structural approach; this is, of course, not the only viable analysis. Maynard (1986) looks at conversational fluidity and interactiveness from the viewpoint of the distribution of themes and rhemes (see section 2.6) across speaker turns in conversation, a method equally applicable to interview data.

On how cultural factors influence interactional style, with special reference to German and English, Byrnes (1986) is very interesting. A paper by Brown (1990), in which she advocates helping learners to develop a range of strategies for interpreting L2 culture rather than simply 'teaching' it, lends support to our view that cultural competence should be incorporated in the discourse strategies that are part of general discourse competence.

In the area of materials evaluation, Cunningsworth (1984) is a good general introduction, but more specifically oriented to spoken discourse is Cunningsworth's paper in the collection on materials evaluation and development edited by Sheldon (1987). Data-referenced evaluation of materials is becoming increasingly important; some studies include interesting comparisons between real data and what is found in course-books, for example Holmes's work on modality (1988) and O'Connor di Vito's (1991) study of features of French discourse in relation to course-book models. Williams (1990) stresses the importance of examining native speaker data before jumping to conclusions about learner usage.

The importance of looking at real data when assessing particular linguistic features is underlined by Smith and Frawley (1983), Morrow (1989) and Rudolph (1989), all of whom look at how conjunctions and other connectors are used in different genres, which is relevant to our discussion about the naturalness of concocted written texts. Lintermann-Rygh (1985) looks at connector density as a measure of essay quality.

Bibliography

Abbs B, Freebairn I 1989 *Blueprint Intermediate*. London: Longman

Adaskou K, Britten D, Fahsi B 1990 Design decisions on the cultural content of a secondary English course for Morocco. *English Language Teaching Journal* **44** (1): 3–10

Aijmer K 1989 Themes and tails: the discourse functions of dislocated elements. *Nordic Journal of Linguistics* **12** (2): 137–54

Akram A M 1989 Text development and Arabic–English negative interference. *Applied Linguistics* **10** (1) 36–51

Alexander R J 1978 Fixed expressions in English: a linguistic, psycholinguistic and didactic study. *Anglistik und Englischunterricht* 6: 171–88

Alexander R J 1984 Fixed expressions in English: reference books and the teacher. *English Language Teaching Journal* **38** (2): 127–32

Algeo J 1989 British–American lexical differences: a typology of interdialectal variation. In Garcia O, Otheguy R (eds) *English Across Cultures; Cultures Across English*. Berlin: Mouton de Gruyter, pp. 219–41

Allison D 1991 Textual explicitness and pragmatic inferencing: the case of 'hypothetical–real' contrasts in written instructional scientific discourse in English. *Journal of Pragmatics* **15**: 373–93

Andrews R (ed) 1989 *Narrative and Argument*. Milton Keynes: Open University Press

Aston G (ed) 1988a *Negotiating Service: Studies in the Discourse of Bookshop Encounters*. Bologna: Editrice CLUEB

Aston G 1988b *Learning Comity*. Bologna: Editrice CLUEB

Aziz Y Y 1988 Theme-rheme organization and paragraph structure in standard Arabic. *Word* **39** (2): 117–28

Bachman L F 1991 *Fundamental Considerations in Language Testing*. Oxford: Oxford University Press

Bailey C J 1985 Irrealis modalities and the misnamed 'present simple tense' in English. *Language and Communication* **5** (4): 297–314

Bailey R W 1992 *Images of English: a Cultural History of the Language*. Cambridge: Cambridge University Press

Bain R, Fitzgerald B, Taylor M (eds) 1992 *Looking into Language*. Sevenoaks: Hodder & Stoughton

Bardovi-Harlig K, Hartford B, Mahan-Taylor R, Morgan M, Reynolds D 1991 Developing pragmatic awareness: closing the conversation. *English Language Teaching Journal* **45** (1): 4–15

Barrs M 1987 Mapping the World. *English in Education* Summer 1987: 10–15

Becker A L 1984 The linguistics of particularity: interpreting superordination in a Javanese text. In *Proceedings of the Tenth Annual Meeting of the Berkeley Linguistics Society*. Berkeley: University of California, pp. 425–36

Bellos D M 1978 The narrative absolute tense. *Language and Style* II: 231–7

Belton A 1988 Lexical naturalness in native and non-native discourse. *English Language Research Journal* (ns) 2: 79–105

Benson J D, Greaves W S 1981 Field of Discourse: theory and application. *Applied Linguistics* 2 (1): 45–55

Berry M 1989 Thematic options and success in writing. In Butler C S, Cardwell R A, Channell J (eds) *Essays in Honour of Walter Grauberg from his Colleagues and Friends*. Nottingham Linguistics Circular Special Issue in association with Nottingham Monographs in the Humanities. Nottingham: University of Nottingham, pp. 62–80

Bhatia, V K 1993 *Analysing Genre: Language Use in Professional Settings*. London: Longman

Bialystok E 1982 On the relationship between knowing and using linguistic forms. *Applied Linguistics* 3 Vol 3, no 3 : 181–206

Biber D 1988 *Variation Across Speech and Writing*. Cambridge: Cambridge University Press

Biber D 1991 Oral and literate characteristics of selected primary school reading materials. *Text* 11 (1): 73–96

Biber D, Finegan E 1989 Drift and the evolution of English style: a history of three genres. *Language* 65 (3): 487–517

Blum-Kulka S 1983 The dynamics of political interviews. *Text* 3 (2): 131–54

Blum-Kulka S 1987 Indirectness and politeness in requests: same or different? *Journal of Pragmatics* 11: 131–46

Blum-Kulka S 1989a *Cross-cultural Pragmatics – Requests and Apologies*. Norwood: Ablex

Blum-Kulka S 1989b Playing it safe: the role of conventionality in indirectness. In Blum-Kulka S, House J, Kaspar G (eds) *Cross-cultural Pragmatics: Requests and Apologies*. Norwood, N J: Ablex, pp. 37–70

Blum-Kulka S, House J, Kasper G (eds) 1989 *Cross-cultural Pragmatics: Requests and Apologies*. Norwood, N J: Ablex

Bond J M 1987 *First Year Assessment Papers in English*. Walton on Thames: Nelson

Bonelli E T 1992 'All I'm saying is . . .': the correlation of form and function in pseudo-cleft sentences. *Literary and Linguistic Computing* 7 (1): 30–42

Breen M 1984 Process in syllabus design. In Brumfit C (ed) *General English Syllabus Design*. Oxford: Pergamon Press

Breen M 1987 Learner contributions to task design. In Candlin C, Murphy D (eds) *Language Learning Tasks*. Englewood Cliffs, NJ: Prentice-Hall

Brimley Norris C 1991 Evaluating English oral skills through the technique of writing as if speaking. *System* 19 (3): 203–16

British Council 1983; 1986 *English Teaching Profile on Malaysia*. London: British Council

Brown G 1990 Cultural values: the interpretation of discourse. *English Language Teaching Journal* 44 (1): 11–17

Brown G, Yule G 1983 *Discourse Analysis*. Cambridge: Cambridge University Press

Brown P, Levinson S 1978 Universals in language use: politeness phenomena. In Goody E (ed) *Questions and Politeness: Strategies in Social Interaction.* Cambridge: Cambridge University Press, pp. 56–289

Brown P, Levinson S 1987 *Politeness. Some Universals in Language Usage.* Cambridge: Cambridge University Press

Brown R 1991 Group work, task difference and second language acquisition. *Applied Linguistics* **12** (1): 1–12

Brumfit C J and Carter R A (eds) 1986 *Literature and Language Teaching.* Oxford: Oxford University Press

Burton D 1980 *Dialogue and Discourse.* London: Routledge

Butler C S 1988 Politeness and the semantics of modalised directives in English. In Benson J D, Cummings M J, Greaves W S (eds) *Linguistics in a Systemic Perspective.* Amsterdam: John Benjamins, pp. 119–53

Buttjes D, Byram M (eds) 1990 *Mediating Languages and Cultures.* Clevedon: Multilingual Matters

Button G 1987 Moving out of closings. In Button G and Lee J R *Talk and Social Organisation.* Clevedon: Multilingual Matters, pp. 101–51

Bygate M 1987 *Speaking.* Oxford: Oxford University Press

Byram M 1989 *Cultural Studies in Foreign Language Education.* Clevedon: Multilingual Matters

Byrnes H 1986 Interactional style in German and American conversations. *Text* **6** (2): 189–206

Canale M 1983 From communicative competence to communicative language pedagogy. In Richards J C, Schmidt R (eds) *Language and Communication.* London: Longman, pp. 2–27

Canale M, Swain M 1980 Theoretical bases of communicative approaches to second language teaching and testing *Applied Linguistics* 1: 1 – 47

Candlin C N 1976 Communicative language teaching and the debt to pragmatics. In Rameh C (ed) *Georgetown University Round Table on Languages and Linguistics.* Washington DC: Georgetown University Press, pp. 237–56

Candlin C N 1984 Syllabus design as a critical process. *ELT Documents 118*: *General English Syllabus Design* London: Modern English Publications/The British Council, pp. 29–46

Candlin C N 1987 Beyond description and explanation in cross-cultural discourse. In Smith L (ed) *Discourse Across Cultures.* London: Prentice-Hall, pp. 22–35

Candlin C N 1989 Language, culture and curriculum. In Candlin C N, McNamara T F (eds) *Language, Learning and Community.* Sydney: NCELTR (National Centre for English Language Teaching and Research), pp. 1–24

Candlin C N 1990 What Happens when Applied Linguistics goes critical? In Halliday, M A K, Gibbons J, Nicholas H (eds) *Learning, Keeping and Using Language* Vol 11. Amsterdam: John Benjamins pp. 461–86

Carter R A 1987a Is there a literary language? In Steele R, Threadgold T (eds) *Language Topics: Essays in Honour of Michael Halliday.* Amsterdam: John Benjamins, pp. 431–50

Carter R A 1987b *Vocabulary: Applied Linguistic Perspectives.* London: Allen and Unwin/Routledge

Carter R A 1990a When is a report not a report? In Nash W (ed) *The Writing Scholar: Written Communication Annual 3*. Los Angeles: Sage Publications, pp. 171–91

Carter R A (ed) 1990b *Knowledge about Language and the Curriculum: the LINC Reader*. Sevenoaks: Hodder & Stoughton

Carter R A 1990c Towards Discourse-Sensitive Cloze Procedures: The Role of Lexis. In Halliday M A K, Gibbons J, Nicholas H (eds) *Learning, Keeping and Using Language* Vol 1. Amsterdam: John Benjamins, pp. 445–53

Carter R A, Burton D (eds) 1982 *Literary Text and Language Study*. London: Edward Arnold

Carter R A, Long M 1991 *Teaching Literature*. London: Longman

Carter R A, McCarthy M J 1988 *Vocabulary and Language Teaching*. London: Longman

Carter R A, Nash W 1990 *Seeing Through Language: a Guide to Styles of English Writing*. Oxford: Basil Blackwell

Carter R A, Simpson P (eds) 1989 *Language, Discourse and Literature: an Introductory Reader in Discourse Stylistics*. London: Unwin Hyman/ Routledge

Chafe W 1982 Integration and involvement in speaking, writing, and oral literature. In Tannen D (ed) *Spoken and Written Language: Exploring Orality and Literacy*. Norwood, NJ: Ablex, pp. 35–53

Chafe W 1986 Evidentiality in English conversation and academic writing. In Chafe W, Nichols J (eds) *Evidentiality: the Linguistic Coding of Epistemology*. Norwoood NJ: Ablex, pp. 261–72

Chafe W 1991 Grammatical subjects in speaking and writing. *Text* 11 (1): 45–72

Cherry R D 1988 Politeness in written persuasion. *Journal of Pragmatics* 12: 63–81

Chiaro D 1992 *The Language of Jokes*. London: Routledge

Chomsky N 1965 *Aspects of the Theory of Syntax*. Cambridge, Mass.: MIT Press

Christie F 1985 Language and schooling. In Tchudi S (ed) *Language, Schooling and Society*. New Jersey: Boynton Cook

Christie F 1986 Writing in schools: generic structures as ways of meaning. In Couture B (ed) *Functional Approaches to Writing Research Perspectives*. London: Frances Pinter, pp. 221–39

Christie F 1990 Young Childrens' Writing: From Spoken to Written Language. In Carter R A (ed) *Knowledge About Language and the Curriculum: the LINC Reader*. Sevenoaks: Hodder and Stoughton, pp. 234–47

Christie F, Rothery J 1989 Genres and Writing: A response to Michael Rosen. *English in Australia* no 90, pp. 3–13

Clarke D F 1991 The negotiated syllabus: what is it and how is it likely to work? *Applied Linguistics* 12 (1): 13–28

Clayman S E 1991 News interview openings: aspects of sequential organisation. In Scannell P (ed) *Broadcast Talk*. London: Sage Publications, pp. 48–75

Clews H 1985 *The Only Teller: Readings in the Monologue Novel*. Victoria, British Columbia: Sono Nis Press

Coates J 1983 *The Semantics of the Modal Auxiliaries.* London: Croom Helm
Coates J 1990 Modal meaning: the semantic-pragmatic interface. *Journal of Semantics* 7 (1): 53–63
Collie J, Slater S 1987 *Literature in the Language Classroom.* Cambridge: Cambridge University Press
Collins P 1991 Pseudocleft and cleft constructions: a thematic and informational interpretation. *Linguistics* 29: 481–519
Cook G 1989 *Discourse.* Oxford: Oxford University Press
Corner J 1991 The interview as social encounter. In Scannell P (ed) *Broadcast Talk.* London: Sage Publications, pp. 31–47
Coulthard R M 1985 *An Introduction to Discourse Analysis.* London: Longman
Couper-Kuhlen E 1989 Foregrounding and temporal relations in narrative discourse. In Schopf A (ed) *Essays on Tensing in English. Volume 2: Time, Text and Modality.* Tübingen: Max Niemeyer Verlag, pp. 7–29
Coupland N (ed) 1988 *Styles of Discourse.* London: Routledge
Cowie A P 1981 The treatment of collocations and idioms in learners' dictionaries. *Applied Linguistics* 2 (3): 223–35
Crismore A 1984 The rhetoric of text books: metadiscourse. *Journal of Curriculum Studies* 16: 279–96
Crystal D, Davy D 1969 *Investigating English Style.* London: Longman
Crystal D, Davy D 1975 *Advanced Conversational English.* London: Longman.
Cunningsworth A 1984 *Evaluating and Selecting EFL Teaching Materials.* London: Heinemann

Daneš F 1974 Functional sentence perspective and the organisation of the text. In Daneš F (ed) *Papers on Functional Sentence Perspective.* Prague: Academia, pp. 106–28
Davies A 1978 Textbook situations and idealised language. *Work in Progress* no 11. Edinburgh: Department of Linguistics, Edinburgh University, pp. 120–33
Davies E E 1987 A contrastive approach to the analysis of politeness formulas. *Applied Linguistics* 8 (1): 75–93
Delin J 1991 Towards a model for generating cleft sentences. In J Verschueren (ed) *Pragmatics at Issue.* Amsterdam: John Benjamins, pp. 113–32
Derewianka B 1990 *Exploring How Texts Work.* Rozelle: New South Wales, Primary English Teaching Association
DES (Department of Education and Science) 1989 Report of the English Working Party. *The Cox Report.* London: HMSO, pp. 5–16
Dixon J 1975 *Growth through English.* Oxford: Oxford University Press
Dixon J 1987 The question of genres. In Reid I (ed) *The Place of Genre in Learning: Current Debates.* Victoria (Australia): Deakin University Press, pp. 58–82
Dixon J, Stratta L 1986 Argument and the teaching of English: A Critical Analysis. In Wilkinson A (ed) *The Writing of Writing.* Milton Keynes: Open University Press, pp. 8–21
Donmall G (ed) 1985 *Language Awareness.* London: Centre for Information on Language Teaching

Downing A 1991 An alternative approach to theme: a systemic-functional perspective. *Word* **42** (2) 119–43

Dubois B L 1987 A reformulation of thematic progression typology. *Text* **7** (2): 89–116

Duff A 1990 *Translation*. Oxford: Oxford University Press

Dudley-Evans A (ed) 1987 Genre Analysis and ESP. Special edition of *English Language Research Journal* (ns) 1. University of Birmingham: English Language Research

Durant A, Fabb N 1990 *Literary Studies in Action*. London: Routledge

Duranti A 1991 Four properties of speech-in-interaction. In Verschueren J (ed) *Pragmatics at Issue*. Amsterdam: John Benjamins, pp. 133–50

Edmondson W, House J, Kasper G, Stemmer B 1984 Learning the pragmatics of discourse: a project report. *Applied Linguistics* **5** (2): 113–27

Ehrlich S 1987 Aspect, foregrounding and point of view. *Text* **7** (4): 363–76

Ehrlich S 1988 Cohesive devices and discourse competence. *World Englishes* **7** (2): 111–18

Ehrlich S 1990 Referential linking and the interpretation of tense. *Journal of Pragmatics* **14**: 57–75

Eisenstein M, Bodman J W 1986 'I very appreciate': expressions of gratitude by native and non-native speakers of American English. *Applied Linguistics* **7** (2): 167–85

Ellis G, Sinclair B 1989 *Learning to Learn English*. Cambridge: Cambridge University Press

El Sayed A 1990 Politeness formulas in English and Arabic: a contrastive study. *ITL* **89/90**: 1–23

Erdman P 1981 Preposed *ing*-forms in English. *Folia Linguistica* **XV** (3/4): 363–86

Fairclough N 1985 Critical and Descriptive Goals in Discourse Analysis. *Journal of Pragmatics* **9**: 139 – 63

Fairclough N 1988 Register, Power and Sociosemantic Change. In Birch D, O'Toole M (eds) *Functions of Style*. London: Francis Pinter pp. 113–25

Fairclough N 1989 *Language and Power*. London: Longman

Fairclough N (ed) 1992 *Critical Language Awareness*. London: Longman

Farrell T B 1985 Narrative in natural discourse: on conversation and rhetoric. *Journal of Communication* **35** (4): 109–27

Fernando C, Flavell R 1981 *On Idiom: Critical Views and Perspectives*. Exeter: University of Exeter

Ferrara K, Brunner H, Whittemore G 1991 Interactive written discourse as an emergent register. *Written Communication* **8** (1): 8–34

Firbas J 1972 On the interplay of prosodic and non-prosodic means of functional sentence perspective. In Fried V (ed) *The Prague School of Linguistics and Language Teaching*. London: Oxford University Press, pp. 77–94

Fleischman S 1985 Discourse functions of tense-aspect oppositions in narrative: towards a theory of grounding. *Linguistics* **23**: 851–82

Fleischman S 1990 *Tense and narrativity*. London: Routledge

Fleischman S, Waugh L R (eds) 1991 *Discourse Pragmatics and the Verb: the Evidence from Romance*. London: Routledge

Fludernik M 1991 The historical present tense yet again: tense switching and narrative dynamics in oral and quasi-oral storytelling. *Text* **11** (3): 365–98

Folia Linguistica 1987 Special issue on Modality. **XXI** (1)

Fowler R, Hodge B, Kress G, Trew T 1979 *Language and Control*. London: Routledge Kegan Paul

Fowler R 1991 *Language in the News: Discourse and Ideology in the Press*. London: Routledge

Fox B 1986 Local patterns and general principles in cognitive processes: anaphora in written and conversational English. *Text* **6** (1): 25–51

Fox B 1987a Morpho-syntactic markedness and discourse structure. *Journal of Pragmatics* **11**: 359–75

Fox B 1987b *Discourse Structure and Anaphora*. Cambridge: Cambridge University Press

Francis G 1986 *Anaphoric Nouns*. Birmingham: English Language Research, University of Birmingham

Francis G 1989 Thematic selection and distribution in written discourse. *Word* **40** (1/2): 201–21

Francis G, Hunston S 1992 Analysing everyday conversation. In Coulthard R M (ed) *Advances in Spoken Discourse Analysis*. London: Routledge, pp. 123–61

Fraser B 1990 An approach to discourse markers. *Journal of Pragmatics* **14**: 383–95

Fries P H 1983 On the status of theme in English: arguments from discourse. In Petöfi J S, Sözer E (eds) *Micro and Macro Connexity of Texts*. Hamburg: Helmut Baske, pp. 116–52

Fries P H 1986 Lexical patterns in a text and interpretation. In Jankowsky K R (ed) *Scientific and Humanistic Dimensions of Language*. Amsterdam: John Benjamins, pp. 483–90

Fries P H 1991 Patterns of information in initial position in English. In Fries P H, Gregory M (eds) *Discourse in Society: Functional Perspectives*. Norwood, NJ: Ablex

Gairns R, Redman S 1986 *Working with Words*. Cambridge: Cambridge University Press

Garcia C 1989 Apologies in English: politeness strategies used by native and non-native speakers. *Multilingua* **8** (1): 3–20

Garfinkel H 1967 *Studies in Ethnomethodology*. Englewood Cliffs, NJ: Prentice-Hall

Ghadessy M 1983 Information structure in Letters to the Editor. *International Review of Applied Linguistics* **21**: 46–56

Ghadessy M 1984 Going beyond the sentence: implications of discourse analysis for the teaching of the writing skill. *International Review of Applied Linguistics* **XXII** (3): 213–18

Gibbs R W, Mueller R A 1988 Conversational sequences and preference for indirect speech acts. *Discourse Processes* **11** (1): 101–16

Giora R 1983a Segmentation and segment cohesion. On the thematic organisation of the text. *Text* **3** (2): 155–82

Giora R 1983b Functional sentence perspective. In Petöfi J S, Sözer E (eds) *Micro and Macro Connexity of Texts*. Hamburg: Buske, pp. 53–182

Grady K, Potter J 1985 Speaking and clapping: a comparison of Foot and Thatcher's oratory. *Language and Communication* 5 (3): 173–83

Greatbatch D 1988 A turn-taking system for British news interviews. *Language in Society* 17 (3): 401–30

Grice H P 1975 Logic and conversation. In Cole P, Morgan J (eds) *Syntax and Semantics, Volume 9: Pragmatics.* New York: Academic Press, pp. 41–58

Haegeman L 1987 Register variation in English: some theoretical observations. *Journal of English Linguistics* 20 (2): 230–48

Haegeman L 1990 Understood subjects in English diaries. On the relevance of theoretical syntax for the study of register variation. *Multilingua* 9 (2): 157–99

Hakulinen A 1989 Some notes on thematics, topic and typology. In Conte M E, Petöfi J, Sözer E (eds) *Text and Discourse Connectedness.* Amsterdam: John Benjamins, pp. 53–63

Halliday M A K 1978 *Language as Social Semiotic.* London: Edward Arnold

Halliday M A K 1985 *An Introduction to Functional Grammar.* London: Edward Arnold

Halliday M A K 1987 Some basic concepts of educational linguistics. In Bickley V (ed) *Languages in Education in a Bi-lingual or Multi-lingual Setting.* Hong Kong: ILE, pp. 5–17

Halliday M A K 1989 *Spoken and Written Language.* 2nd ed. Oxford: Oxford University Press

Halliday M A K, Hasan R 1976 *Cohesion in English.* London: Longman

Halliday M A K, Hasan R 1989 *Language Context and Text: Aspects of Language in a Social Semiotic Perspective.* 2nd ed. Oxford: Oxford University Press

Hamp-Lyons E, Heasley B 1987 *Study Writing.* Cambridge: Cambridge University Press

Harley B, Allen P, Cummins J, Swain M (eds) 1990 *The Development of Second Language Proficiency.* Cambridge: Cambridge University Press

Harris J, Wilkinson J (eds) 1986 *Reading Children's Writing: A Linguistic View.* London: Unwin Hyman/Routledge

Harris S 1991 Evasive action: how politicians respond to questions in political interviews. In Scannell P (ed) *Broadcast Talk.* London: Sage Publications, pp. 76–99

Harrison B (ed) 1990 *Culture and the Language Classroom.* ELT Documents. London: Macmillan

Hasan R 1978 Text in the systemic-functional model. In Dressler W V (ed) *Current Trends in Text Linguistics.* Berlin: de Gruyter

Hasan R 1984 Coherence and cohesive harmony. In Flood J (ed) *Understanding Reading Comprehension.* Newark, Delaware: International Reading Association, pp. 181–219

Hasan R, Martin J R (eds) 1989 *Language Development: Learning Language, Learning Culture: Studies for Michael Halliday.* Norwood NJ: Ablex

Hatch E 1992 *Discourse and Language Education.* Cambridge: Cambridge University Press

Hatim B 1991 The pragmatics of argumentation in Arabic: the rise and fall of a text type. *Text* 11 (2) 189–99

Held G 1989 On the role of maximisation in verbal politeness. *Multilingua* 8 (2/3): 167–206

Heritage J C, Watson D R 1979 Formulations as conversational objects. In Psathas G (ed) *Everyday Language: Studies in Ethnomethodology*. New York: Irvington, pp. 123–62

Herman V 1991 Dramatic dialogue and the systematics of turn-taking. *Semiotica* 83 (1/2): 92–121

Hermerén L 1978 *On Modality in English*. Lund: CWK Gleerup.

Hewings M, McCarthy M J 1988 An alternative approach to the analysis of text. *Praxis des Neusprachlichen Unterrichts* 1: 3–10

Hicks D 1990 Narrative skills and genre knowledge: ways of telling in the primary school grades. *Applied Psycholinguistics* 11: 83–104

Hietaranta P S 1984 A functional note on topicalization. *English Studies* 1: 48–51

Hinds J 1977 Paragraph structure and pronominalisation. *Papers in Linguistics* 10: 77–97

Hockett C F 1977 Jokes. In *The View From Language: Selected Essays 1948 – 1964*. Allens: Georgia, pp. 257–89

Hoey M P 1983 *On the Surface of Discourse*. London: Allen & Unwin

Hoey M P 1988 The discourse properties of the criminal statute. In Nixon G, Honey J (eds) *An Historic Tongue: Studies in English Linguistics in Memory of Barbara Strang*. London: Routledge, pp. 154–66

Hoey M P 1991a *Patterns of Lexis in Text*. Oxford: Oxford University Press

Hoey M P 1991b Some properties of spoken discourse. In Bowers R, Brumfit C (eds) *Applied Linguistics and English Language Teaching*. Basingstoke: Macmillan/MEP, pp. 65–84

Hofmann T R 1989 Paragraphs and anaphora. *Journal of Pragmatics* 13: 239–50

Holborrow M 1991 Linking language and situation: a course for advanced learners. *English Language Teaching Journal* 45 (1): 24–33

Holmes J 1983 Speaking English with the appropriate degree of conviction. In Brumfit C (ed) *Learning and Teaching Languages for Communication: Applied Linguistic Perspectives*. London: Centre for Information on Language Teaching, pp. 100–13

Holmes J 1988 Doubt and certainty in ESL textbooks. *Applied Linguistics* 9 (1): 21–44

Hong B 1985 Politeness in Chinese: impersonal pronouns and personal greetings. *Anthropological Linguistics* 27 (2) 204–13

Hopper P J 1979 Aspect and foregrounding in discourse. In Givón T (ed) *Syntax and Semantics, Volume 12: Discourse and Syntax*. New York: Academic Press, pp. 213–41

Hopper P J 1982 Aspect between discourse and grammar. In Hopper P J (ed) *Tense-Aspect: Between Semantics and Pragmatics*. Amsterdam: John Benjamins, pp. 3–18

Hudson T 1990 The discourse of advice giving in English: 'I wouldn't feed until spring no matter what you do'. *Discourse Processes* 10 (4): 285–97

Hymes D 1971 On communicative competence. In Pride J, Holmes J (eds) *Sociolinguistics*. 1972. Harmondsworth: Penguin, pp. 269–93

Iarovici E, Amel R 1989 The strategy of the headline. *Semiotica* 77 (4): 441–59

ICC (International Certificate Conference) 1986 *Foreign Languages in Adult and Continuing Education: Specifications for Stage 3 Level of the International Certificate Conference Language Certificate System.* Bonn-Frankfurt: Deutscher Volkshochschul-Verband e.v.

Ishikawa M 1991 Iconicity in discourse: the case of repetition. *Text* **11** (4): 553–80

Ivanič R 1991 Nouns in search of a context: a study of nouns with both open- and closed-system characteristics. *International Review of Applied Linguistics* **XXIX** (2): 93–114

James C, Garrett P (eds) 1992 *Language Awareness in the Classroom.* London: Longman

Jaworski A 1990 The acquisition and perception of formulaic language and foreign language teaching. *Multilingua* **9** (4): 397–411

Johns A M 1986 Coherence and academic writing: some determinants and suggestions for teaching, *TESOL Quarterly* **20**, 2, 247–65

Johns C M, Johns T F 1977 Seminar discussion strategies. In Cowie A P, Heaton J B (eds) *English for Academic Purposes.* Reading: BAAL/SELMOUS, pp. 99–107

Johnstone B 1987 'He says . . . so I said': verb tense alternation and narrative depictions of authority in American English. *Linguistics* **25** (1): 33–52

Jones L B, Jones L K 1985 Discourse functions of five English sentence types. *Word* **36** (1): 1–21

Jordan M P 1984 *Rhetoric of Everyday English Texts.* London: Allen & Unwin

Journal of Pragmatics 1982 Special issue: Stories. **6** (5)

Journal of Pragmatics 1990 Special issue: Politeness. **14** (2)

Jucker A H 1986 *News Interviews: a Pragmalinguistic Analysis.* Amsterdam: John Benjamins

Källgren G, Prince E F 1989 Swedish VP-topicalization and Yiddish verb-topicalization. *Nordic Journal of Linguistics* **12**: 47–58

Kaplan R B 1966 Cultural thought patterns in intercultural education. *Language Learning* **16**: 1–20

Kaplan R 1972 Cultural thought patterns in intercultural education. In Croft K (ed) *Readings on English as a Second Language.* Cambridge, Mass: Winthrop pp. 245–62

Kasper G 1984 Pragmatic Comprehension in Learner – Native Speaker Discourse *Language Learning* **34**: pp.1–20

Kehe D, Kehe P D 1989 Maintaining teacher control during pair/group work. *Muinteoir Teanga* **2** (2): 35–9

Khanittanan W 1988 Some observations on expressing politeness in Thai. *Language Sciences* **10** (2): 353–62

Knapp M L, Hart R P, Friedrich G W, Shulman G M 1973 The rhetoric of goodbye: verbal and nonverbal correlates of human leave-taking. *Speech Monographs* **40**: 182–98

Knowles G M, Malmkjaer K (eds) 1989 Language and Ideology. Special issue of *English Language Research Journal* (ns) **3**

Kress G 1982 *Learning to Write.* London: Routledge & Kegan Paul

Kress G 1987 Genre in a social theory of language: a reply to John Dixon. In Reid I (ed) *The Place of Genre in Learning: Current Debates.* Victoria (Australia): Deakin University Press, pp. 35–45

Kress G 1989 *Linguistic Processes in Sociocultural Practice.* Oxford: Oxford University Press

Kress G, Hodge R 1981 *Language as Ideology.* London: Routledge & Kegan Paul

Kurzon D 1985 Signposts for the reader: a corpus-based study of text deixis. *Text* **5** (3) 187–200

Labov W 1972 *Language in the Inner City.* Oxford: Basil Blackwell

Lakoff R 1973 The logic of politeness; or minding your p's and q's. *Papers from the 9th Regional Meeting, Chicago Linguistics Society.* Chicago: Chicago Linguistics Society, pp. 292–305

Lambrecht K 1988 Presentational cleft constructions in spoken French. In Haiman J, Thompson S (eds) *Clause Combining in Grammar and Discourse.* Amsterdam: John Benjamins, pp. 135–79

Laver J 1975 Communicative functions of phatic communion. In Kendon A, Harris R M, Key M R (eds) *Organisation of Behaviour in Face-to-Face Interaction.* The Hague: Mouton, pp. 215–38

Le Page R 1975 Sociolinguistics and the problem of competence. *Language Teaching and Linguistics: Abstract* **8** (3): 137–56

Lebra T S 1987 The cultural significance of silence in Japanese. *Multilingua* **6** (4): pp. 343–57

Leech G 1969 *A Linguistic Guide to English Poetry.* London: Longman

Leith R, Myerson G 1989 *The Power of Address: Explorations in Rhetoric.* London: Routledge

Linguistics and Philosophy 1986 Special issue: Tense and Aspect in Discourse. **9** (1)

Lintermann-Rygh I 1985 Connector density: an indicator of essay quality? *Text* **5** (4): 347–58

Littlefair A 1991 *Reading All Types of Writing.* Milton Keynes: Open University Press

Livingstone S M 1990 Interpreting a television narrative: how different viewers see a story. *Journal of Communication* **40** (1): 72–85

Lonergan J, Gordon K 1986 *New Dimensions 1: Student's Book.* London: Macmillan

Long M H, Crookes G 1992 Three approaches to task-based syllabus design. *TESOL Quarterly* **26** (1): 27–56

Longacre R 1976 *An Anatomy of Speech Notions* Lisse: Peter de Ridder Press

Longacre R 1979 The paragraph as a grammatical unit. In Givón T (ed) *Syntax and Semantics. Volume 12: Discourse and Syntax.* New York: Academic Press, pp. 115–34

Longacre R 1983 *The Grammar of Discourse.* New York: Plenum Press

Loveday L J 1982 Communicative interference: a framework for contrastively analysing L2 communicative competence exemplified with the linguistic behaviour of Japanese performing in English. *International Review of Applied Linguistics* **XX**: 1–16

Loveday L J 1983 Rhetoric patterns in conflict: The sociocultural relativity of discourse – organising processes *Journal of Pragmatics* **7**, 169–90

Low G 1988 On teaching metaphor. *Applied Linguistics* **9** (2): 125–47

Luetkemeyer J, Van Antwerp C, Kindell G 1984 An annotated bibliography of spoken and written language. In Tannen D (ed) *Coherence in Spoken and Written Discourse.* Norwood, NJ: Ablex, pp. 265–81

Macken M, Rotherey J 1991 *A Model for Literacy in Subject Learning* Metropolitan East Region Disadvantaged Schools Program. Erskineville, NSW: NSW Department of Education

Makkai A 1978 Idiomaticity as a language universal. In Greenberg J H, Ferguson C A, Moravcsik E A (eds) *Universals of Human Language, Volume 3: Word Structure.* Stanford, California: Stanford University Press, pp. 401–48

Macolm L 1987 What rules govern tense usage in scientific articles? *English for Specific Purposes* 6 (1): 31–43

Martin J R 1986 Intervening in the process of writing development. In Painter C, Martin J R (eds) *Writing to Mean: Teaching Genres Across the Curriculum.* Occasional Papers no. 9, Applied Linguistics Association of Australia, pp. 11–43

Martin J R 1989 *Factual Writing: Exploring and Challenging Social Reality.* 2nd edn. Oxford: Oxford University Press

Martin J R, Rothery J 1981 Writing project reports: 1980 and 1981. *Working Papers in Linguistics 1/2.* Sydney: University of Sydney

Martin J, Christie F, Rothery J 1987 Social processes in education: a reply to Sawyer and Watson (and others). In Reid I (ed) *The Place of Genre in Learning: Current Debates.* Victoria (Australia): Deakin University Press, pp. 58–82

Matsumoto Y 1988 Re-examination of the universality of face: politeness phenomena in Japanese. *Journal of Pragmatics* 12 (4) 403–26

Maynard S 1986 Interactional aspects of thematic progression in English casual conversations. *Text* 6 (1): 73–106

Maynard S K 1990 Conversation management in contrast: listener response in Japanese and American English. *Journal of Pragmatics* 14: 397–412

Mazzie C 1987 An experimental investigation of the determinants of implicitness in spoken and written discourse. *Discourse Processes* 10 (1): 31–42

McCarthy M J 1984 A new look at vocabulary in EFL. *Applied Linguistics* 5 (1): 12–22

McCarthy M J 1988a Some vocabulary patterns in conversation. In Carter R A, McCarthy M J *Vocabulary and Language Teaching.* London: Longman, pp. 181–200

McCarthy M J (ed) 1988b Naturalness. Special issue of *English Language Research Journal* (ns) 2. Birmingham: English Language Research

McCarthy M J 1990 *Vocabulary.* Oxford: Oxford University Press

McCarthy M J 1991 *Discourse Analysis for Language Teachers.* Cambridge: Cambridge University Press

McCarthy M J 1992a Interactive lexis: prominence and paradigms. In Coulthard R M (ed) *Advances in Spoken Discourse Analysis.* London: Routledge, pp. 197–208

McCarthy M J 1992b Grammar, discourse and the fanzine. In Ikegami Y (ed) *Varieties of English: Proceedings of the British Council Conference Kyoto 1990.* Tokyo: Maruzen, pp. 181–95

McConvell P 1988 *To be* or double *be?* Current changes in the English copula. *Australian Journal of Linguistics* **8** (2): 287–305

McRae J 1991 *Literature with a Small 'l'*. London: Macmillan

McRae J, Pantaleoni L 1990 *Chapter and Verse*. Oxford: Oxford University Press

Melrose R 1991 *The Communicative Syllabus: a Systemic-functional Approach to Language Teaching*. London: Pinter

Mitchell T F 1957 The language of buying and selling in Cyrenaica: a situational statement. *Hespéris* **44**: 31–71. Reprinted in Mitchell T F 1975 *Principles of Firthian Linguistics*. London: Longman, pp. 167–200

Moeran B 1984 Advertising sounds as cultural discourse. *Language and Communication* **4** (2): 147–58

Moffett J 1968 *Teaching the Universe of Discourse*. Boston, Mass.: Houghton Miflin

Moller A, Whiteson V 1981 *Cloze in Class: Exercises in Developing Reading and Comprehension Skills*. Oxford: Pergamon

Mohideen H 1991 An error analysis of the written English of Malay students at pre-university level. Unpublished PhD thesis. Cardiff: University of Wales

Monroe J 1990 Idiom and cliché in T S Eliot and John Ashbery. *Contemporary Literature* **31**: 17–36

Montgomery M 1986 *An Introduction to Language and Society*. London: Methuen

Moon R 1992 Textual aspects of fixed expressions in learners' dictionaries. In Arnaud P J, Béjoint H (eds) *Vocabulary and Applied Linguistics*. Basingstoke: Macmillan, pp. 13–27

Morrow P 1989 Conjunct use in business news stories and academic journal articles: a comparative study. *English for Specific Purposes* (New York) **8** (3): 239–54

Mulkay M 1985 Argument and disagreement in conversations and letters. *Text* **5** (3): 201–28

Munby J 1978 *Communicative Syllabus Design*. Cambridge: Cambridge University Press

Murphy R 1985 *English Grammar in Use*. British edition. Cambridge: Cambridge University Press

Murphy R 1989 *English Grammar in Use*. US edition. New York: Cambridge University Press

Murry D 1988 The context of oral and written language: a framework for mode and medium switching. *Language in Society* **17** (3): 351–73

Myers G 1989 The pragmatics of politeness in scientific articles. *Applied Linguistics* **10** (1): 1–35

Myers Scotton C, Bernsten J 1988 Natural conversations as a model for textbook dialogue. *Applied Linguistics* **9** (4): 372–84

Myhill J, Hibiya J 1988 The discourse function of clause-chaining. In Haiman J, Thompson S (eds) *Clause Combining in Grammar and Discourse*. Amsterdam: John Benjamins. pp. 361–98

Nagy J F 1989 Representations of oral tradition in Medieval Irish literature. *Language and Communication* **9** (2/3): 143–58

Nash W 1989 *Rhetoric: the Wit of Persuasion*. Oxford: Basil Blackwell

Niyi Akinnaso F 1982 On the differences between spoken and written language. *Language and Speech* 25 (2): 97–125
Nolasco R, Arthur L 1987 *Conversation*. Oxford: Oxford University Press
Norrick N R 1987 Functions of repetition in conversation. *Text* 7 (3): 245–64
Nunan D 1988 *Syllabus Design*. Oxford: Oxford University Press
Nunan D 1989 *Designing Tasks for the Communicative Classroom*. Cambridge: Cambridge University Press
Nunan D 1990 Using learner data in curriculum development. *English for Specific Purposes* 9 (1): 17–32
Nystrand M 1983 The role of context in written communication. *Nottingham Linguistic Circular* 12 (1): 55–65
Nystrand M 1986 *The Structure of Written Communication: Studies in Reciprocity between Writers and Readers*. London: Academic Press.
Nystrand M, Wiemelt J 1991 When is a text explicit? Formalist and dialogical conceptions. *Text* 11 (1) 25–41

O'Connor di Vito N 1991 Incorporating native speaker norms in second language materials. *Applied Linguistics* 12 (4): 383–96
O'Faoláin S 1985 *Bird Alone*. Oxford: Oxford University Press
Olesky W (ed) 1989. *Contrastive Pragmatics* Amsterdam: John Benjamins

Paprotté W 1988 A discourse perspective on tense and aspect in standard modern Greek and English. In Rudzka-Ostyn B (ed) *Topics in Cognitive Linguistics*. Amsterdam: John Benjamins, pp. 447–505
Paulston C B 1992 *Linguistic and Communicative Competence: Topics in ESL*. Clevedon, Avon: Multilingual Matters
Pearson E 1986 Agreement/disagreement: an example of results of discourse analysis applied to the oral English classroom. *ITL Review of Applied Linguistics* 74: 47–61
Phillipson R 1992 *Linguistic Imperialism*. Oxford: Oxford University Press
Polanyi L 1981 Telling the same story twice. *Text* 1 (4): 315–36
Pomerantz A 1978 Compliment responses: notes on the co-operation of multiple constraints. In Schenkein J (ed) *Studies in the Organisation of Conversational Interaction*. New York: Academic Press, pp. 79–112
Pomerantz A 1984 Agreeing and disagreeing with assessments: some features of preferred/dispreferred turn shapes. In Atkinson J, Heritage J (eds) *Structure of Social Action*. Cambridge: Cambridge University Press, pp. 57–101
Powell M J 1992 Semantic/pragmatic regularities in informal lexis: British speakers in spontaneous conversational settings. *Text* 12 (1): 19–58
Prabhu N 1987 *Second Language Pedagogy: a Perspective*. Oxford: Oxford University Press
Psathas G 1986 The organisation of directions in interaction. *Word* 37 (1/2): 83–91
Psathas G, Kozloff M 1976 The structure of directions. *Semiotica* 17: 111–30

Quirk R, Greenbaum S, Leech G, Svartvik J 1985 *A Comprehensive Grammar of the English Language*. London: Longman

Rader M 1982 Context in written language: the case of imaginative fiction. In Tannen D (ed) *Spoken and Written Language: Exploring Orality and Literacy*. Norwood, NJ: Ablex, pp. 185–98

Ranney S 1992 Learning a new script: an exploration of sociolinguistic competence. *Applied Linguistics* 13 (1): 25–50

Redeker G 1984 On differences between spoken and written language. *Discourse Processes* 7: 43–55

Redeker G 1990 Ideational and pragmatic markers of discourse structure. *Journal of Pragmatics* 14: 367–81

Reid I (ed) 1987 *The Place of Genre in Learning: Current Debates*. Victoria (Australia): Deakin University Press

Riddle E 1986 The meaning and discourse function of the past tense in English. *TESOL Quarterly* 20 (2): 267–86

Riley P 1987 'Who do you think you're talking to?' Perception, categorisation and negotiation processes in exolinguistic interaction. In Bickley V (ed) *Languages in Education in a Bi-lingual or Multi-lingual Setting*. Hong Kong: ILE, pp. 118–33

Riley P 1992 Having a good gossip: sociolinguistic dimensions of language use. In Bowers R, Brumfit C J (eds) *Applied Linguistics and English Language Teaching*. Basingstoke: Macmillan/Modern English Publications, pp. 53–64

Robinson G 1985 *Crosscultural Understanding*. Oxford: Pergammon Press

Rosen M 1988 Will Genre Theory Change the World? *English in Australia* 86 (Dec): 4–12

Rudolph E 1989 The role of conjunctions and particles for text connexity. In Conte M E, Petöfi J, Sözer E (eds) *Text and Discourse Connectedness*. Amsterdam: John Benjamins. pp. 175–90

Rutherford W 1987 *Second Language Grammar*. London: Longman

Sacks H, Schegloff E A, Jefferson G 1974 A simplest systematics for the organisation of turn-taking for conversation. *Language* 50 (4): 696–735

Salager-Meyer F 1992 A text-type and move analysis study of verb tense and modality distribution in medical English abstracts. *English for Specific Purposes* 11 (2): 93–113

Samraj B 1989 Exploring current issues in genre theory. *Word* 40 (1/2): 189–200

Scarcella R, Brunak J 1981 On speaking politely in a second language. *International Journal of the Sociology of Language* 27: 59–75

Schachter J, Rutherford W 1983 Discourse function and language transfer. In Robinett B W, Schachter J (eds) *Second Language Learning: Contrastive Analysis, Error Analysis and Related Aspects*. Ann Arbor, Mich.: University of Michigan Press, pp. 303–15

Schachter J 1990 Communicative competence revisited. In Harley B, Allen P, Cummins J, Swain M (eds) *The Development of Second Language Proficiency*. Cambridge: Cambridge University Press, pp. 39–49

Schegloff E A 1979 Identification and recognition in telephone conversation openings. In Psathas G (ed) *Everyday Language: Studies in Ethnomethodology*. New York: Irvington, pp. 23–78

Schegloff E A 1986 The routine as achievement. *Human Studies* 9 (2/3): 111–51

Schegloff E A, Sacks H 1973 Opening up closings. *Semiotica* 8 (4): 289–327

Schenkein J (ed) 1978 *Studies in the Organisation of Conversational Interaction*. London: Academic Press

Schiffrin D 1981 Tense variation in narrative. *Language* 57 (1): 45–62

Schiffrin D 1987 *Discourse Markers*. Cambridge: Cambridge University Press

Schourup L 1985 *Common Discourse Particles in English Conversation*. New York: Garland

Shaw P 1992 Variation and universality in communicative competence: Coseriu's model. *TESOL Quarterly* 26 (1): 9–25

Sheldon L (ed) 1987 *ELT Textbooks and Materials: Problems in Evaluation and Development*. ELT Documents 126. London: Modern English Publications/The British Council

Short M (ed) 1988 *Reading, Analysing and Teaching Literature*. London: Longman

Short M, Candlin C N 1986 Teaching study skills for English literature. In Brumfit C J, Carter R A (eds) *Literature and Language Teaching*. Oxford: Oxford University Press, pp. 89–109

Silva-Corvalán C 1983 Tense and aspect in oral Spanish narrative: context and meaning. *Language* 59 (4): 760–80

Sinclair J McH, Renouf A 1988 A lexical syllabus for language learning. In Carter R A, McCarthy M J *Vocabulary and Language Teaching*. London: Longman, pp. 140–60

Sinclair J McH, Coulthard R M 1975 *Towards an Analysis of Discourse*. Oxford: Oxford University Press

Smith E L 1985 Text type and discourse framework. *Text* 5 (3) 229–47

Smith E L 1986 Achieving impact through the interpersonal component. In Couture B (ed) *Functional Approaches to Writing Research Perspectives*. London: Frances Pinter, pp. 108–19

Smith L E (ed) 1987 *Discourse Across Cultures: Strategies in World Englishes*. London: Prentice-Hall

Smith R N, Frawley W J 1983 Conjunctive cohesion in four English genres. *Text* 3 (4): 347–74

Soga M 1983 *Tense and Aspect in Modern Colloquial Japanese*. University of British Columbia Press

Stainton C 1989 Review of genre and genre study. Working paper. Nottingham: University of Nottingham

Stainton C 1992 Language Awareness: Genre awareness. A focused review of the literature. *Language Awareness* 1 (2), pp. 109–22

Stern H H 1992 *Issues and Options in Language Teaching* Oxford: Oxford University Press

Strässler J 1982 *Idioms in English: a Pragmatic Analysis*. Tübingen: Gunter Narr Verlag

Strevens P 1987 Cultural Barriers to Language Learning. In Smith L (ed) *Discourse Across Cultures: Strategies in World Englishes*. Prentice Hall: Hemel Hempstead U.K., pp. 169–78

Stubbs M 1983 *Discourse Analysis*. Oxford: Basil Blackwell

Stubbs M 1986a Lexical density: a computational technique and some findings. In Coulthard R M (ed) *Talking About Text*. Birmingham: English Language Research, pp. 27–42

Stubbs M 1986b 'A matter of prolonged fieldwork'; notes towards a modal grammar of English. *Applied Linguistics* **7** (1): 1–25
Svartvik J, Quirk R 1980 *A Corpus of English Conversation.* Lund: Liberläromedel
Swales J 1981 *Aspects of Article Introductions.* ESP Research Reports no. 1. Birmingham: University of Aston
Swales J 1985 *Episodes in ESP.* London: Pergamon Press
Swales J 1988 Mini-texts: resources for advanced ESL and discourse analysis training. In Jha A K, Bhargava R (eds) *New Directions in Language Teaching.* Jaipur: Pointer Publishers, pp. 1–11
Swales J 1990 *Genre Analysis.* Cambridge: Cambridge University Press
Swan M, Walter C 1984 *The Cambridge English Course.* Volume 1. Cambridge: Cambridge University Press

Tannen D 1982a Oral and literate strategies in spoken and written discourse. *Language* **58**: 1–20
Tannen D (ed) 1982b *Spoken and Written Language: Exploring Orality and Literacy.* Norwood, NJ: Ablex
Tannen D (ed) 1984 *Coherence in Spoken and Written Discourse.* Norwood, NJ: Ablex
Tannen D 1987a Repetition in conversation as spontaneous formulaicity. *Text* **7** (3): 215–43
Tannen D 1987b Repetition in conversation: toward a poetics of talk. *Language* **63** (3): 574–605
Tannen D 1989 *Talking Voices: Repetition, Dialogue and Imagery in Conversational Discourse.* Cambridge: Cambridge University Press
Taylor G, Chen T 1991 Linguistic, cultural, and subcultural issues in contrastive discourse analysis: Anglo-American and Chinese scientific texts. *Applied Linguistics* **12** (3): 319–36
Thomas J 1983 Cross-cultural pragmatic failure. *Applied Linguistics* **4** (2): 91–112
Thompson S 1985 Grammar and written discourse: initial versus final purpose clauses in English. *Text* **5** (1/2): 55–84
Threadgold T 1988 The Genre Debate *Southern Review.* **21** (3) 315–330
Threadgold T 1989 Talking about Genre: Ideologies and Incompatible Discourses. *Cultural Studies* **3** (1) 101–127
Tolson A 1991 Televised chat and the synthetic personality. In Scannell P (ed) *Broadcast Talk.* London: Sage Publications, pp. 178–200
Toolan M J 1988 *Narrative: a Critical Linguistic Introduction.* London: Routledge
Tottie G, Bäcklund I (eds) 1986 *English in Speech and Writing: a Symposium.* Uppsala: Studia Anglistica Uppsaliensia
Tripp S D 1990 The idea of a lexical meta-syllabus *System* **18** (2): 209–20
Trosborg A 1987 Apology strategies in natives/non-natives. *Journal of Pragmatics* **11**: 147–67

Ure J 1971 Lexical density and register differentiation. In Perren G E, Trim J L M (eds) *Applications of Linguistics: Selected Papers of the Second International Congress of Applied Linguistics, Cambridge, 1969.* Cambridge: Cambridge University Press, pp. 443–52

Valdes J M (ed) 1986 *Culture Bound: Bridging the Gap in Language Teaching*. Cambridge: Cambridge University Press

Van de Kopple W J 1985a Some exploratory discourse on metadiscourse. *College Composition and Communication* 36: 82–93

Van de Kopple W J 1985b Sentence topics, syntactic subjects and domains in texts. *Written Communication* 2: 339–57

Van Dijk T A (ed) 1985 *Handbook of Discourse Analysis*. 4 Vols. London: Academic Press

Van Peer W (ed) 1988 *The Taming of the Text*. London: Routledge

Ventola E 1987 *The Structure of Social Interaction: A Systematic Approach to the Semiotics of Service Encounters*. London: Frances Pinter

Ventola E 1989 Problems of modelling and applied issues within the framework of genre. *Word* 40 (1/2): 129–61

Virtanen T 1992 Given and new information in adverbials: clause-initial adverbials of time and place. *Journal of Pragmatics* 17: 99–115

Walters J (ed) 1979 The perception of politeness in English and Spanish. In Yorio C A, Perkins K et al (eds) *On TESOL '79: EFL Policies, Programs, Practices*. Washington DC: TESOL (Teachers of English to Speakers of Other Languages), pp. 257–87

Watabe M, Brown C, Ueta Y 1991 Transfer of discourse function: passives in the writing of ESL and JSL learners. *International Review of Applied Linguistics* XXIX (2): 115–34

Watts R J 1984 An analysis of epistemic possibility and probability. *English Studies* 65: 129–40

Watts R J 1989a Taking the pitcher to the 'well': native speakers' perception of their use of discourse markers in conversation. *Journal of Pragmatics* 13: 203–37

Watts R J 1989b Relevance and relational work: linguistic politeness as politic behaviour. *Multilingua* 8 (2/3): 131–66

Waugh L R, Monville-Burston M 1986 Aspect and discourse function: the French simple past in newspaper usage. *Language* 62 (4): 846–77

Werlich E 1976 *A Text Grammar of English*. Heidelberg: Quelle and Meyer

Werlich E 1986 The relevance of a text (type) grammar to foreign language teaching – with a note on text type switches. In Leitner G (ed) *The English Reference Grammar: Language and Linguistics, Writers and Readers*. Tübingen: Max Niemeyer, pp. 65–88

Westney P 1986 How to be more or less certain in English: scalarity in epistemic modality. *International Review of Applied Linguistics* XXIV (4): 311–20

White S 1989 Backchannels across cultures: a study of Americans and Japanese. *Language in Society* 18 (1): 59–76

Widdowson H G 1979 *Explorations in Applied Linguistics 1*. Oxford: Oxford University Press

Widdowson H G 1983 Talking Shop: Literature and ELT. *English Language Teaching Journal* 37 (1): 30–36

Widdowson H G 1984 *Explorations in Applied Linguistics 2*. Oxford: Oxford University Press

Widdowson H G 1987 The roles of teacher and learner. *English Language Teaching Journal* 41: 83–8

Widdowson H G 1990 *Aspects of Language Teaching.* Oxford: Oxford University Press

Wilkinson A (ed) 1986 *The Writing of Writing.* Milton Keynes: Open University Press

Williams J 1990 Another look at yes/no questions: native speakers and non-native speakers. *Applied Linguistics* **11** (2) 159–82

Willis D 1990 *The Lexical Syllabus.* London: Collins

Winter E O 1977 A clause-relational approach to English texts: a study of some predictive lexical items in written discourse. *Instructional Science* **6** (1): 1–92

Winter E O 1978 A look at the role of certain words in information structure. In Jones K P, Horsnell V (eds) *Informatics* **3** (1): 85–97. London: ASLIB (Association of Special Libraries and Information Bureaux)

Wodak R 1981 How do I put my problem? Problem presentation in therapy and interview. *Text* **1** (2): 191–213

Wolfson N 1978 A feature of performed narrative: the conversational historical present. *Language in Society* **7**: 215–237

Wolfson N 1979 The conversational historical present alternation. *Language* **55**: 168–82

Yalden J 1983 *The Communicative Syllabus: Evolution, Design and Implementation.* New York: Pergamon

Yule G 1990 Interactive conflict resolution in English. *World Englishes* **9** (1): 53–62

Zwicky A M, Zwicky E D 1986 Imperfect puns, markedness, and phonological similarity: with fronds like these, who needs anenomes? *Folia Linguistica* **XX** (3/4): 493–503

Zydatiss W 1986 Grammatical categories and their text functions – some implications for the content of reference grammars. In Leitner G (ed) *The English Reference Grammar: Language and Linguistics, Writers and Readers.* Tübingen: Max Niemeyer, pp. 140–155

Index